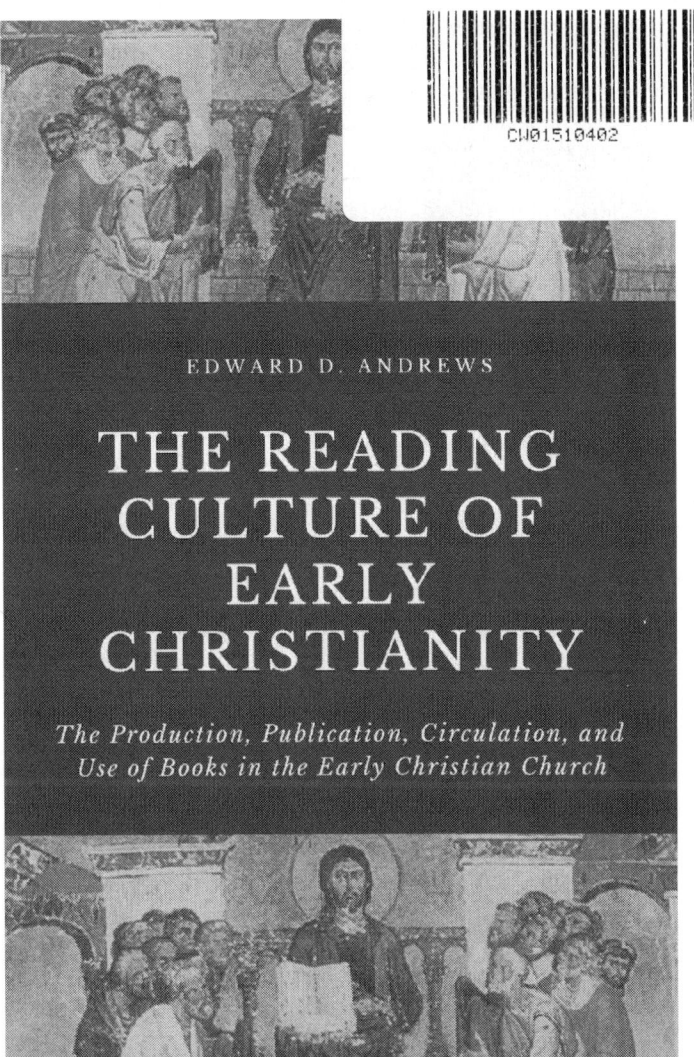

EDWARD D. ANDREWS

THE READING CULTURE OF EARLY CHRISTIANITY

The Production, Publication, Circulation, and Use of Books in the Early Christian Church

i

THE READING CULTURE OF EARLY CHRISTIANITY

The Production, Publication, Circulation, and Use of Books in the Early Christian Church

Edward D. Andrews

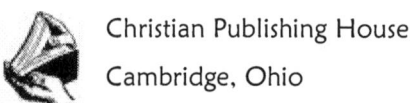

Christian Publishing House

Cambridge, Ohio

Christian Publishing House

Professional Conservative Christian Publishing of the Good News!

CPH Since 2005

Unless otherwise stated, Scripture quotations are from Updated American Standard Version (UASV) Copyright © **2019** by Christian Publishing House

THE READING CULTURE OF EARLY CHRISTIANITY: The Production, Publication, Circulation, and Use of Books in the Early Christian Church by Edward D. Andrews

ISBN-13: **978-1-949586-84-8**

ISBN-10: **1-949586-84-7**

Significant English Bible Translations

Unless otherwise indicated, Scripture quotations are from the *New American Standard Bible* (NASB) Copyright © 1960, 1962, 1963, 1968, 1971, 1972, 1973, 1975, 1977, 1995 by The Lockman Foundation

Below are some of the most significant English Bible translation of the twentieth and now twenty-first centuries. The word significant is used broadly and does not necessarily suggest a preferred or accurate translation.

ASV American Standard Version, 1901 Public Domain

CEV Contemporary English Version, 1995 by American Bible Society

CSB Christian Standard Bible, 2017 by Holman Bible Publishers

ESV English Standard Version, 2001 by Crossway Bibles, a publishing ministry of Good News Publishers

GNT Good News Translation, 1992 by American Bible Society

KJV King James Version, 1611 Public Domain

REB Revised English Bible, 1989 by Oxford University Press and Cambridge University Press

RSV Revised Standard Version, 1946, 1952, and 1971 the Division of Christian Education of the National Council of the Churches of Christ in the United States of America

NASB New American Standard Bible, 1960, 1962, 1963, 1968, 1971, 1972, 1973, 1975, 1977, 1995 by the Lockman Foundation

NEB New English Bible, 1961 by Oxford University Press and Cambridge University Press

NIV New International Version, 2011 973, 1978, 1984, 2011 by Biblica, Inc.®

NKJV New King James Version, 1982 by Thomas Nelson

NLT New Living Translation (second edition), 2004 by Tyndale House Foundation

NRSV New Revised Standard Version, 1990 by the Division of Christian Education of the National Council of the Churches of Christ in the United States of America

TNIV Today's New International Version, 2005 by Biblica (Formerly International Bible Society)

UASV Updated American Standard Version, NT 2017 OT, 2018 by Christian Publishing House

Publication Abbreviations

AA Aland-Aland = *The Text of the New Testament, An Introduction to the Critical Editions and to the Theory and Practice of Modern Textual Criticism*, by Kurt Aland and Barbara Aland (Grand Rapids, 1987; 2nd ed., 1989).

BAA *Griechisch-Deutsches Wörterbuch zu den Schriften des Neuen Testaments und der frühchristlichen Literatur*, by W. Bauer, K. Aland, and B. Aland (6th ed.; Berlin: de Gruyter, 1988)

BAGD *A Greek-English Lexicon of the New Testament and Other Early Christian Literature*, by W. Bauer, W. F. Arndt, F. W. Gingrich, and F. W. Danker (2d ed.; Chicago: University of Chicago Press, 1979)

BDB *A Hebrew and English Lexicon of the Old Testament*, by F. Brown, S. R. Driver, and C. A. Briggs (Oxford: Clarendon, 1907)

BDF *A Greek Grammar of the New Testament and Other Early Christian Literature*, by F. Blass, A. Debrunner, and R. W. Funk (Chicago: University of Chicago Press, 1961)

BDR *Grammatik des neutestamentlichen Griechisch*, by F. Blass, A. Debrunner, and F. Rehkopf (Göttingen: Vandenhoeck & Ruprecht, 1984)

FJAH F. J. A. Hort's "Notes on Select Readings," in *The New Testament in the Original Greek*, the Text Revised by Brooke Foss Westcott and Fenton John Anthony Hort; [vol. ii] *Introduction [and] Appendix* (Cambridge and London, 1881; 2nd ed., 1896).

GMAW *Greek Manuscripts of the Ancient World* (2nd ed., E. G. Turner)

GELNTBSD Johannes P. Louw and Eugene Albert Nida, *Greek-English Lexicon of the New Testament: Based on Semantic Domains* (New York: United Bible Societies, 1996).

HIBD Brand, Chad, Charles Draper, and England Archie. *Holman Illustrated Bible Dictionary*. Revised, Updated and Expanded. Nashville, TN: Holman, 2003.

ISBE *International Standard Bible Encyclopedia* (4 vols., Bromiley) [1979–1988]

LSJ *A Greek-English Lexicon*, by H. G. Liddell, R. Scott, and H. S. Jones (Oxford: Clarendon, 1968)

LXX *Septuaginta*: With Morphology, electronic ed. (Stuttgart: Deutsche Bibelgesellschaft, 1979)

LXX Swete Henry Barclay Swete, The Old Testament in Greek: According to the Septuagint (Cambridge, UK: Cambridge University Press, 1909)

MCEDONTW Mounce, William D. *Mounce's Complete Expository Dictionary of Old & New Testament Words.* Grand Rapids, MI: Zondervan, 2006.

MM *The Vocabulary of the Greek Testament: Illustrated from the Papyri and Other Non-literary Sources,* by J. H. Moulton and G. Milligan (repr. Grand Rapids: Eerdmans, 1980)

(MT) Masoretic Text

NA²⁶ *Novum Testamentum Graece* (26th ed., Nestle-Aland) [1979]

NA²⁷ *Novum Testamentum Graece* (27th ed., Nestle-Aland) [1993]

NA²⁸ *Novum Testamentum Graece* (27th ed., Nestle-Aland) [2012]

NBD Wood, D R W. *New Bible Dictionary* (Third Edition). Downers Grove: InterVarsity Press, 1996.

NIDNTT *The New International Dictionary of New Testament Theology,* edited by L. Coenen, E. Beyreuther, and H. Bietenhard; English translation edited by C. Brown (4 vols.; Grand Rapids: Zondervan, 1975–86)

NU text of Nestle-Aland 26th/27th/28th [N] and the United Bible Societies 3rd/4th/5th [U]

TCGNT A TEXTUAL COMMENTARY ON THE GREEK NEW TESTAMENT by Bruce M. Metzger (German Bible Society, 1970; 2ⁿᵈ ed., 1994)

TDNT *Theological Dictionary of the New Testament,* edited by G. Kittel and G. Friedrich; translated and edited by G. W. Bromiley (10 vols.; Grand Rapids: Eerdmans, 1964–76)

TENTGM THE TEXT OF THE EARLIEST NEW TESTAMENT MANUSCRIPTS A Corrected, Enlarged Edition of The Complete Text of the Earliest New Testament Manuscripts by Philip W. Comfort and David P. Barrett (Tyndale House Publishers, 1999, 2ⁿᵈ ed., 2001)

TTNT-A *The Text of the New Testament, An Introduction to the Critical Editions and to the Theory and Practice of Modern Textual Criticism,* by Kurt Aland and Barbara Aland (Grand Rapids, 1987; 2nd ed., 1989).

TTNT-M *The Text of the New Testament, Its Transmission, Corruption, and Restoration*, by Bruce M. Metzger (Oxford, 1964; 3rd ed., 1992).

TNTCR The Text of the New Testament in Contemporary Research: Essays on the Status Quaestionis (New Testament Tools, Studies, and Documents, by Bart D. Ehrman and Michael W. Holmes (Brill, 1995; 2nd ed., 2012)

UBS³ United Bible Societies' *Greek New Testament* (3rd ed., Metzger et al) [1975]

UBS⁴ United Bible Societies' *Greek New Testament* (4th corrected ed., Metzger et al) [1993]

UBS⁵ United Bible Societies' *Greek New Testament* (4th corrected ed., Metzger et al) [2014]

VCEDONTW Vine, W E. *Vine's Expository Dictionary of Old and New Testament Words.* Nashville: Thomas Nelson, 1996.

WHI Westcott and Hort, *Introduction = The New Testament in the Original Greek*, the Text Revised by Brooke Foss Westcott and Fenton John Anthony Hort; [vol. ii] *Introduction [and] Appendix* (Cambridge and London, 1881; 2nd ed., 1896).

WPNT Robertson, A.T. *Word Pictures in the New Testament.* Oak Harbor, MI: Logos Research Systems, 1933, 1997.

WSNT Vincent, Marvin. Word Studies in the New Testament. Bellingham: Logos Research Systems, 2002.

WWSGNT Wuest, Kenneth S. *Wuest's Word Studies from the Greek New Testament: For the English Reader.* Grand Rapids: Eerdmans, 1997, c1984.

ABBREVIATIONS: Manuscripts and Ancient Versions

Textual scholars employ a symbol (called sigla; singular siglum), which indicate a manuscript and to identify the copyist or corrector of a text. Below are the sigla used in THE READING CULTURE OF EARLY CHRISTIANITY, as well as the content to the nearest book (sometimes chapter) and its date. We are only providing a few examples each. For the complete list, please see the introduction and appendixes to UBS5 and NA[28].

- Dates are given to the nearest 25-50-year increment.

- A small cross (†) shows the content the nearest chapter, while other times the verses are sometimes listed. For example, P11 would read 1 Corinthians 1-7 † because it has many verses throughout chapters 1-7: 1:17-22, 25-27; 2:6-8, 9-12, 14; 3:1-3, 5-6, 8-10, 20, 4:3-5; 5:7-8; 6:5-9, 11-18; 7:3-6, 10-14.

- Symbol c. for "circa," or "about."

- Exact dates, like 316 C.E. for P[10] are the result of being found with, being tied to a document with an exact date, or having an exact date on the manuscript.

- Abbreviation for text families is as follows: Alexandrian Alex.; Western West.; Caesarean Caes.; Byzantine Byz.

- Independent text is abbreviated as Ind.

PAPYRI

Papyrus, Papyri: named for the Egyptian plant from which it is made, in the proper climate this is a very durable writing material that was made by bonding vertical strips of the papyrus pith to horizontal strips. Writing could easily be done on the side with the horizontal strips, and with some difficulty on the other side (called an "opisthograph" when written on both sides). The oldest manuscripts of the NT were written on papyrus; some of them are as early as the second century.

P[4]+ Luke 1–6; same as P[64]+P[67] Matt 3; 5; 26; c. 160-180 C.E. (Alex. esp. P[75])

P[45] Gospels and Acts †; c. 200 C.E. (Mark Caes.; Matt, Luke and John Alex. and West.; Acts Alex. esp. ℵ A B and C)

P[46] Rom 5-6; 8-16; 1 Cor.; 2 Cor.; Gal.; Eph.; Php; Col.; 1 Thess.; Heb.; c. 200 C.E. (Proto-Alex. esp. B in Eph., Col., and Heb.) P46 and P13 are nearly the same text. There are only seventeen disagreements out of eighty-eight variation units.

P[52] John 18:31-34, 37-38; c. 110-125 C.E. (Seems to be Alex.)

P[66] John 1:1-6:11; 6:35-14:26, 29-30; 15:2-26; 16:2-4, 6-7; 16:10-20:20, 22-23; 20:25-21:9, 12, 17; c. 150 C.E. (Alex. esp. close to P[75], B, 016) Because P[66] is an early Papyrus near complete codex of the Gospel of John, we are adding more here. Fee studied the corrections (i.e., **P**[66c]) of P[66] in John 1-9 with P[75]. He found that the corrections are in more of an agreement with P[75] than the original scribe of P[66], which means that P[66] was corrected with a manuscript akin to P[75], as far as John 1-9 goes. The agreement is increased significantly when the corrections (P[66c]) of John 10:1-15:8 are compared to P[75] and 15:9-21:22 with B (this section is missing from P[75]).

P[66c1] this corrector is designated as the original scribe by Comfort and Barrett.

P[66c2] this corrector is designated as a second scribe in the scriptorium by Comfort and Barrett.

P[66c3] this corrector is designated as a third scribe who was also the paginator by Comfort and Barrett.[1]

P[75] Luke 3:18-24:53 and John †; c. 175-200 C.E. (Alex.) The Christian scribe of P[75] was a professional. This was the kind of text that was used to make Codex Vaticanus. Porter shows that there is an 87% agreement between P[75] and B.

UNCIALS

Uncial: a term commonly used to refer to majuscule (q.v.) letters (4th to 8th centuries C.E.). It is agreed, however, that the term, taken from Latin and meaning "one-twelfth," should be applied only to a particular type of Latin script or document.

א (Sinaiticus) most of NT; c. 330–360 C.E.

א[a] designates corrections that were done by several scribes before the manuscript left the scriptorium.

---

[1] James Royse states that other than John 13:19, the corrections are all by the hand of the original scribe. (Royse 2008, pp. 409-21)

ℵ^{ca} designates a group of correctors working at Caesarea in about the sixth or seventh century C.E., who corrected the manuscript in both the Old and New Testament.

A (Alexandrinus) most of NT; c. fifth century C.E.

B (Vaticanus) most of NT; c. 300–325

B[1] designates a corrector who was contemporary with the original scribe.

B[2] designates a tenth or eleventh century corrector, who also retraced the original writing, as well as adding accents and punctuation marks.[2]

C (Ephraemi Rescriptus) most of NT with many lacunae; fifth century C.E.

D (Bezae) Gospels, Acts; fifth century C.E.

D (Claromontanus) Paul's Epistles; sixth century C.E. (different MS than Bezae)

E (Laudianus 35) Acts; sixth century C.E.

MINUSCULES

Minuscule: from a Latin word meaning "somewhat smaller," a set of small, cursive Greek letters as opposed to majuscules (q.v.). In a loose sense, minuscules are often thought of as lowercase Greek letters. They seem to have been invented in the ninth century to speed and lower the cost of book production, usually on vellum or parchment

1 Gospels, Acts, Paul's Epistles; twelfth century C.E.

20 Gospels; eleventh century C.E.

22 Gospels; twelfth century C.E.

28 Gospels; eleventh century C.E.

33 All NT except Rev; ninth century C.E.

2344 Rev; eleventh century C.E.

f[1] (a family of manuscripts including 1, 118, 131, 209) Gospels; twelfth-fourteenth century C.E.

---

[2] Bruce M. Metzger, *Manuscripts of the Greek Bible: An Introduction to Greek Palaeography*, New York, Oxford: Oxford University Press, 1991, p. 74.

f[13] (a family of manuscripts that include 13, 69, 124, 174, 230, 346, 543, 788, 826, 828, 983, 1689, 1709, known as the Ferrar group) Gospels; eleventh-fifteenth c.

Maj The **Majority Text**: a text of the NT in which variant readings are chosen that are found in the majority of all Greek NT manuscripts (cf. "Byzantine Family" above). One could consider this external (objective) evidence and maintain that it is the leading criterion for establishing the text. Credit for this text is due primarily to Zane Hodges and Arthur Farstad, though the latter once humbly told me (Wilkins) that the text was mainly Hodges' work. Hodges maintained that mathematical probabilities pointed to the text with the greatest number of surviving manuscripts as the one closest to the original. Thus, the name is an accurate description, though Hodges' theory about the text's relation to the original is arguable at best. Of greater value and importance, the Majority Text has essentially purged the Byzantine text of its negative association with the Textus Receptus. Nevertheless, most textual critics maintain that those favoring the MT rely heavily on theological arguments and thin objective evidence in their defense of the text. In particular, easier readings tend to prevail over harder in the MT and BT.

Maj[a] This siglum only occurs in Revelation and indicates a large group of manuscripts which contain a commentary on Revelation by Andreas of Caesarea.

Maj[k] This siglum also occurs only in Revelation and indicates the large group of manuscripts which do not contain Andreas's commentary.

LECTIONARIES

Lectionaries: books of NT passages chosen by the Christian church for reading at services. For the most part, they represent the Byzantine text and are of use in reconstructing the history of that text. Below are some of the lectionaries cited in the critical editions. At present, there are 2,412 lectionaries extant.

ℓ 1 Evangelistarion (uncial); tenth century C.E.

ℓ 2 Evangelistarion (uncial); tenth century C.E.

ℓ 3 Evangelistarion (uncial); eleventh century C.E.

ANCIENT VERSIONS

Syriac (syr)

syr[c] (Syriac Curetonianus) Gospels; fifth century C.E.

syr[h] (Syriac Harclean) All NT; 616 C.E.

syr[h**] This siglum denotes a reading in syr[h] that is set off by asterisks, which questions its originality.

syr^{hmg} This siglum denotes a reading from the margin of syr^h.

syr^p (Peshitta) All NT except Revelation and shorter General Epistles; fourth-fifth century C.E.

syr^{pal} (Palestinian Syriac) Gospels; fifth-sixth century C.E.

syr^s (Syriac Sinaiticus) Gospels; fourth century C.E.

Old Latin (it)

it^a (Vercellensis) Gospels; fourth century C.E.

it^{aur} (Aureus) Gospels; seventh century C.E.

it^b (Veronensis) Gospels; fifth century C.E.

it^c (Colbertinus) Gospels; twelfth century C.E.

it^d (Cantabrigiensis, the Latin text of Bezae) Gospels, Acts, 3 John; fifth century C.E.

it^e (Palatinus) Gospels; fifth century C.E.

it^f (Brixianus) Gospels; sixth century C.E.

it^{ff2} (Corbeiensis II) Gospels; fifth century C.E.

it^{g1} (Sangermanensis) Matthew; eighth-ninth century C.E.

it^{gig} (Gigas) Gospels; Acts; thirteenth century C.E.

it^h (Fleury palimpsest) Matt 3–14; 18–28; Acts; Revelation; Peter's Epistles; 1 John; fifth century C.E.

itⁱ (Vindobonensis) Mark 2–15; Luke 10–23; fifth century C.E.

it^k (Bobbiensis) Matthew, Mark; c. 400 C.E.

it^l (Rehdigeranus) Gospels; Acts 8-11; 15; James; 1 Peter; John's Epistles; eighth century C.E.

it^q (Monacensis) Gospels; sixth-seventh century C.E.

it^r (Usserianus) Gospels, Paul's Epistles, Peter's Epistles, 1 John; seventh century C.E.

it^w (Wernigerodensis) Acts; 14th–15th c.; Peter's Epistles; 1 John; sixth century C.E.

Vulgate

The following sigla represent the major editions of the Vulgate.

vg^{cl} (Clementine) *Biblia Sacra Vulgatae Editionis Sixti Quinti Pont. Max. iussu recognita atque edita*; 1592

vgst (Stuttgart) *Biblia sacra iuxta Vulgatam versionem*; 1969

vg^{ww} (Wordsworth and White) *Novum Testamentum Domini nostri Iesu Christi latine secundum editionem Sancti Hieronymi*; 1889–1954

lat Indicates a reading supported by the Vulgate and some of the Old Latin MSS.

Coptic

The Coptic translations of the New Testament date from the 3rd century onward.

cop^{ach} (Akhmimic) John; James; fourth century C.E.

cop^{ach2} (Subakhmimic) John; fourth century C.E.

cop^{bo} (Bohairic = north Egypt) All NT; ninth century C.E.

cop^{fay} (Fayyumic = central Egypt) John; fourth-fifth century C.E.

cop^{G67} (a Middle Egyptian ms) Acts; fifth century C.E.

cop^{mae} (Middle Egyptian) Matthew; fourth-fifth century C.E.

cop^{sa} (Sahidic = southern Egypt) All NT; fourth-fifth century C.E.

Armenian

arm All NT; twelfth century C.E.

Ethiopic

eth All NT; fourteenth century C.E.

Georgian

geo All NT; eleventh century C.E.

Slavonic

slav All NT; tenth- twelfth century C.E.

Ancient Authors

The following abbreviations are used for ancient works.

1 Apol. Justin Martyr, *First Apology*

1 Clem. *1 Clement*

Ann. Tacitus, *Annals*

Ant. Josephus, *Jewish Antiquities*

b. Ber. Babylonian tractate *Berakot*

Bacch. Euripides, *Bacchanals*

Cels. Origen, *Against Celsus*

Claud. Suetonius, *Claudius*

Comm. Jo. Origen, *Commentary on John*

Comm. Matt. Origen, *Commentary on Matthew*

Comm. Rom. Origen, *Commentary on Romans*

Cons. Augustine, *De consensus evangelistarum*(Harmony of the Gospels)

Dial. Justin Martyr, *Dialogue with Trypho*

Dial. Pseudo-Athanasius, *Dialogue with Zaccheus*

Did. *Didache*

Epist. Jerome, *Epistulae*

Fel. Augustine, *Against Felix*

Geogr. Ptolemy, *Geography*

Gos. Pet. Gospel of Peter

Haer. Irenaeus, *Against Heresies*

Hist. eccl. Eusebius, *Ecclesiastical History*

J.W. Josephus, *Jewish War*

Life Josephus, *The Life*

LXX Septuagint

Marc. Tertullian, *Against Marcion*

Onom. Eusebius, *Onomasticon*

Or.Bas. Gregory of Nazianzus, *Oratio in laudem Basilii*

Pan. Epiphanius, *Panarion (Refutation of all Heresies)*

Phaen. Aratus, *Phaenomena*

Prom. Aeschylus, *Prometheus Bound*

Pyth. Pindar, *Pythian Odes*

Quaest. Mar. Eusebius, *Quaestiones ad Marinum*

Tg. Ps.-J. Targum Pseudo-Jonathan

PREFACE

THE READING CULTURE OF EARLY CHRISTIANITY provides the reader with the production process of the New Testament books, the publication process, how they were circulated, and to what extent they were used in the early Christian church. It examines the making of the New Testament books, the New Testament secretaries and the material they used, how the early Christians viewed the New Testament books, and the literacy level of the Christians in the first three centuries. It also explores how the gospels went from an oral message to a written record, the accusation that the apostles were uneducated, the inspiration and inerrancy in the writing process of the New Testament books, the trustworthiness of the early Christian copyists, and the claim that the early scribes were predominantly amateurs. Andrews also looks into the early Christian's use of the codex [book form], how did the spread of early Christianity affect the text of the New Testament, and how was the text impacted by the Roman Empire's persecution of the early Christians?

INTRODUCTION The Making of New Testament Books

As Luke, Paul, Peter, Matthew, James, or Jude handed their authorized text off to be copied by others, i.e., published, what would it have looked like? What is the process that the New Testament writers would have followed to get their book ready to be published, that is, copied by others? Once they were prepared for publication, how would they be copied throughout the centuries, up until the time of the printing press of 1455 C.E.?[3] As we open our Bible to the Gospel of Matthew, or the letter to the Romans, or any of the 27 books of the New Testament, how can we have confidence that what we are reading is a reflection of the original in our language? If we were to bring home from a bookstore a copy of the CSB, ESV, GNB, NLT, MSG, NASB, UASV or any of the other one hundred and fifty plus English translations, could we have confidence that what we are reading is, in fact, the Word of God? Some translations have footnotes throughout that say, "Other ancient MSS[4] read .... What exactly does that mean, and which is the Word of God: the words in the main text of our Bible, or the others below in the footnote?

The science and art of textual criticism has answered these questions, and more. It is a science because there are rules and principles, as well as a method or process that is to be followed if the textual scholar is to get back to the original reading.[5] It is an art because the human agent needs to be balanced with his use of those rules and principles. It is like driving a car. The driver needs to follow all driving rules as he stays between the lines of his side of the road to reach his destination. So too, the textual scholar needs to stay within the rules to reach his destination. However, the designers of the roads were not rigid to the point of making those two lines so narrow that there was no room for the driver to miss obstructions, which might be in his path. This extra room would help the driver to avoid objects that could result in a crash. The same holds true for the textual scholar

---

[3] B.C.E. means "before the Common Era," which is more accurate than B.C. ("before Christ"). C.E. denotes "Common Era," often called A.D., for *anno Domini*, meaning "in the year of our Lord."

[4] Manuscripts, MS would be singular manuscript

[5] When we use the term "original" reading or "original" text in this publication, it is a reference to the exemplar manuscript by the New Testament author (e.g. Paul) and his secretary, if he used one (e.g. Tertius), from which other copies was made for publication and distribution to the Christian communities.

having room within the lines of his field, to prevent a wreck, causing him not to be able to reach his desired destination, i.e., the original reading.

From ancient times until 1455 C.E., anything that was penned was done so literally, by hand. A "manuscript" is a handwritten text. It did not matter if it was a poem, letter, receipt, book, or a marriage certificate; it would still have been produced and copied by hand. In addition, it would mostly have been done one copy at a time in the early decades of Christianity. In the second century C.E., it may have been copied in a scriptorium, i.e., a room in a monastery for storing, copying, illustrating, or reading manuscripts. In the scriptorium, there would have a lector who would have read aloud slowly as multiple scribes or copyists took down what he was saying.

Dead Sea Scroll of Isaiah

The Scroll or Roll Book

A scroll is a roll of papyrus, parchment, or other material, used for a written document. The scroll was generally divided up into pages, even though it was continuous, by gluing separate sheets at the edges. Usually, the reader or lector, as well as the writer unrolled, the scroll one page at a time, leaving it rolled up on both sides of the current page that was showing. The scroll is unrolled from side to side, with the text being written or read, from lines of text, from the top to the bottom of the pages. If it were Hebrew for example, it would be written from right to left, and one would open that scroll by rolling to the right. On the other hand, if it were Greek, it would be written from left to right, or even an alternating direction with other languages. Boustrophedon is an ancient method of inscribing and writing in which lines are written alternately from right to left and from left to right. Usually, professional scribes would justify the pages on both sides, with both left and right margins aligned. On the papyrus scroll, Harold Greenlee writes,

> Papyrus scrolls are mentioned several times in the New Testament; references are usually translated as "book." Luke 4: 17 speaks of the scroll (*biblion*) of the prophet Isaiah. John uses the same word to refer to his gospel in John 20:30. The "books" or "scrolls" mentioned in 2 Tim 4:13 may be either parchment scrolls or leather scrolls of the Old Testament. Rev 6:14 describes the sky as vanishing like "a scroll when it is rolled up."[6]

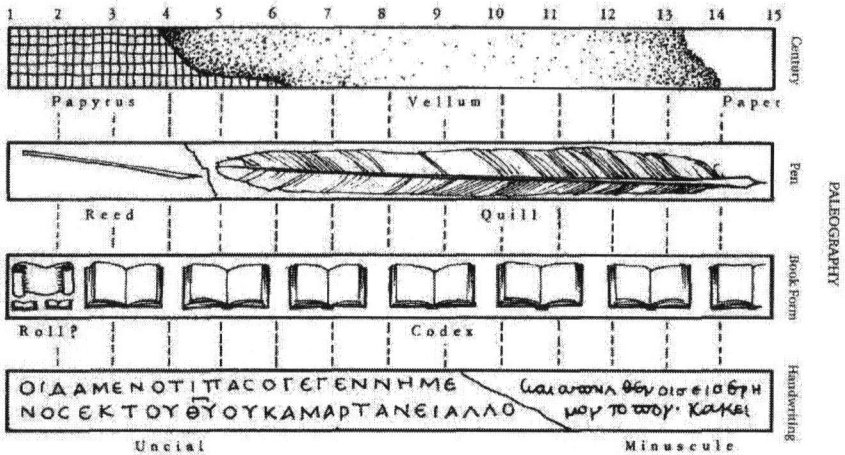

Harold Greenlee, Introduction to New Testament Textual Criticism, (p. 23)

The scroll was the first form to receive writing which was in a format that could be edited by the author or scribe and was used in the Eastern Mediterranean ancient Egyptian civilizations. The parchment scroll that was used by Moses to pen the first five books of the Old Testament, which goes back to about the late sixteenth-century B.C.E. The codex (bound book) got its start by Latin authors in the first-century C.E. (widely used in the second-century), some 1,500 years after the scroll. The early Christians popularized the codex in the second-century C.E. Some would even argue that it was the Christians who invented the codex. However, it appears that Christians mainly used the roll, or scroll, at least until about the end of the first century C.E. However, from the close of the first to the third century C.E., there was a struggle between those who encouraged the use of the codex and those preferring scrolls. Traditionalists, familiar and comfortable with using the scroll, were unwilling to give up deep-rooted conventions

---

[6] Greenlee, J. Harold (2008-06-01). *Text of the New Testament, The: From Manuscript to Modern Edition* (pp. 13-14). Baker Publishing Group. Kindle Edition.

20

and traditions. Nevertheless, the popularization of the codex played a significant role in the displacement of the scroll. Nevertheless, the scroll continued to be used for centuries.

Scrolls were used for literary works: continuous rolls twenty or thirty feet long, and nine to ten inches high. (Psa. 40:7) The text was written in columns, which formed the pages. (Jer. 36:23) Our English word "volume" literally means *something rolled up*. Imagine being in the synagogue of Nazareth, when Jesus was handed the scroll of the prophet Isaiah, where he skillfully unrolled with one hand while simultaneously rolling it up with the other hand until he reached the place he wanted to read. (Lu 4:16-17; Isa. 61:1-2) The ink that was used on the surface of the scrolls had to withstand being rolled and unrolled. Therefore, special ink was developed. In addition, the Jews would discard any scroll that had too many letters missing from wear and tear. It was not until about the fifth-century C.E. that the codex finally outnumbered the scroll by a ten to one margin in Egypt. When we consider the surviving examples, we also see that the scroll had almost vanished by the sixth-century C.E.

The Codex Book

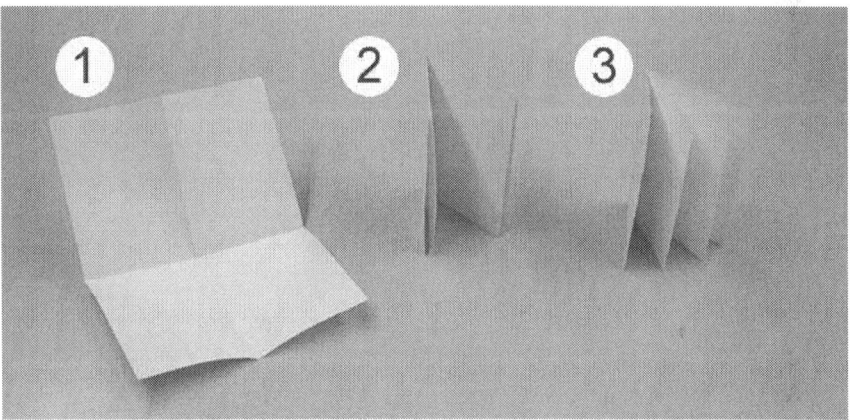

A typical four-leaf quire can be formed from a single sheet of papyrus, parchment, or paper by folding and then cutting the sheet

A codex is a collection of ancient manuscript texts, especially of the Biblical Scriptures, in book form.[7] It is made up of sheets of papyrus or parchment inscribed with handwritten material, which is created by folding a single sheet of standard-sized pages, giving the scribe two leaves or four pages.

---

[7] [Late 16th century: < Latin, "block of wood, book, set of statutes"]

The first codices were made with waxed-coated wooden tablets. The people of Greece and Rome used waxed tablets before the Christian era. Schoolboys were sometimes given waxed tablets on which the teacher had written letters in model script with a stylus. Today, we have the blackboard (UK) or chalkboard (US), which was originally made of smooth, thin sheets of black or dark gray slate stone. In the early part of the 20th century, schoolchildren even had smaller slate tablets. They had a reusable writing surface on which text or drawings could be made with sticks of calcium carbonate, i.e., chalk.

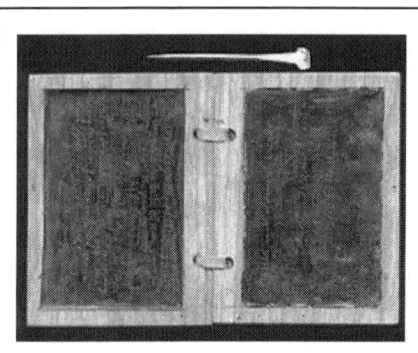

Roman wax tablet and stylus

To make the waxed tablets of Jesus' day, one would slightly hollow out a flat piece of wood and fill that void with wax. These tablets were also used for temporary writing like modern chalkboards. They were also commonly used for corresponding with others. Greenlee writes, "They were also used at times for legal documents, in which case two tablets would be placed face to face with the writing inside and fastened together with leather thongs run through holes at the edges of the tablets. In one of his writings St. Augustine mentions some tablets he owned, although his were made of ivory instead of wood."[8] An example of temporary writing is found in the Gospel of Luke. Zechariah, the father of John the Baptist, who had temporarily lost the ability to speak, was asked what name he wanted his son to have. Luke 1:63 (NASB) reports, "And he asked for a tablet and wrote as follows, 'His name is John.'"

Polyptychs [pol·yp·tych ˈpälipˌtik] is an arrangement of three or more panels with a painting or carving on each, usually hinged together. Some were discovered at Herculaneum, an ancient Roman town near modern Naples that was destroyed along with Pompeii by the eruption of Mount Vesuvius in 79 C.E.

In time, sheets of foldable material replaced rigid tablets. The codex has been viewed as the most significant advancement in the development of the book, aside from the printing press.[9] Some of the earliest surviving codices were made of papyrus, being preserved in the dry sands of Egypt.

---

[8] (Greenlee, Introduction to New Testament Textual Criticism 1995, pp. 8-9)

[9] Colin H. Roberts; T. C. Skeat, (1983), *The Birth of the Codex*, London: Oxford University Press, p. 1.

When we consider the thought of unrolling and using a scroll as opposed to the codex, we can likely think of many advantages of one over the other. The codex can contain far more written material; it is much easier to carry and more convenient. Some in the early days of the codex even mentioned these advantages but were slow to move away from the long use of the scroll. Again, the Christians played a major part in the eventual death of the scroll. Their evangelism would have been far more cumbersome without the codex.

The Codex Gigas, 13th century, Bohemia.

In comparison to the scroll, the codex was also far more affordable, because both sides of the pages could be written on, getting more value for one's money. Moreover, instead of having one book with each scroll, one could have the whole of the old or New Testament. The fact that one could find Bible passages far easier and faster added to the codex's success. This was true for Christians, but also lawyers and the like. When we think of the early Christians, we are reminded that they evangelized to the point of going from 120 disciples in the upper room, to more than one million Christians spread throughout the Roman Empire at the beginning of the second century C.E. In addition, early Christians were evangelists, who used pre-evangelism, i.e., apologetics. They could have what we now call proof texts, easily located, to make their arguments to pagans and Jews alike. Then, the fact that the codex book had a wooden cover, making it more durable than the scroll, added to its advantages. Codices were useful,

23

sensible, and likely practical for personal reading. The Christians of the third century C.E. had parchment pocket Gospels.

Larry Hurtado, in his blog (*The Codex and Early Christians: Clarification & Corrections*), writes,

> Bagnall offered figures (pp. 72-74) comparing the number of non-Christian and Christian codices from Egypt datable to the early centuries, also giving the percentages of Christian codices of the total. His own data show, e.g., that Christian codices amount to somewhere between 22-34% of the total for the 2nd-3rd centuries CE. Yet Christian books overall amount to only ca. 2% of the total number of books (codices and rolls) of these centuries. Of course, there are more non-Christian codices, but the first point to note is that Christian codices comprise a vastly disproportionate percentage of the total number of codices in this period.
>
> The very data provided by Bagnall clearly show that Christians invested in the codex far more than is reflected in the larger book-culture of the time. That is, the early Christian *preference* for the codex is undeniable, and this preference is quite distinctive in that period. Bagnall actually reached the same judgment, stating, "Christian books in these centuries (2nd/3rd) are far more likely to be codices than rolls, quite the reverse of what we find with classical literature." (p. 74)
>
> My second point also stands, and is supported by Bagnall: the early Christian preference for the codex seems to have been especially keen when it came to making copies of texts used as scripture (i.e. read in corporate worship). For example, 95+% of Christian copies of OT writings are in codex form. As for the writings that came to form the NT, they're all in codex form except for a very few instances of NT writings copied on the back of a re-used roll (which were likely informal and personal copies made by/for readers who couldn't afford a copy on unused writing material). Here again, Bagnall grants the same conclusion, judging that, although they were ready to copy "the Christians adopted the codex as the normative format of deliberately produced public copies of scriptural texts" (p. 78), but were ready to use rolls for other texts (76).

The Making of a Codex

The process of making a codex began with a dried and treated sheepskin, goatskin, or another animal hide. "The pelts were first soaked in

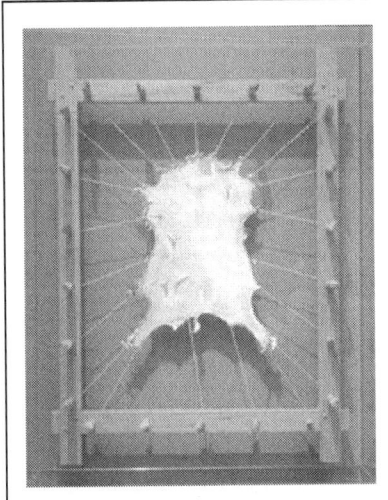

Skin of a stillborn goat on a stretcher (modern) – The J. Paul Getty Museum

a lime solution to loosen the fur, which was then removed. While wet on a stretcher, the skin was scraped using a knife with a curved blade. As the skin dried, the parchment maker would adjust the tension so that the skin remained taut. This cycle of scraping and stretching was repeated over several days until the desired thinness had been achieved. Here, the skin of a stillborn goat, prized for its smoothness, is stretched on a modern frame to illustrate the parchment making process."[10] The first step for preparing the pages to receive writing was to set up the quires, i.e. a bundle of sheets of parchment folded together for binding into a book, especially a four-sheet bundle, folded once to make eight leaves or sixteen pages. Raymond Clemens and Timothy Graham point out that "the quire was the scribe's basic writing unit throughout the Middle Ages."[11]

The Craft of the Scribe

The *recto* is the front side of a sheet of papyrus or parchment while the *verso* is the back of a page. If the scribe were writing on a sheet of papyrus, he would write his script on the horizontal lines of the fibers on the recto side of his sheet. If the scribe were using a sheet of parchment, the manuscript had pinpricks placed in it, so that it could be ruled with lines, to accommodate writing better. In some of the manuscripts, we can still see faintly visible lines. It was similar to modern-day tablet paper, with horizontal lines running across the page to receive text, and vertical lines, which served to mark the boundaries, to have justification on both sides. The scribal schools had different techniques for ruling manuscripts, and sometimes a textual scholar can identify the school of a particular manuscript, based on how it was ruled, giving us the place of its origin. The hair side of the parchment was darker than that of the flesh side, so scribes

---

[10] "*The Making of a Medieval Book*" The J. Paul Getty Trust. Retrieved Monday September 15, 2014.

http://www.getty.edu/art/exhibitions/making/

[11] Raymond Clemens, Timothy Graham. *Introduction to Manuscript Studies*. Ithaca: Cornell University Press, 2008, 14.

placed the quires so that the hair side faced the hair side of the corresponding page, making it more reader-friendly.

Study of Ancient Handwriting

The study of ancient handwriting and manuscripts is an essential skill for paleographers, but also for the textual scholar as well. The style of the characters that make up an alphabet change every fifty years or so; thus, it is essential to know the eras of different styles. Moreover, scribes use abbreviations and contractions for various reasons. Therefore, the student of ancient handwriting must know how to interpret them. For example, various contractions and abbreviations are found in our earliest manuscripts of the Christian Greek New Testament.[12]

The abbreviations that are most relevant to this discussion are what have become known as the sacred names, or nomina sacra (nomen sacrum, singular), such as Lord ($\overline{KC}$),[13] Jesus ($\overline{IH}$, $\overline{IHC}$), Christ ($\overline{XP}$, $\overline{XC}$, $\overline{XPC}$), God ($\overline{\Theta C}$), and Spirit ($\overline{\Pi NA}$). These sacred names are abbreviated or contracted by keeping the first letter or two and the last letter. Another important feature is the horizontal bar placed over these letters to help readers recognize that they are encountering a contraction. The early Christian writers had three different ways that they would pen a sacred name: (1) suspension, (2) contraction, and (3) longer contraction. The suspension was accomplished by writing only the first two letters of "Jesus," for example (ιησους = ιη), and suspending the remaining letters (σους). The contraction was accomplished by writing only the first and last letter of Jesus (ιησους = ις) and removing the remaining letters (ησου).

The longer contraction would simply keep the first two letters instead of just one, as well as the last letter (ιης). After penning the suspension or contraction, the scribe would place a bar over the $\overline{name}$. This practice of placing a bar over the name was likely carried over from the common practice of scribes placing bars above contractions, especially numbers, which were represented by letters, e.g. $\overline{IA}$ = eleven.

---

[12] It should be noted that the early manuscripts were written in what we consider all uppercase letters, known as majuscule, the large rounded letters used in ancient manuscripts. Moreover, there were no breaks between the letters, so a phrase like GODISNOWHERE could be divided as GOD IS NO WHERE or GOD IS NOW HERE.

[13] In the fourth and third centuries B.C.E., the sigma form of Σ was simplified into a C-like shape in koinē Greek.

When students of ancient handwriting have knowledge of these individual letterforms, ligatures,[14] punctuation, and abbreviations, it enables them to read and understand the text. Of course, textual scholars must know the language of the manuscripts they are studying—in our case, Greek. They need to be an expert in the forms of the language, the various styles of handwriting, writing customs, and able to identify different hands within the same manuscript, and scribal notes and abbreviations. They also need to study the development of the language over the years and its history, to better analyze the texts. As we have discussed, students of ancient handwriting must have knowledge of the writing materials as well, which will enable them better to identify the period in which a document was copied.[15] One of the primary goals of paleographers is to ascertain the date of the text and its place of origin. For these reasons alone, they must consider the style and formation of a manuscript, as well as the style of handwriting used therein.

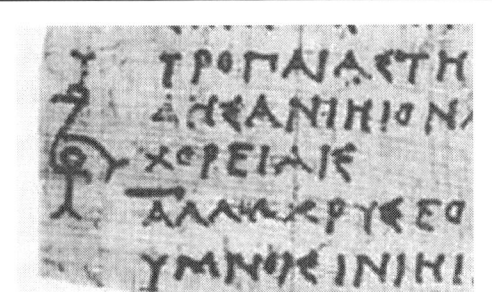

Detail of the Berlin Papyrus 9875 showing the 5th column of Timotheus' Persae, with a coronis symbol, to mark the end.

We have, for example, what is known as the **Ptolemaic Book Hand**, and how it developed is difficult to say because we have so few examples, which are not datable. It is not until we reach the third century B.C.E. that we can have confidence. The hands of this period are stiff, awkward, and sharply defined (e.g., **E, Σ,** and **Ω**). Moreover, the letters evidenced no consistency in size. At times, there was a fineness, and pleasing subtlety attained. When we arrive at the second century B.C.E., we find the letters becoming more rounded, as well as more uniform in size. However, one can detect a loss of unity in the first century. On this, Comfort writes, "Paleographers date the emergence of the Roman Uncial as coming on the heels of the Ptolemaic period, which ended in 30 BC. Thus, early Roman Uncial begins around 30 BC, and the Roman Uncial hand can be seen throughout the first two to three centuries of the Christian era. The Roman Uncial script, generally speaking, shares the

---

[14] A ligature is a character that consists of two or more letters joined together, e.g. "æ". We do not normally find ligatures in majuscule manuscripts. In the minuscule manuscripts, it can be difficult to determine a ligature due to the fact it is a manuscript with a running hand.

[15] Robert P. Gwinn, "Paleography" in the Encyclopaedia Britannica, Micropædia, Vol. IX, 1986, p. 78.

characteristics of literary manuscripts in the Roman period (as distinct from the Ptolemaic period) in that these manuscripts show a greater roundness and smoothness in the forms of letters and are somewhat larger than what was penned in the Ptolemaic period. Furthermore, the Roman Uncial typically displays decorative serifs in several letters, but not all. (By contrast, the Decorated Rounded style aims at making the decorations rounded and replete.)"[16]

Majuscule Hand

During the Byzantine period (300-650 C.E.), the dominant type of book-hand became known as the biblical hand. It had its earliest beginnings toward the end of the second-century C.E., being used by all, not necessarily having any connection to Christian literature. In addition, manuscripts from Egypt, of vellum or papyrus dating to around the fourth century C.E., contained other forms of script, i.e., a sloping rather unpolished hand resulting from the literary hand, which continued until about the fifth century C.E. The three early great codices, Vaticanus and Sinaiticus of the fourth century C.E. and Alexandrinus of the fifth century C.E., were penned in majuscules of the biblical hand. The hand that produced Vaticanus is the least demonstrated, as the letters are characteristic of the biblical hand but do not possess the heavy look of the later manuscripts, with a greater roundness to them. Sinaiticus, which was copied shortly after that, has larger, heavier letters. In Alexandrinus, we notice a development in the form, a definite distinction between thick and thin strokes.

Vaticanus, From Page Matthew 1:22-2:18

[16] Philip Comfort, *Encountering the Manuscripts: An Introduction to New Testament Paleography & Textual Criticism* (Nashville, TN: Broadman & Holman, 2005), 110.

Sinaiticus, From Page Matthew 2:5-3:7

Codex Alexandrinus of the fifth century, The Center for the Study of New Testament Manuscripts

Once we enter the sixth century C.E., we notice in the manuscripts, vellum or papyrus, that the heavier hand became the standard, but still possessed an attractive appearance. However, in the centuries to come there was a steady decline, as the writing appears to be done artificially, i.e., as a matter of duty or custom, without thought, attention. The thick strokes became heavier; the cross strokes of T and Θ and the bottom of Δ were equipped with sagging spurs. This era of an unpleasant hand followed in sequence, morphing from sloping to upright.

Publishing Industry of the Ancient World

Most people today would not imagine the ancient world's having a large publishing industry, yet this was the case. The ancient writings of famous authors were great pieces of literature that were highly sought after from the moment they were penned, much as today. Thus, there was a need for the scriptorium[17] to fill orders for both pagan and civil literature, as well as the Bible books. There was a need for hundreds of copies, and as Christianity displaced paganism, the demand would grow exponentially.

The **Autograph** ("self-written") was the text written by a New Testament author or the author and scribe as the author dictated to him. If the scribe was taking down dictation (Rom. 16:22; 1 Pet. 5:12), he might have done so in shorthand.[18] Whether by shorthand or longhand, we can

---

[17] A scriptorium was a room for storing, copying, illustrating, or reading manuscripts.

[18] "The usual procedure for a dictated epistle was for the amanuensis (secretary) to take down the speaker's words (often in shorthand) and then produce a transcript, which the

29

assume that both the scribe and the author would check the scribe's work. The author would have authority over all corrections since the Holy Spirit did not inspire the scribe. If the inspired author wrote everything down himself as the Spirit moved him, the finished product would be the autograph. This text is also often referred to as the **Original**. Hence, the terms *autograph* and *original* are often used interchangeably. Sometimes textual critics prefer to make a distinction, using "original" as a general reference to the text that is correctly attributed to a biblical author. This designation does not focus on the process of how a book or letter was written.

The *original* can also be referred to as the first **Authorized Text (Archetypal Manuscript)**, i.e., the text first used to make other copies. We should also point out that some textual critics debate whether the original or autograph of any given book was actually the first text used to make copies, and they prefer to call the latter the **Initial Text** instead, not requiring that it actually be the autograph. Conservative critics would maintain that they are the same. Neither term should be confused with what is known as an ordinary **Exemplar**, any authorized text of the book from which other copies were made. The original text necessarily was the very first exemplar used to make copies, but after that additional copies of high quality were used as exemplars. We will frequently use this term to refer to any copy that a scribe employed as his text for making another copy. Usually, a scribe would have a main or primary exemplar from which he makes most of his copies and one or more secondary exemplars with which to compare what he found in his main exemplar. Scribes sometimes substituted text from other exemplars for what they found in their main exemplars.

We have mentioned the **Scriptorium**, a room where multiple scribes or even one scribe worked to produce the manuscript(s). A lector would read aloud from the exemplar, and the scribe(s) would write down his words. The **Corrector** was one who checked the manuscripts for needed corrections. Corrections could be by three primary persons: **(1)** the copyist himself, **(2)** the official corrector of the scriptorium, or **(3)** a person who had purchased the copy. When textual scholars speak of the **Hand**, this primarily refers to a person who is making the copy, distinguishing his level of training. Paleographers have set out four basic levels of handwriting. First, there was the *common hand* of a person who was untrained in making copies. Second, there was the *documentary hand* of an

author could then review, edit, and sign in his own handwriting. Two New Testament epistles provide the name of the amanuensis: Tertius for (Romans 16:22) and Silvanus (another name for Silas) for 1 Peter 5:12." Philip Comfort, *Encountering the Manuscripts: An Introduction to New Testament Paleography & Textual Criticism* (Nashville, TN: Broadman & Holman, 2005), 06.

individual who was trained in preparing documents. The third level was the *reformed documentary* hand of a copyist who was experienced in the preparation of documents and copying literature; and fourth was the *professional hand*, the scribe experienced in producing literature.[19]

We must keep in mind that we are dealing with an oral society. Therefore, the apostles, who had spent three and a half years with Jesus, first published the Good News orally. The teachers within the newly founded Christian congregations would repeat this information until it was memorized. After that, those who had heard this gospel would, in turn, share it with others (Acts 2:42, Gal 6:6). In time, they would see the need for a written record, so Matthew, Mark, Luke, and John would pen the Gospels, and other types of New Testament books would be written by Paul, James, Peter, and Jude. We can see from the first four verses of Luke that Theophilus[20] was being given a written record of what he had already been taught orally. In verse 4, Luke says to Theophilus, "[My purpose is] that you may know the exact truth about the things you have been taught."

The appearance of the written record did not mean the end of the oral publication. Both oral and written would be used together. Many did not read the written documents themselves, as they would hear them read in the congregational meetings by the lector. This would apply to those that could read as well because they may not have been able to afford to have copies made for themselves. Paul and his letters came to be used in the same way as he traveled extensively but was just one man and could only be in one place at a time. It was not long before he took advantage of the fact that he could be in one place and dispatch letters to other locations through his traveling companions. These traveling companions would not only deliver the letters but would know the issues well enough to address questions that might be asked by the leaders of the congregation to which they had been dispatched. In summary, the first century saw the life and ministry of Jesus Christ, the Son of God, as well as his death, resurrection, and ascension. After that, his disciples spread this gospel orally for at least 15 years before Matthew penned his gospel. The written was used in conjunction with the oral message.

---

[19] Philip Comfort, *Encountering the Manuscripts: An Introduction to New Testament Paleography & Textual Criticism* (Nashville, TN: Broadman & Holman, 2005), 17-20.

[20] Theophilus means "friend of God," was the person to whom the books of Luke and Acts were written (Lu 1:3; Ac 1:1). Theophilus was called "most excellent," which may suggest some position of high rank. On the other hand, it simply may be Luke offering an expression of respect. Theophilus had initially been orally taught about Jesus Christ and his ministry. Thereafter, it seems that the book of Acts, also by Luke, confirms that he did become a Christian. The Gospel of Luke was partially written to offer Theophilus assurances of the certainty of what he had already learned by word of mouth.

In the first-century C.E., the Bible books were being copied individually. In the late first century or the beginning of the second century, they began to be copied in groups. At first, it was the four gospels and then the book of Acts with the four gospels, as well as a collection of the Apostle Paul's writings. Each of the individual books of the New Testament were penned, edited, and published between 44 and 98 C.E. A group of the apostle Paul's letters and the gospels were copied and published between 90 to 125 C.E. The entire 27 books of the New Testament were not published as a whole until about 290 to 340 C.E.

Thus, we have the 27 books of the New Testament that were penned individually in the second half of the first century. Each of these would have been copied and recopied throughout the first century. Copies of these copies would, of course, be made as well. Some of the earliest manuscripts that we now have indicate that a professional scribe copied them. Many of the other papyri provide evidence that a semi-professional hand copied them, while most of these early papyri give evidence of being made by a copyist who was literate and experienced at making documents. Therefore, either literate or semi-professional copyists produced the vast majority of our early papyri, with some being made by professionals.

Sadly, we do not have the autographs. Even if we did, we would have no way to authenticate them. We do however have copies of New Testament manuscripts that go back to the second and third centuries C.E. Over the centuries this copying of copies continued. The authors were inspired so that the originals were error-free. However, this is not the case with those who made copies; they were not under the influence of the Holy Spirit while making their copies. Therefore, these copies must have contained unintentional mistakes, as well as intentional changes, differing from the originals and each other. However, this is not as disconcerting as it may first appear. By far, most of the copyist errors are trivial, such as differences in spelling, word order and such. Moreover, they are easily analyzed and corrected, so that we know what the original contained. It is true that other copyist errors, a very small portion, are noteworthy, arising from the copyist's desire to correct something in the text that he perceived as erroneous or problematic. However, these changes have little to no effect on doctrines because other passages addressing the same beliefs provide the means to analyze and correct the copyist's "corrections."

In the language of textual criticism, changes to the original text introduced by copyists are called "variant readings." A variant reading is a different reading in the extant [existing] manuscripts for any given portion of the text. The process of textual criticism is an examination of variant readings in various ancient manuscripts to reconstruct the original wording of a written text. These variants in our copies of the New Testament manuscripts are largely the reason for the rise of the science of textual criticism in the 16th century. After that, we have had hundreds of scholars working very hard over the following five centuries to restore the New Testament text to its original state. Keep in mind that textual criticism is not just performed on the Old and New Testament texts, but in all other ancient literature as well: Plato (428/427–348/347 B.C.E.), Herodotus (c. 484–c. 425 B.C.E.), Homer (Ninth or Eighth Century B.C.E.), Livy (64or 59 B.C.E.–17 C.E.), Cicero (106–43 B.C.E.), and Virgil (70–19 B.C.E.). However, as the Bible is the greatest work of all time, which has directly influenced the lives of countless Christians, it is the most crucial field.

It is here that we should also expound a little more on the "criticism" portion of the term textual criticism. It may be helpful if for a moment we address biblical criticism in general, which is divided into two branches: lower criticism and higher criticism. Lower criticism, also known as textual criticism, is an investigation of manuscripts by those who are known as textual scholars, seeking to establish the original reading, which is only available in the thousands of extant copies. Higher criticism, also known as literary criticism, is the investigation of the restored text to identify any sources that may lie behind it. Therefore, we can say the following:

Lower criticism (i.e., textual criticism), has been the bedrock of scholarship over the last 500 years. It has given us a master text, i.e., a critical text, which is a reflection of the original published Greek New Testament. It has done nothing but contribute to the furtherance of Bible scholarship, removing interpolations, correcting scribal errors, and giving us a restored text, allowing us to produce better translations of the New Testament.

In contrast, **higher criticism** (i.e., literary criticism) has attempted to provide rationalized explanations for the composition of Bible books, ignoring the supernatural element and very often eliminating the traditional authorship of the books. Late dating of the composition of Bible books is widespread, and the historicity of biblical accounts is called into question. It would not be an overstatement to say that the effect has often been to challenge and undermine the Christian's confidence in the New Testament. Fortunately, some conservative scholars[21] have rightly criticized higher critics for their illogical or unreasonable approaches in dissecting God's Word.

Importance of Textual Criticism

Christian Bible students need to be familiar with Old and New Testament textual criticism as two of the most essential foundational studies. Why? If we fail to establish what was originally penned with

---

[21] Such Bible scholars as Robert L. Thomas, Norman L. Geisler, Gleason L. Archer, F. David Farnell, and the late Gleason L. Archer Jr. among many others have fought for decades to educate readers about the dangers of higher criticism.

reasonable certainty, how are we to do a translation, or even to interpret what we think is the actual Word of God? We are fortunate in that there are far more existing New Testament manuscripts today than any other book from ancient history. This gives New Testament textual scholars vastly more to work with in establishing the original words of the text. Some ancient Greek and Latin classics are based on one existing manuscript, while with others there are just a handful and a few exceptions that have a few hundred available. However, for the New Testament over 5,838 Greek manuscripts have been cataloged,[22] 10,000 Latin manuscripts, and an additional 9,300 other manuscripts in such languages as Syriac, Slavic, Gothic, Ethiopic, Coptic, and Armenian.

The other difference between the New Testament manuscripts and those of the classics is that the existing copies of the New Testament date much closer to the originals. In the case of the Greek classics, some of the manuscripts are dated about a thousand years after the author had penned the book. Some of the Latin classics are dated from three to seven hundred years after the time the author wrote the book. When we look at the Greek copies of the New Testament books, some portions are within decades of the original author's book. Sixty-two Greek papyri, along with five majuscules[23] date from 110 C.E. to 300 C.E.

Distribution of Greek New Testament Manuscripts

- The **Papyrus** is a copy of a portion of the New Testament made on papyrus. At present, we have 127-cataloged New Testament papyri, many dating between 110-350 C.E., but some as late as the 6th century C.E.

- The **Majuscule** or **Uncial** is a script of large letters commonly used in Greek and Latin manuscripts written between the 3rd and 9th centuries C.E. that resembles a modern capital letter but is more rounded.

- The **Minuscule** is a small cursive style of writing used in manuscripts from the 9th to the 16th centuries.

- The **Lectionary** is a schedule of readings from the Bible for Christian church services during the year, in both majuscules and minuscules, dating from the 4th to the 16th centuries C.E.

We should clarify that of the approximate 24,000 total manuscripts of the New Testament, not all are complete books. There are fragmented

---

[22] As of January 2016

[23] Large lettering, often called "capital" or uncial, in which all the letters are usually the same height.

manuscripts which have just a few verses; but there are manuscripts that contain an entire book, others that contain numerous books, and some that have the entire New Testament, or nearly so. This is to be expected since the oldest manuscripts we have were copied in an era when copying the whole New Testament was not the norm, but rather a single book or a group of books (i.e., Paul's letters). This still does not negate the vast riches of manuscripts that we possess.

What can we conclude from this short introduction to textual criticism? There is some irony here, in that secular scholars have no problem accepting the wording of classic authors, with their minuscule amount of evidence. However, they discount the treasure trove of evidence that is available to the New Testament textual scholar. Still, this should not surprise us as the New Testament has always been under-appreciated and attacked in some way, shape, or form over the past 2,000 years.

On the contrary, in comparison to classical works, we are overwhelmed by the quantity and quality of existing New Testament manuscripts. We should also keep in mind that seventy-five percent[24] of the New Testament does not even require the help of textual criticism because that much of the text is unanimous and thus, we know what it says. Of the other twenty-five percent, about twenty percent make up trivial scribal mistakes that are easily corrected. Therefore, textual criticism focuses mainly on a small portion of the New Testament text. The facts are clear: the Christian, who reads the New Testament, is fortunate to have so many manuscripts, with so many dating so close to the originals, with 500 hundred years of hundreds of textual scholars who have established the text with a level of certainty unimaginable for ancient secular works.

Atheist commentator Bob Seidensticker, after discussing the amount of New Testament manuscripts available, writes, "The first problem is that more manuscripts at best increase our confidence that we have the original version. That does not mean the original copy was history ...."[25] That is, Seidensticker is forced to acknowledge the reliability of the New Testament text as we have it today and can only try to deny what it says. He also says of the New Testament, "Compare that with 2000 copies of the Iliad, the second-best represented manuscript."[26] Of those 2,000 copies of the Iliad, how far removed are they from the alleged originals? The Iliad is dated to about 1260–1180 B.C.E. The most notable Iliad manuscripts are from the

---

[24] The numbers in this paragraph are rounded for simplicity purposes.

[25] 25,000 New Testament Manuscripts? Big Deal. - Patheos, http://www.patheos.com/blogs/crossexamined/2013/11/25000-new-testament-manuscrip (accessed November 28, 2015).

[26] Ibid

9th, 10th, and 11th centuries C.E. That would make these manuscripts over 2,000 years removed from their original.

The Range of Textual Criticism

The Importance and scope of New Testament textual criticism could be summed up in the few words used by J. Harold Greenlee; it is "the basic biblical study, a prerequisite to all other biblical and theological work. Interpretation, systemization, and application of the teachings of the NT cannot be done until textual criticism has done at least some of its work. It is, therefore, deserving of the acquaintance and attention of every serious student of the Bible." (Greenlee, *Introduction to New Testament Textual Criticism* 1995, 7)

It is only reasonable to assume that the original 27 books written first-hand by the New Testament authors have not survived. Instead, we only have what we must consider being imperfect copies. Why the Holy Spirit would miraculously inspire 27 fully inerrant texts, and then allow human imperfection into the copies, is not explained for us in Scripture. We do know that imperfect humans have tended to worship relics that traditions hold to have been touched by the miraculous powers of God or to have been in direct contact with one of his special servants of old. Ultimately, though, all we know is that God had his reasons for allowing the New Testament autographs to be worn out by repeated use. From time to time we hear of the discovery of a fragment possibly dated to the first century, but even if such a fragment is eventually verified, the dating alone can never serve as proof of an autograph; it will still be a copy in all likelihood.

As for errors in all the copies, we have, however, we can say is that the vast majority of the Greek text is not affected by errors at all. The errors occur in the form of variant readings, i.e., portions of the text where different manuscripts disagree. Of the **small amount** of the text that is affected by variant readings, the vast majority of these are minor slips of the pen, misspelled words, etc., or intentional but quickly analyzed changes, and we are certain what the original reading is in these places. A **far smaller number** of changes present challenges to establishing the original reading. It has always been said and remains true that no major doctrine is affected by a textual problem. Only rarely does a textual issue change the meaning of a verse.[27] Still, establishing the original text wherever there are variant readings is vitally important. Every word matters!

---

[27] Leading textual scholar Daniel Wallace tells us, after looking at all of the evidence, that the percentage of instances where the reading is uncertain and a well-attested alternative reading could change the meaning of the verse is a quarter of one percent, i.e., 0.0025%

CHAPTER 1 The New Testament Secretaries and Their Materials

One of the greatest tragedies in the modern-day history of Christianity [1880 - present] is that churchgoers have not been educated about the history of the New Testament text. They are so misinformed that many do not even realize that the Hebrew text lies behind our English Old Testament, and the Greek text lies behind our English New Testament. Sadly, many seminaries that train the pastors of today's churches have also required little or no studies in the history of the Old or New Testament texts.

Textual Criticism Defined

Again, New Testament textual criticism is the study of families[28] of manuscripts, especially the Greek New Testament, as well as versions,[29] lectionaries,[30] and patristic quotations,[31] along with internal evidence, in order to determine which reading is the original. Comparing any two copies of a document even a few pages long will reveal variant readings. "A textual variant is simply any difference from a standard text (e.g. a printed text, a particular manuscript, etc.) that involves spelling, word order, omission, addition, substitution, or a total rewrite of the text."[32]

When we use the term "textual *criticism*," we are not referring to something negative. In this instance, "criticism" is a reference to a careful,

---

[28] (Wilkins) A different position on manuscript families has won the support of most textual scholars and will be discussed in the later chapters by Wilkins. Nevertheless, it is indispensable to have an understanding of these families as background, and the conclusions drawn about individual manuscripts largely remain the same.

[29] A version is a translation of the New Testament into another language, such as Latin, Syriac, Coptic, Armenian, Georgian, and so on.

[30] A Lectionary is a book containing readings from the Bible for Christian church services during the course of the year.

[31] Patristic quotations are New Testament quotations from early Christian writers, such as the Apostolic Fathers, including Clement of Rome, Ignatius of Antioch, Polycarp of Smyrna, Hermas, and Papias. There were also the Apologists: Justin Martyr, Theophilus of Antioch, Clement of Alexandria, and Tertullian, to name a few. After them came the Church Fathers, e.g. St. Augustine or St. Ambrose whose works have helped to shape the Christian Church.

[32] The Number of Textual Variants: An Evangelical Miscalculation .., https://bible.org/article/number-textual-variants-evangelical-miscalculation (accessed December 01, 2015).

measured or painstaking study and analysis of the internal and external evidence for producing our New Testament Greek text, generally called a "critical text." The goal of many New Testament textual scholars today is to recover the earliest text *possible*, while the objective of the remaining few, such as the author of this book, is to get back to the *ipsissima verba* ("the very words") of the original author.[33]

> Variant readings occur only in about 5 percent of the Greek NT text, and so all the manuscripts agree about 95 percent of the time. Only about 2,100 variant readings may be considered "significant" and in no instance is any point of Christian doctrine challenged or questioned by a variant reading. Only about 1.67 percent of the entire Greek NT text still is questioned at all. We may be confident that our current eclectic, or critical, Greek NT text (an eclectic, or critical text is one based on the study of as many manuscripts as possible), is far beyond 99 percent established. In fact, there is more variation among some English translations of the Bible than there is among the manuscripts of the Greek NT. God's Word is infallible and inerrant in its original copies (autographs), all of which have perished. Textual critics of the Greek NT will continue their work until, if possible, the original of every questioned reading is firmly established. (Brand, Draper and Archie 2003, 1575)

An investigation of the enormous supply of Greek manuscripts, as well as the ancient versions in other languages, shows that they have preserved for us the very Word of God.

Throughout the period of the first five books of the Bible being penned by Moses (beginning in the late sixteenth century B.C.E.), and down to the time of the printing press (1455 C.E.)–almost 3,000 years–many forms of material have been used to receive writing. Material such as bricks, sheets of papyrus, animal skin, broken pottery, metal, wooden tablets with or without wax, and much more have been used to pen or copy God's Word. The following are some of the tools and materials.

Stylus: The stylus was used to write on a waxed codex tablet. The stylus could be made of bone, metal, or ivory. It would be sharpened at one end for the purpose of writing and have a

---

[33] (Wilkins) This goal, which will be mentioned in passing throughout the book, is a philosophical difference with some implications for TC practice. Both groups of critics will arrive at what they consider the earliest form of the text, but the authors take this to be the autograph as a matter of faith. One of the implications for practice is that conjectures are not considered viable options for variant readings. Another is that every word of the autograph can be found in some extant Greek NT manuscript. – THE TEXT OF THE NEW TESTAMENT.

rounded knob on the other for making corrections. The stylus could also be used to write on soft metal or clay.

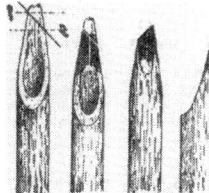

Reed Pen: The reed pen was used with ink to write on papyrus or parchment manuscripts. Καλαμος (kalamos) is the Greek word for "pen." (2 John 12; 3 John 13) There is no doubt that all the early extant papyrus manuscripts were copied with a reed pen, which can produce an impressive and pleasing script.

Quill Pen: The quill[34] pen came into use long after the reed pen. Quill would have been unsatisfactory for writing on papyrus, but parchment would have been an excellent surface for receiving writing from a quill pen. Of course, history shows that as parchment more fully displaced papyrus, the quill pen likewise replaced the reed pen. The quill was sharpened for use much like the reed, by having the tip sharpened and slit.

The first page of papyrus 66, showing John 1:1-13 and the opening words of v.14

Papyrus: Papyrus was the writing material used by the ancient Egyptians, Greeks, and Romans that was made from the pith of the stem of a water plant. It was cut into strips, with one layer laid out horizontally and the other vertically. Sometimes it was covered with a cloth and then beaten with a mallet. Scholarship has also suggested that paste may have been used between layers, and then a large stone would be placed on top until the materials were dry. Typically, a sheet of papyrus would be between 6–9 inches in width and 12–15 inches long. These sheets were then glued end to end until scribes had enough length to copy the book they were working on. The writing was done only on the horizontal side, and it was rolled so that the writing would be on the inside. If one were to attempt to write across the vertical side, it would be difficult because of the direction of the papyrus fibers. The scribe or copyist would have used a reed pen to write on the papyrus sheets (cf. 3 John 13). Papyrus was the main material used for writing until about 300

---

[34] The quill pen was the principal writing instrument in the Western world from the 6th to the 19th centuries C.E.

C.E. It was used with a *roll* or *scroll* (a document that is rolled up into itself), as well as the *codex* (book) form.

Writing on the papyrus sheet, even the correct side, was no easy task by any means because the surface was rough and fibrous. "Defects sometimes occurred in the making through retention of moisture between the layers or through the use of spongy strips which could cause ink to run; such flaws necessitated the remaking of the sheet." (Abbot, 1938, p. 11) The back pain from long periods of sitting cross-legged on the ground bent over a papyrus sheet on a board, dealing with running ink, the reed pen possibly snagging and tearing the papyrus sheet, having to erase illegible characters, all were a deterrent from personally writing a letter.

Early papyrus manuscripts, such as P[45], P[46], P[47], P[52], P[66], P[73] and P[75] (to mention a few), all date before 300 C.E., from as early as 110 C.E. On the other hand, the larger manuscripts, such as Codex Sinaiticus and Vaticanus from about 350 C.E., were written on parchment: creamy or yellowish material made from dried and treated sheepskin, goatskin, or other animal hides.

One may wonder why more New Testament manuscripts have not survived. It must be remembered that the Christians suffered intense persecution during intervals in the first 300 years from Pentecost 33 C.E. With this persecution from the Roman Empire came many orders to destroy Christian texts. In addition, these texts were not stored in such a way as to secure their preservation; they were actively used by the Christians in the congregation and were subject to wear and tear. Furthermore, moisture is the enemy of papyrus, and it causes them to disintegrate over time. This is why, as we will discover, the papyrus manuscripts that have survived have come from the dry sands of Egypt. Moreover, it seems not to have entered the minds of the early Christians to preserve their documents, because their solution to the loss of manuscripts was just to make more copies. Fortunately, the process of making copies transitioned to the more durable animal skins, which would last much longer. Those that have survived, especially from the fourth century C.E. and earlier, are the path to restoring the original Greek New Testament.[35]

Animal Skin: About the fourth century C.E., Bible manuscripts made of papyrus began to be superseded by the use of vellum, a high-quality parchment made from calfskin, kidskin, or lambskin. Manuscripts such as the famous Codex Sinaiticus (01) and Codex Vaticanus (03, also known as B) of the fourth century C.E. are parchment, or vellum, codices. This use of parchment as the leading writing material continued for almost a thousand years until it was replaced by paper. The advantages of parchment over papyrus were many, such as (1) it was much easier to write on smooth parchment, (2) one could write on both sides, (3) parchment lasted much longer, and (4) when desired, old writing could be scraped off and the parchment reused.

A 2,000-year-old Dead Sea Isaiah Scroll. It matches closely the Masoretic text and what is in the Bible today

Scroll or Roll: The scroll dominated until the beginning of the second century C.E., at which time the papyrus codex was replacing it. Papyrus enjoyed another two centuries of use until it was replaced with animal skin (vellum), which proved to be a far better writing material.

The writing on a scroll was done in 2- to 3-inch columns, which allowed the reader to have it opened, or unrolled, only partially. Although movies and television have portrayed the scroll being opened while holding it vertically, this was not the case; scrolls were opened horizontally. For the Greek or Latin reader, it would be rolled to the left as those languages were written left to right. The Jewish reader would roll it to the right as Hebrew was written right to left.

---

[35] Cf. J. H. Greenlee, *Introduction to New Testament Textual Criticism* (Peabody: Hendrickson, 1995), 11.

The difficulty of using a scroll should be apparent. If one had a long book (such as Isaiah) and were to attempt to locate a particular passage, it would not be user-friendly. An ancient saying was "A great book, a great evil." The account in the book of Luke tells us:

> And he [Jesus] came to Nazareth, where he had been brought up. And as was his custom, he went to the synagogue on the Sabbath day, and he stood up to read. And the scroll of the prophet Isaiah was given to him. He unrolled the scroll and found the place where it was written, 'The Spirit of the Lord is upon me because he has anointed me to proclaim good news to the poor. He has sent me to proclaim liberty to the captives and recovering of sight to the blind, to set at liberty those who are oppressed, to proclaim the year of the Lord's favor.' And he rolled up the scroll and gave it back to the attendant and sat down. And the eyes of all in the synagogue were fixed on him. And he began to say to them, 'Today this Scripture has been fulfilled in your hearing.' – Luke 4:16–21; Isaiah 61:1-2, ESV.

Codex: The trunk of a tree that bears leaves only at its apex was called a *caudex* in Latin. This name–modified to *codex*–would be applied to a tablet of wood that had raised edges, with a coat of wax placed within those raised edges. The dried wax would then be used to receive writing with a stylus. We might compare it to the schoolchild's slate such as seen in some Hollywood Western movies. Around the fifth century B.C.E., some of these were being used and attached by strings that were run through the edges. It is because these bound tablets resembled a tree trunk that they were to take on the name "codex."

Codex Vaticanus ("Book from the Vatican"), Facsimile, Fourth century. It is one of the earliest manuscripts of the Bible, which includes the Greek translation of the bulk of the Hebrew Scriptures as well as most of the Christian Greek Scriptures

As we can imagine, this bulky item also was not user-friendly! Sometime later, it would be the Romans who would develop a lighter, more flexible material, the parchment notebook, which would fill the need before the development of the later book-form codex. The Latin word *membranae* (skins) is the name given to such notebooks of parchment. In fact, at 2 Timothy 4:13 the apostle Paul requested of Timothy that he "bring the cloak that I left with Carpus at Troas, also the books [scrolls], and above all the parchments [*membranas,* Greek spelling]." One might ask why Paul used a Latin word (transliterated in Greek)? Undoubtedly it was due to the fact that there was no Greek word that would serve as an equivalent to what he was requesting. It was only later that the transliterated "codex" was brought into the Greek language as a reference to what we would know as a book.

The ink of ancient manuscripts was usually one of two kinds. There was ink made of a mixture of soot and gum. These were sold in the form of a bar, which was dissolved in water in an inkwell, and produced a very black ink. There was also ink made out of nutgalls, which resulted in a rusty-brown color. Aside from these materials, the scribe would have had a knife to sharpen his reed pen, as well as a sponge to erase errors. With the semi-professional and professional scribe, each character was written with care. Thus, writing was a slow, tedious, and often difficult task.

'I, Tertius, Greet You in the Lord'

Tertius is among the many greetings that we find at the end of the letter of Paul to the Romans, wherein he writes, "I am greeting you, I, Tertius, the one having written this letter, in the Lord." (Rom. 16:22) Of Paul's fourteen letters, this is the only occurrence where we find a clear reference to one of his secretaries.

Little is known of Tertius, who must have been a faithful Christian, based on the greeting "in the Lord." He may have been a member of the Corinthian congregation who likely knew many Christians in Rome, which is suggested by the fact his name is Latin for "third." Quartus for "fourth" is one of the other two who added their greetings: "Erastus the city treasurer greets you, and Quartus the brother, i.e., a member of the Corinthian congregation. (16:23b) Some scholars have suggested that Quartus could have been the younger brother of Tertius. (Brand, Draper and Archie 2003,

1574) Others have suggested that Tertius was a slave or a freedman.[36] This is also suggested by his Latin name and the fact that slaves were commonly involved in the scribal activity. From this we could conjecture that Tertius likely had experience as a professional scribe, who became a fellow worker with the apostle Paul, helping compile the longest of Paul's letters. It was common for Bible authors to use a scribe, as for example Jeremiah used Baruch in a similar way, just as Peter used Silvanus (Jer. 36:4; 1 Pet. 5:12). Of Paul's fourteen letters, it is certain that six involved the use of a secretary: Romans (16:22), 1 Corinthians (16:21), Galatians (6:11), Colossians (4:18), 2 Thessalonians (3:17), and Philemon (19).

Penning the Book of Romans

The letter of Paul to the Romans was written while he was on his third missionary journey as a guest of Gaius in Corinth, about 55-56 C.E.. (Ac 20:1-3; Rom. 16:23). We do know for a certainty that Paul used Tertius as his secretary to pen the book of Romans. However, we cannot say with absolute certainty how he was used. Some have argued, "from evidence outside of the New Testament that it was common practice for authors to dictate their letters to an amanuensis or secretary."[37] (McRay 2003, 270) Did the secretary take that dictation down in shorthand, and then go on to compose the letter, even contributing content, with the New Testament author giving the final approval? Alternatively, was the secretary used in a more limited fashion, such as editing spelling, grammar, and syntax? Otto Roller makes the point that for an author to dictate a letter to a scribe verbatim would require the author to speak very slowly, i.e., syllable by syllable.[38] There will be more on this later. For now, whatever method was used, the work of a secretary was no easy job. What we do know is that the sixty-six books of the Bible were "inspired by God," and "men spoke from God as they were carried along by the Holy Spirit." – 2 Timothy 3:16; 2 Peter 1:21.

---

[36] When the Roman Empire was in power, one who was released from slavery was called a "freedman" (Gr *apeleutheros*), while a "freeman" (Gr *eleutheros*) was free from birth, having full citizenship rights, as was the case with the apostle Paul – Ac 22:28 (Balz and Schneider 1978, Vol. 1, P 121).

[37] See Gordon J. Bahr, "*Paul and Letter Writing in the First Century*," Catholic Biblical Quarterly 28 (1966): 465-77.

[38] Otto Roller, *Das Formular der Paulinischen Briefe: Ein Beitrag zur Lehre vom antiken Briefe* (Stuttgart: W. Kohlhammer, 1933), p. 333.

CHAPTER 2 The Book Writing Process of the New Testament: Authors and Early Christian Scribes

The Place of Writing

When we think of the apostle Paul penning his books that would make up most of the New Testament, some have had the anachronistic tendency to impose their modern way of thinking about him, such as presupposing where he would have written. As I am writing this page, I am tucked away in my home office, seeking privacy from the hustle and bustle of our modern world. This was not the case in the ancient world where Paul lived and traveled. People of that time favored a group setting, not isolation. The apostle Paul probably would have been of this mindset. Paul would not have necessarily sought a quiet place to pen his letters, to escape the noise of those around him. As for myself, I struggle to get back on track if I am interrupted for more than a couple of minutes.

Most during Paul's day would have been surprised by this way of thinking, i.e., seeking quiet and solitude to focus all of one's energy on the task of writing. Those of Paul's day, including himself, would not have even noticed people talking around them, nor would they have been troubled by what we perceive as interruptions, such as the discussions of others, which were neither relevant nor applicable to the subject of their letter writing.

The Scribe of the New Testament Writer

Ancient Greco-Roman society employed secretaries or scribes for various reasons. Of course, the government employed some scribes, working for chief administrators. Then, there were the scribes who were employed in the private sector. These latter scribes (often slaves) usually were employed by the wealthy. However, even high-ranking slaves and freed slaves employed scribes. Many times, one would find scribes who would pen letters for their friends. According to E. Randolph Richards, the skills of these unofficial secretaries "could range from a minimal competency with the language and/or the mechanics of writing to the highest proficiency at rapidly producing an accurate, proper, and charming letter."[39] Scribes carried out a wide range of administrative, secretarial, and

---

[39] (Richards, The Secretary in the Letters of Paul 1990, 11)

literary tasks, including administrative bookkeeping, shorthand and taking dictation, letter-writing, and copying literary texts.

The most prominent ways that a scribe would have been used in the first century C.E. would have been as (1) a recorder, (2) an editor, and (3) as a secretary for an author. At the very bottom of the writing tasks, he would be used to record information, i.e. as a record keeper. The New Testament scribes, when they were needed or desired, were being used as secretaries, writing down letters by dictation. Tertius, in taking down the book of Romans with its 7,000+ words, would have simply written out the very words that the apostle Paul spoke. Some have argued that longhand in dictation was not feasible in ancient times because the author would have to slow down to the point of speaking syllable-by-syllable. They usually cite Cicero as evidence for this argument because of the numerous references to dictation in his writings. Cicero stated in a letter to his friend Varro that he had to slow down his dictation to the point of "syllable by syllable" for the sake of the scribe. However, the scribe he was using at that time was inexperienced, not his regular scribe. Of course, it would be very difficult to retain one's line of thought in such a dictation process. It should be noted that Cicero had experienced scribes who could take down dictation at a normal pace of speaking, even rapid speech.[40] Therefore, since there is evidence that there were scribes in those days who were skilled enough to take down dictation at the normal rate of speech, we should not assume that the apostles would not have had access to such scribes in the persons of Tertius, Silvanus, or even Timothy.

In fact, Marcus Fabius Quintilianus (b. 35 C.E. d. 100 C.E.) complained that a scribe who could write at the speed of normal speech can lead to the speaker feeling rushed, to the point of not having time to ponder his thoughts.

> On the other hand, there is a fault which is precisely the opposite of this, into which those fall who insist on first making a rapid draft of their subject with the utmost speed of which their pen is capable, and write in the heat and impulse of the moment. They call this their rough copy. They then revise what they have written, and arrange their hasty outpourings. But while the words and the rhythm may be corrected, the matter is still marked by the superficiality resulting from the speed with which it was thrown together. The more correct method is, therefore, to exercise care from the very beginning, and to form the work from the outset in such a manner that it merely requires being chiseled into shape, not fashioned anew. Sometimes, however,

---

[40] (Richards, Paul And First-Century Letter Writing: Secretaries, Composition and Collection 2004, 29-30); Murphy-O'Connor, *Paul the Letter-Writer*, 9–11; Shorthand references Plutarch, *Cato Minor*, 23.3–5; Caesar, 7.4–5; Seneca, *Epistles*, 14.208.

we must follow the stream of our emotions since their warmth will give us more than any diligence can secure. The condemnation which I have passed on such carelessness in writing will make it pretty clear what my views are on the luxury of dictation which is now so fashionable. For, when we write, however great our speed, the fact that the hand cannot follow the rapidity of our thoughts gives us time to think, whereas the presence of our amanuensis hurries us on, and at times we feel ashamed to hesitate or pause, or make some alteration, as though we were afraid to display such weakness before a witness. As a result, our language tends not merely to be haphazard and formless, but in our desire to produce a continuous flow we let slip positive improprieties of diction, which show neither the precision of the writer nor the impetuosity of the speaker. Again, if the amanuensis is a slow writer or lacking in intelligence, he becomes a stumbling-block, our speed is checked, and the thread of our ideas is interrupted by the delay or even perhaps by the loss of temper to which it gives rise.[41]

Therefore, again, we do have evidence that some scribes were capable, skilled to the point of writing at the normal speed of speech. While Richards says that this is by way of shorthand, saying it was more widespread than originally thought, where the secretary uses symbols in place of words, forming a rough draft that would be written out fully,[42] this need not be the case. True, there is some evidence that shorthand existed a hundred years before Christ. However, it was still rare, with few scribes having the ability. Whether this was true of the scribes that assisted our New Testament authors is an unknown. It is highly unlikely but not necessarily impossible.

Who in the days of the New Testament authors would use the services of scribes? Foremost would be those who did not know how to read and write. Within ancient contracts and business letters, one can find a note by the scribe (illiteracy statement), who penned it, stating he had done so because his employer could not read or write. For example, an ancient letter concludes with, "Eumelus, son of Herma, has written for him because he does not know letters."[43] It may be that they were able to read, but struggled with writing. Then again, it may simply be that they wrote slowly, and were not willing to spend the time on improving their skills. An ancient letter from Thebes, Egypt, penned for a certain Asklepiades, concludes,

---

[41] Institutio Oratoria, 10.3.17–21

[42] (Richards, Paul And First-Century Letter Writing: Secretaries, Composition and Collection 2004, 72)

[43] See examples in Francis Exler, *The Form of the Ancient Greek Letter: A Study In Greek Epistolography* (Washington D.C.: Catholic University of America, 1922), pp. 126-7

"Written for him hath Eumelus the son of Herma ..., being desired so to do for that he writeth somewhat slowly." (Deissmann 1910, 166-7)

On the other hand, whether one knew how to read and write was not always the decisive issue in the use of a secretary. John L. McKenzie writes, "Even people who could read and write did not think of submitting their readers to unprofessional penmanship. It was probably not even a concern for legibility, but rather a concern for beauty, or at least for neatness," (McKenzie 1975, 14) which moved the ancients to turn to the services of a secretary. Although the educated could read and write, some likely very well, writing was tedious, trying, and frustrating, particularly where lengthy and elaborate texts were concerned. It seems that if one could avoid the tremendous task of penning a lengthy letter, entrusting it to a scribe, so much the better.

The apostle Paul had over 100 traveling companions; like Aristarchus, Luke and Timothy served by the apostle's side for many years. Then, there are others such as Asyncritus, Hermas, Julia, or Philologus, of whom we barely know more than their names. Many of Paul's friends traveled for the sake of the gospel, such as Achaicus, Fortunatus, Stephanas, Artemas, and Tychicus. We know that Tychicus was used by Paul to carry at least three letters now included in the Bible canon: the epistles to the Ephesians, the Colossians, and to Philemon. Tychicus was not simply some mail carrier. He was a well-trusted carrier for the apostle, Paul. The final greeting from Paul to the Colossians reads,

Colossians 4:7-8 New American Standard Bible (NASB)

[7] As to all my affairs, Tychicus, *our* beloved brother and faithful servant and fellow bond-servant in the Lord, will bring you information. [8] *For* I have sent him to you for this very purpose, that you may know about our circumstances and that he may encourage your hearts;

Richards offers the following about a letter carrier, saying he "was often a personal link between the author and the recipients in addition to the written link. . . . [One purpose] for needing a trustworthy carrier was, he often carried additional information. A letter may describe a situation briefly, frequently with the author's assessment, but the carrier is expected to elaborate for the recipient all the details." (Richards, The Secretary in the Letters of Paul 1990, 7) Many of Paul's letters deal with teachings, as well as one crisis after another; the carrier was expected to be aware of these on a much deeper level so that he could orally explain, and answer any questions. Therefore, he needed to be a highly trusted messenger who was literate.

Tertius was the scribe Paul used to pen his letter to the Romans. We cannot assume that all of Paul's companions were proficient readers and writers, but we can infer that Paul would task coworkers, who were able to carry and read letters, as well as understand the condition of the people or congregation where they were being sent or stationed. In addition, the scribes whom Paul used, such as Tertius, would very likely have been semi-professional or professional. It would have been simply senseless to entrust the secretarial work of taking down the monumental words of the book of Romans, for example, to an inexperienced scribe. What skills would Tertius need to carry out the task of penning the book of Romans?

The ordinary coworker of Paul would likely have been able to read proficiently, but barely be able to write. Paul would have chosen workers whose skills would have equipped them to carry out their assignments. Tertius would have been the exception to the rule, most likely having been a professional scribe. He would have to have been able to glue the sheets together if it was to be a roll or stitch the pages together if a codex. He would need to know the appropriate mixture of soot and gum to make ink and to be able to use his knife to make his own reed pen. Richards writes that a professional scribe would also "draw lines on the paper. Small holes were often pricked down each side, and then a straight edge and a lead disk were used to lightly draw evenly spaced lines across the sheet."[44] If Tertius had not been trained as a copyist of documents, he would have made many minor errors because his attention would have been on the sense of what he was penning, as opposed to the exact words, as is typical of the unconscious mind.

Did Tertius take Paul's exact dictation, word for word? Robert H. Mounce writes,

> The only legitimate question about authorship relates to the role of Tertius, who in 16:22 writes, 'I Tertius, who wrote down this letter, greet you in the Lord.' We know that at that time in history an amanuensis [scribe] that is, one hired to write from dictation, could serve at several levels. In some cases, he would receive dictation and write it down immediately in longhand. At other times, he might use a form of shorthand (*tachygraphy* [ancient shorthand]) to take down a letter and then later write it out in longhand. In some cases, an amanuensis would simply get the gist of what a person wanted to say and then be left on his own to formulate the ideas into a letter. (R. H. Mounce 2001, 22)

It might seem quite the task for Tertius to take down Paul's words in longhand. However, this is not to say that it was impossible, just difficult. Paul might have had to speak in a slow to a normal rate of speech, **but not**

---

[44] (Richards, Paul And First-Century Letter Writing: Secretaries, Composition and Collection 2004, 29)

syllable-by-syllable. It is true that Tertius would have been writing on a papyrus sheet with a reed pen, with the intention of being legible; however, he would have been very skilled in his trade. Then again, there is the slight possibility of Tertius taking it down in shorthand and thereafter making out a full draft, which would have been reviewed by both Paul and Tertius. The last option by Mounce in the above is contrary to the attitudes that both the scribes and the New Testament authors would have had toward what was being penned. God chose to convey a message through Matthew, Mark, Luke, John, Peter, Jude, James, and Paul, not Tertius and Silvanus, or others. We cannot say with any certainty whether Tertius or Silvanus took their authors' words down in shorthand or longhand. We can say, however, that the Word of God was being dictated by the human author to the scribe, and in no way composed by the scribe.

Inspiration and Inerrancy in the Writing Process

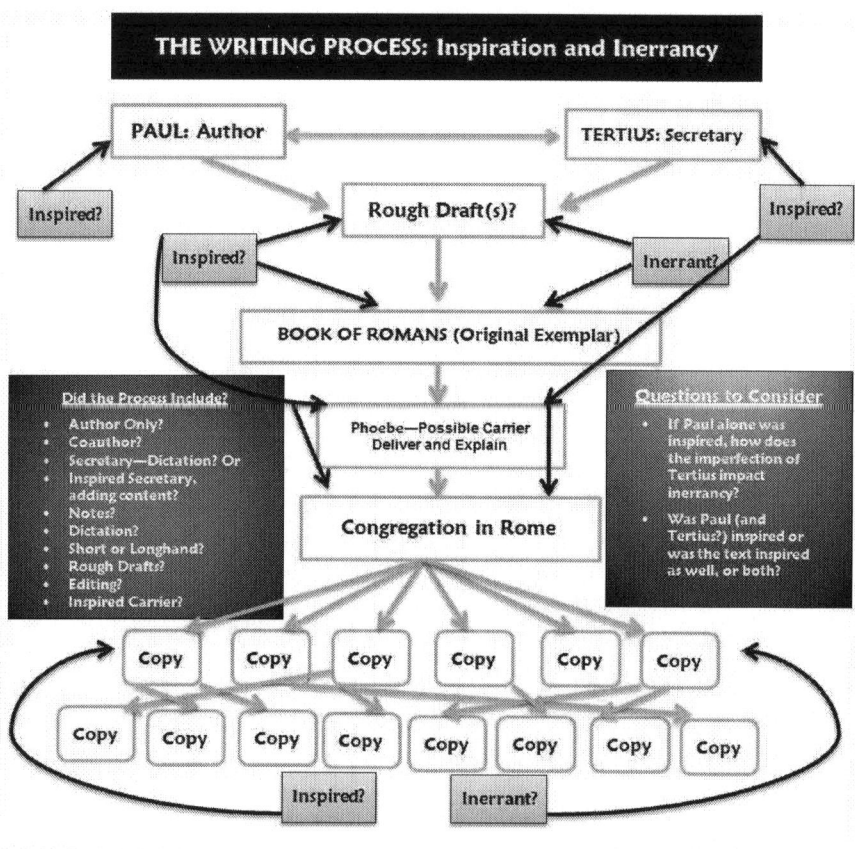

All Scripture is Inspired by God

In this context, inspiration is **the state** of a human being moved by the Holy Spirit, which results in an inspired, fully inerrant written Word of God.

Chicago Statement on Biblical Inerrancy ICBI

Article VII

We affirm that **inspiration** was the work in which God by His Spirit, through human writers, gave us His Word. The origin of Scripture is divine. The mode of divine **inspiration** remains largely a mystery to us. We deny that **inspiration** can be reduced to human insight, or to heightened states of consciousness of any kind.

Article VIII

We affirm that God in His Work of **inspiration** utilized the distinctive personalities and literary styles of the writers whom He had chosen and prepared. We deny that God, in causing these writers to use the very words that He chose, overrode their personalities.

Article IX

We affirm that **inspiration**, though not conferring omniscience, guaranteed true and trustworthy utterance on all matters of which the Biblical authors were moved to speak and write. We deny that the finitude or fallenness of these writers, by necessity or otherwise, introduced distortion or falsehood into God's Word.

Article X

We affirm that **inspiration**, strictly speaking, applies only to the autographic text of Scripture, which in the providence of God can be ascertained from available manuscripts with great accuracy. We further affirm that copies and translations of Scripture are the Word of God to the extent that they faithfully represent the original. We deny that any essential element of the Christian faith is affected by the absence of the autographs. We further deny that this absence renders the assertion of Biblical **inerrancy** invalid or irrelevant.

Article XI

We affirm that Scripture, having been given by divine inspiration, is infallible, so that, far from misleading us, it is true and reliable in all the matters it addresses. We deny that it is possible for the Bible to be at the same time infallible and errant in its assertions. Infallibility and inerrancy may be distinguished, but not separated.

Inerrancy of Scripture

Inerrancy of Scripture is **the result** of the state of a human being moved by Holy Spirit from God, which results in an inspired, fully inerrant written Word of God.

Article XII

We affirm that Scripture in its entirety is **inerrant**, being free from all falsehood, fraud, or deceit. We deny that Biblical infallibility and **inerrancy** are limited to spiritual, religious, or redemptive themes, exclusive of assertions in the fields of history and science. We further deny that scientific hypotheses about earth history may properly be used to overturn the teaching of Scripture on creation and the flood.

Article XIII

We affirm the propriety of using **inerrancy** as a theological term with reference to the complete truthfulness of Scripture. We deny that it is proper to evaluate Scripture according to standards of truth and error that are alien to its usage or purpose. We further deny that **inerrancy** is negated by Biblical phenomena such as a lack of modern technical precision, irregularities of grammar or spelling, observational descriptions of nature, the reporting of falsehoods, the use of hyperbole and round numbers, the topical arrangement of material, variant selections of material in parallel accounts, or the use of free citations.

Article XV

We affirm that the doctrine of **inerrancy** is grounded in the teaching of the Bible about **inspiration**. We deny that Jesus' teaching about Scripture may be dismissed by appeals to accommodation or to any natural limitation of His humanity.

Article XVI

We affirm that the doctrine of **inerrancy** has been integral to the Church's faith throughout its history. We deny that inerrancy is a doctrine invented by Scholastic Protestantism, or is a reactionary position postulated in response to negative higher criticism.

Authoritative Word of God

The **authoritative** aspect of Scripture is that God by way of inspiration gives the words the authors chose to use power and authority, so that the outcome (i.e., originals) is the very Word of God, as though God were speaking to us himself.

Article I

We affirm that the Holy Scriptures are to be received as the **authoritative** Word of God. We deny that the Scriptures receive their authority from the Church, tradition, or any other human source.

2 Timothy 3:16-17 New American Standard Bible (NASB)

[16] All Scripture is inspired by God and profitable for teaching, for reproof, for correction, for training in righteousness; [17] so that the man of God may be adequate, equipped for every good work.

What does this mean? The phrase "inspired by God" (Gr., *theopneustos*) literally means, "Breathed out by God." A related Greek word, *pneuma*, means "wind," "breath," life, "Spirit." Since *pneuma* can also mean "breath," the process of "breathing out" can rightly be said to be the work of the Holy Spirit inspiring the Scriptures. The result is that the originals were accurate, fully inerrant and authoritative. Thus the Holy Spirit moved human writers so that the result can truthfully be called the Word of *God*, not the word of man.

2 Peter 1:21 New American Standard Bible (NASB)

[21] for no prophecy was ever made by an act of human will, but men moved by the Holy Spirit spoke from God.

The Greek word here translated "men moved by (NASB)," *phero*, is used in another form at Acts 27:15, 17, which describes a ship that was driven along by the wind. So the Holy Spirit, by analogy, 'navigated the course' of the Bible writers. While the Spirit did not give them each word by dictation,[45] it certainly kept the writers from inserting any information that did not convey the will and purpose of God.

The heart of what the International Council on Biblical Inerrancy (ICBI) stood for is apparent in "A Short Statement," produced at the Chicago conference in 1978:

A SHORT STATEMENT

1. God, who is Himself Truth and speaks truth only, has inspired Holy Scripture in order thereby to reveal Himself to lost mankind through Jesus Christ as Creator and Lord, Redeemer and Judge. Holy Scripture is God's witness to Himself.

---

[45] (Wilkins) Exactly how the Spirit guided the writers is a mystery, and the words "thus says the Lord" in prophecy most likely do introduce a dictated message. However, those familiar with Greek can easily see stylistic differences between the NT writers which seem to reflect different personalities and rule out verbatim dictation from a single source.

2. Holy Scripture, being God's own Word, written by men prepared and superintended by His Spirit, is of infallible divine authority in all matters upon which it touches: it is to be believed, as God's instruction, in all that it affirms, obeyed, as God's command, in all that it requires; embraced, as God's pledge, in all that it promises.

3. The Holy Spirit, Scripture's divine Author, both authenticates it to us by His inward witness and opens our minds to understand its meaning.

4. Being wholly and verbally God-given, Scripture is without error or fault in all its teaching, no less in what it states about God's acts in creation, about the events of world history, and about its own literary origins under God, than in its witness to God's saving grace in individual lives.

5. The **authority of Scripture** is inescapably impaired if this total divine **inerrancy** is in any way limited or disregarded or made relative to a view of truth contrary to the Bible's own; and such lapses bring serious loss to both the individual and the Church.

Questions to Consider

We have been using the book of Romans as our example, so we will continue with it. We know that Paul was the author who gave us the inspired content of Romans, Tertius was the secretary who recorded Romans, and Phoebe was likely the one who carried the letter to Rome or else accompanied the one who did. Thus, we have at least three persons: the author, the secretary (scribe), and the carrier.

What is inspiration?

Inspiration is a "theological concept encompassing phenomena in which human action, skill, or utterance is immediately and extraordinarily supplied by the Spirit of God. Although various terms are employed in the Bible, the basic meaning is best served by Gk. *theopneustos* "God-breathed" (2 Tim. 3:16), meaning "breathed forth by God" rather than "breathed into by God" (Warfield)." (Myers 1987, 524) **Verbal plenary inspiration** holds that "every word of Scripture was God-breathed." A significant role was played by the human writers. Their individual backgrounds, personal traits, and literary styles were authentically theirs but had been providentially prepared by God for use as his instrument in producing Scripture. "The Scriptures had not been dictated, but the result was as if they had been (A. A. Hodge, B. B. Warfield)." (Myers 1987, 525)

Benjamin B. Warfield: "Inspiration is, therefore, usually defined as a supernatural influence exerted on the sacred writers by the Spirit of God, by virtue of which their writings are given Divine trustworthiness."[46]

Edward J. Young: "Inspiration is a superintendence of God the Holy Spirit over the writers of the Scriptures, as a result of which these Scriptures possess Divine authority and trustworthiness and, possessing such Divine authority and trustworthiness, are free from error."[47]

Charles C. Ryrie: "Inspiration is ... God's superintendence of the human authors so that, using their own individual personalities, they composed and recorded without error His revelation to man in the words of the original autographs."[48]

Paul P. Enns: "There are several important elements that belong in a proper definition of inspiration: (1) the divine element—God the Holy Spirit superintended the writers, ensuring the accuracy of the writing; (2) the human element—human authors wrote according to their individual styles and personalities; (3) the result of the divine-human authorship is the recording of God's truth without error; (4) inspiration extends to the selection of words by the writers; (5) inspiration relates to the original manuscripts."[49]

Were both Paul and Tertius inspired, or just Paul?

Only Paul and other Old and New Testament authors were inspired. First, as was stated above, **Verbal plenary inspiration** holds that "every word of Scripture was God-breathed." God **did not**, generally speaking, dictate the books of the Bible word by word to the Bible authors as if they were dictating machines.

2 Thessalonians 3:17 New American Standard Bible (NASB)

[17] I, Paul, write this greeting with my own hand, and this is a distinguishing mark in every letter; this is the way I write.

An appended note to every letter with his signature "distinguishing mark" is like a boss signing a letter that he dictated to a secretary. It is unthinkable that Paul would sign or make a distinguishing mark on anything without reading through it and make any necessary corrections. This supposes that Paul looked over all of his letters, which would also suppose

---

[46] B. B. Warfield, *The Inspiration and Authority of the Bible*(Philadelphia: Presbyterian and Reformed, 1948), p. 131.

[47] Edward J. Young, *Thy Word Is Truth* (Grand Rapids: Eerdmans, 1957), p. 27.

[48] Charles C. Ryrie, *A Survey of Bible Doctrine* (Chicago: Moody, 1972), p. 38.

[49] Paul P. Enns, *The Moody Handbook of Theology* (Chicago: Moody Press, 1989), p. 161.

that the scribe could not have been inspired because if he were, then there would have been no mistakes in the document, which means it would not have been needed to be looked over let alone corrected. So again, there would have been no need for Paul to check the work of an inspired secretary. If Tertius had been inspired, the moment he set the pen down, Paul would have had no need to look the text over. There is no need to read into silence and suggest that the secretary was inspired. While the secretary was certainly engaged in his work being that they were coworkers and traveling companions,

However, in some cases, information was transmitted by verbal dictation, word for word. For example, when God delivered the large body of laws and statutes of his covenant with Israel, Jehovah instructed Moses: "Write for yourself these words." (Ex 34:27, LEB) In another example, the prophets were often given specific messages to deliver. (1 Ki 22:14; Jer. 1:7; 2:1; 11:1-5; Eze. 3:4; 11:5) More importantly, the Bible authors did dictate what they received under inspiration to their secretaries, i.e., amanuenses/scribes.

Jeremiah 36:4 New American Standard Bible (NASB)

[4] Then Jeremiah called Baruch the son of Neriah, and Baruch wrote on a scroll at **the dictation of Jeremiah** all the words of the Lord which He had spoken to him. (Bold mine)

If Paul alone was inspired, how does the imperfection of Tertius affect inerrancy?

First, we should state that just because Paul used Tertius, Peter used Silvanus, or Jeremiah used Baruch, to pen the Word of God, they did not thereby detract from or weaken the authority of God's Word or the inerrancy of Scripture. The dictation that Paul gave Tertius was the result of divine inspiration as he, Paul, was moved along by Holy Spirit. Tertius merely recorded Paul's dictation, word by word. Whether Tertius was a professional scribe[50] or had the skills of a semi-professional scribe, he must have made at least a few slips of the pen. Afterward, however, Paul would have reviewed the document with Tertius, correcting any errors before publishing the official, authoritative text.

What about Phoebe, what role did the carrier have in the process?

Those used by New Testament authors to deliver the Word of God to people or congregations would have been some of Paul's most trusted, competent coworkers. Certainly, in the case of congregations contacting

---

[50] In the strictest sense, a professional scribe is one who was specifically trained in that vocation and was paid for his services.

Paul with questions and concerns, to which Paul responded with an inspired letter, the carrier would be made aware of those questions and concerns. Paul would have spoken to the carrier at length about these matters, going over what he meant by what he wrote. This would have provided the carrier sufficient knowledge; in case the person or congregation had any question that the carrier could address. This process is not indicated within the Scriptures; but are we to believe God and Paul for that matter would send a simple carrier who was left in the dark as to what he was carrying, and that no congregational leader would have follow-up questions, which God would have foreseen? Hardly.

The Publishing, Copying and Distributing Process

In the above, we spoke of the initial aspect of the publishing process, i.e., the moment Paul decided to pen a letter to a congregation like the Romans, the Ephesians, the Colossians, or to a person such as Philemon. We discussed the process that Paul went through with his secretary (e.g., Tertius), to the carrier (e.g., Phoebe, Tychicus) and the recipients. Now we turn to the circulation aspect, i.e., getting the book out to more and more readers. Harry Y. Gamble says the following in *The Publication and Early Dissemination of Early Christian Books:*

> The letters of Paul to his communities, the earliest extant Christian texts, were dictated to scribal associates (presumably Christian), carried to their destinations by a traveling Christian, and read aloud to the congregations.[51] But Paul also envisioned the circulation of some of his letters beyond a single Christian group (cf. Gal. 1: 2, 'to the churches of Galatia', Rom. 1:7 'to all God's beloved in Rome'—dispersed among numerous discrete house churches, Rom. 16: 5, 10, 11, 14, 15), and the author of Colossians, if not Paul, gives instruction for the exchange of Paul's letters between different communities (Col. 4: 16), which must indeed have taken place also soon after Paul's time.[52] The gospel literature of early Christianity offers only meager hints of

---

[51] On the dictation of Paul's letters to a scribe, see E. R. Richards, The Secretary in the Letters of Paul (WUNT 42; Tubingen: Mohr, 1991), 169–98; for couriers see Rom. 16: 1, 1 Cor. 16: 10, Eph. 6: 21, Col. 4: 7, cf. 2 Cor. 8: 16–17. Reference to their carriers is common in other early Christian letters (e.g. 1 Pet. 5: 12, 1 Clem. 65: 1, Ignatius, Phil. 11.2, Smyr. 12.1, Polycarp, Phil. 14.1). For the general practice see E. Epp, 'New Testament Papyrus Manuscripts and Letter Carrying in Greco-Roman Times', in B. A. Pearson (ed.), The Future of Early Christianity (Minneapolis: Fortress, 1991), 35–56. Reading a letter aloud to the community, which seems to be presupposed by all the letters, is stipulated only in 1 Thess. 5: 27.

[52] This is shown for an early time by the generalization of the original particular addresses of some of Paul's letters (Rom. 1: 7, 15; 1 Cor. 1: 2; cf. Eph. 1: 1).

intentions or means of its publication and circulation. The prologue to Luke/Acts (Luke 1: 1–4) provides a dedication to 'Theophilus', who (whether or not a fictive figure) by that convention is implicitly made responsible for the dissemination of the work by encouraging and permitting copies to be made. The last chapter of the Gospel of John, an epilogue added by others after the original conclusion of the Gospel (20: 30–1), aims at least in part (21: 24–5) to insure appreciation of the book and to promote its use beyond its community of origin. To take another case, the Apocalypse, addressed to seven churches in western Asia Minor, was almost surely sent in separate copy to each. Even so, the author anticipated its wider copying and dissemination beyond those original recipients, and so warned subsequent copyists to preserve the integrity of the book, neither adding nor subtracting, for fear of religious penalty (Rev. 22: 18–19). The private Christian copying and circulation that is presumed in these early writings continued to be the means for the publication and dissemination of Christian literature in the second and third centuries. It can be seen, for example, in the explicit notice in The Shepherd of Hermas (Vis. 2.4.3) that the book was to be published or released in two final copies, one for local use in Rome, the other for the transcription of further copies to be sent to Christian communities in 'cities abroad'. It can also be seen when Polycarp, bishop of Smyrna, had the letters of Ignatius copied and sent to the Christian community in Philippi, and had copies of letters from them and other churches in Asia Minor sent to Syrian Antioch (Phil. 13). It is evident too in the scribal colophons of the Martyrdom of Polycarp (22.2–4), and must be assumed also in connection with the letters of Dionysius, bishop of Corinth (fl. 170 ce; Eusebius, H.E. 4.23.1–12).

From another angle, the physical remains of early Christian books show that they were produced and disseminated privately within and between Christian communities. Early Christian texts, especially those of a scriptural sort, were almost always written in codices or leaf books—an informal, economical, and handy format—rather than on rolls, which were the traditional and standard vehicle of all other books. This was a sharp departure from convention, and particularly characteristic of Christians. Also distinctive to Christian books was the pervasive use of nomina sacra, divine names written in abbreviated forms, which was clearly an in-house practice of Christian scribes. Further, the preponderance in early Christian papyrus manuscripts of an informal quasi-documentary script rather than a professional bookhand also suggests that Christian writings were privately transcribed with a view to intramural circulation and use.[53]

If Christian books were disseminated in roughly the same way as other books, that is, by private seriatim copying, we might surmise that they spread slowly and gradually in ever-widening circles, first in proximity to their places of origin, then regionally, and then transregionally, and for some books this was doubtless the case. But it deserves notice that some early Christian texts appear to have enjoyed surprisingly rapid and wide circulation. Already by the early decades of the second century Papias of Hierapolis in western Asia Minor was acquainted at least with the Gospels of Mark and Matthew (Eusebius, H.E. 3.39.15–16); Clement of Rome, Ignatius of Antioch, and Polycarp of Smyrna were all acquainted with collections of Paul's letters; and papyrus copies of various early Christian texts were current in Egypt.[54] The Shepherd of Hermas, written in Rome near the mid-second century, was current and popular in Egypt not long after.[55] Equally interesting, Irenaeus' Adversus haereses, written about 180 in Gaul, is shown by papyrus fragments to have found its way to Egypt by the end of the second century, and indeed also to Carthage, where it was used by Tertullian.[56]

The brisk and broad dissemination of Christian books presumes not only a lively interest in texts among Christian communities but also efficient means for their reproduction and distribution. Such interest and means may be unexpected, given that the rate of literacy within Christianity was low, on average no greater than in the empire at large, namely in the range of 10–15 percent.[57] Yet there were some literate members in almost all

---

[53] On these features see H. Gamble, Books and Readers in the Early Church (New Haven: Yale University Press, 1995), 66–81, and L. Hurtado, The Earliest Christian Artifacts (Grand Rapids: Eerdmans, 2006).

[54] For Clement, Ignatius, and Polycarp, see A. F. Gregory and C. M. Tuckett, eds., The Reception of the New Testament in the Apostolic Fathers (Oxford: OUP, 2005), 142–53, 162–72, 201–18, 226–7. For early Christian papyri in Egypt see Hurtado, Earliest Christian Artifacts, appendix 1 (209–29). The most notable case is P52 (a fragment of the Gospel of John, customarily dated to the early 2nd cent.).

[55] Some papyrus fragments of Hermas are 2nd cent. (P.Oxy. 4706 and 3528, P.Mich. 130, P.Iand. 1.4).

[56] For the A.H. in Egypt: P.Oxy. 405; for Tertullian's use of A.H. in Carthage, see T. D. Barnes, Tertullian (Oxford: Clarendon, 1971), 127–8, 220–1.

[57] The fundamental study of literacy in antiquity is still W. V. Harris, Ancient Literacy (Cambridge, Mass.: Harvard University Press, 1989); see now also the essays in J. H. Humphrey, ed., Literacy in the Roman World (Journal of Roman Archaeology, suppl. ser. 3;

Christian communities, and as long as texts could be read aloud by some, they were accessible and useful to the illiterate majority. Christian congregations were not reading communities in the same sense as elite literary or scholarly circles, but books were nevertheless important to them virtually from the beginning, for even before Christians began to compose their own texts, books of Jewish scripture played an indispensable role in their worship, teaching, and missionary preaching. Indeed, Judaism and Christianity were the only religious communities in Greco-Roman antiquity in which texts had any considerable importance, and in this, as in some other respects, Christian groups bore a greater resemblance to philosophical circles than to other religious traditions.[58]

If smaller, provincial Christian congregations were not well-equipped or well-situated for the tasks of copying and disseminating texts, larger Christian centers must have had some scriptorial capacity: already in the second century: Polycarp's handling of Ignatius' letters and letters from other churches shows its presence in Smyrna; the instruction about the publication of Hermas' The Shepherd suggests it for Rome; and it can hardly be doubted for Alexandria, since even in a provincial city like Oxyrhynchus many manuscripts of Christian texts were available.[59] The early third-century Alexandrian scriptorium devised for the production and distribution of the works of Origen (Eusebius, H.E. 6.23.2), though unique in its sponsorship by a private patron and its service to an individual writer, surely had precursors, more modest and yet efficient, in other Christian communities. It also had important successors, not the least of which was the library and scriptorium that flourished in Caesarea in the second half of the third century under the auspices of

---

Ann Arbor: University of Michigan, 1991), and in W. A. Johnson and H. N. Parker, eds., Ancient Literacies (Oxford: OUP, 2009).

[58] M. Beard, 'Writing and Religion: Ancient Religion and the Function of the Written Word in Roman Religion', in Humphrey, Literacy in the Roman World, 353–8, argues that texts played a relatively large role in Greco-Roman religions, yet characterizes that role as 'symbolic rather than utilitarian', which was clearly not the case in early Christianity. The kind of careful reading, interpretation, and exposition of texts that we see in early Christianity and in early Judaism (whether in worship or school settings) provides, mutatis mutandis, an interesting analogy to the activity of elite literary circles.

[59] On the question of early Christian scriptoria (the term may be variously construed), see Gamble, Books and Readers, 121–6. Hurtado, Earliest Christian Artifacts, 185–9, rightly calls attention to corrections by contemporary hands in early Christian papyri as pointing to at least limited activity of a scriptorial kind.

Pamphilus.[60] Absent such reliable intra-Christian means for the production of books, the range of texts known and used by Christian communities across the Mediterranean basin by the end of the second century would be without explanation.[61] (Hill and Kruger 2012, 32-35)

When we think of publishing a book today, there are some similarities to the ancient process, but of course, it was not the same for Christian communities in the ancient world of the Roman Empire. Paul dispatched Tychicus as a carrier with a letter to the Ephesians, to the Colossians, and Philemon, as well as a potential fourth letter to the Laodiceans. Tychicus was a competent, trusted, skilled coworker, who delivered these letters hundreds of miles from an imprisoned Paul, with enough information to bring God's Word to the first-century Christian congregations. However, in the letter to the Colossians, Paul said, "When this letter has been read among you, have it also read in the church of the Laodiceans; and see that you also read the letter from Laodicea." (Col. 4:16) In other words, it was to be a circuit letter. Paul had also stated to the Thessalonians in a letter to them, "I put you under oath before the Lord to have this letter read to all the brothers." (1 Thess. 5:27) Paul encouraged the distribution of his books.

Remember the process from the above; the book would be shared with friends of similar interests, and then the circles grew wider and wider to friends of friends and others. First, Paul's primary level of friends would be his more than one hundred traveling companions and fellow workers, some being the carriers who delivered the books. Second, the friends in the Christian congregation would have the letter read to them, who would then share it with other fellow congregations. In the secular circle of friends, interested readers who wished to have a copy would have their slaves (i.e., scribes) make a copy or copies of a book. The same would have been true within the Christian congregation. When the Laodiceans read the letter that had been sent by Paul to the Colossians, they would have had one of their wealthy members use his literate and trained scribe to make a copy for their congregation and maybe even a few copies for other members. Now the same would hold true when the Colossians received the letter that had been

---

[60] The role of Pamphilus and the Caesarean library/scriptorium in the private production and dissemination of early Christian literature, esp. of scriptural materials, was highlighted by Eusebius in his Life of Pamphilus, as quoted by Jerome in his Apology against Rufinus (1.9).

[61] Beyond the uses of Christian texts in congregational settings, there were already in the 2nd cent. some Christian circles that pursued specialized and technical engagements with texts, usually in the service of theological arguments and exegetical agendas. The 'school-settings' of teachers such as Valentinus and Justin, and a little later of Theodotus, Clement, and Origen, were Christian approximations to the kinds of literary activity associated with 'elite' reading communities in the early empire.

written to the Laodiceans. Eventually, Paul's letters would be gathered together so that they circulated as a group, such as P[46].

The scriptorium was a room for copying manuscripts, where a lector would read aloud from his exemplar with a room full of copyists taking down his dictation. Recent scholarship has suggested that we remove the concept of the scriptorium in the time of Jesus and the apostles of the first century C.E., on the grounds that this was not a practice until the fourth century C.E. Harry Y. Gamble addresses this effectively when he writes,

> It is difficult to determine just when Christian scriptoria came into existence. The problem is partly of definition, partly of evidence. If we think of the scriptorium as simply a writing center where texts were copied by more than a single scribe, then any of the larger Christian communities, such as Antioch or Rome, may have already had scriptoria in the early second century, and in view of Polycarp's activity something of the kind can be imagined for Smyrna. If we think instead of a scriptorium as being more structured, operating, for example, in a specially designed and designated location; employing particular methods of transcription; producing certain types of manuscripts; or multiplying copies on a significant scale, then it becomes more difficult to imagine that such institutions developed at an early date. (Gamble 1995, 121)

Gamble goes on to inform us that Origen's scriptorium of about 230 C.E. was an exception. The scriptorium of Cyprian just a few short years later was a more official version of what we think of when picturing scriptoria. Then, there is the scriptorium that was attached to the Christian library in Caesarea, which we know was commissioned to produce fifty New Testament manuscripts in short order. It may even have been added in the third century when Pamphilus (latter half of the 3rd century–309 C.E.) built the library. It is likely that a more official type of scriptorium could be found in this period at other Christian epicenters, such as Rome, Jerusalem, and Alexandria. Gamble adds, "It was only during the fourth and fifth centuries that the scriptoria on monastic communities came into their own, also in association with monastic libraries." (Gamble 1995, 121-2)

While it is extremely difficult, if not impossible to identify a specific Alexandrian scriptorium for our early manuscripts of the second century, or even if they were produced in a scriptorium at all, we do know that professional scribes produced them. There are many possibilities: (1) the professional scribe could have produced them in a Christian scriptorium. On the other hand, (2) the professional scribe could have been a Christian who worked for a scriptorium, who then used his skills to produce copies.

Then again, (3) it could have been that the scribe formerly worked in a scriptorium, but now was the private scribe of a wealthy Christian, who used his skills to make copies. What we do know is that there were about a million Christians spread throughout the Roman Empire at the beginning of the second century. Therefore, the copying of manuscripts could very well have been within the Christian community, i.e., from Christian congregation to Christian congregation, as well as wealthy Christians acquiring personal copies for themselves.

We have a number of early manuscripts that evidence that they were very likely produced in a scriptorium, even if it was simply a room attached to a Christian library, which had a handful of copyists. For example, P46 (150 C.E.) was certainly done by a professional scribe because it contained stichoi marks, which are notes at the end of sections, stating how many lines were copied. This was a means of calculating how much a scribe should be paid. It is likely that an employee of the scriptorium numbered the pages, indicating the stichoi marks. Moreover, this same scribe made corrections as he went. Another example would be P66, according to Comfort:

> It is also fairly certain that P66 was the product of a scriptorium or writing center. The first copyist of this manuscript had his work thoroughly checked by a diorthotes [corrector], according to a different exemplar—just the way it would happen in a scriptorium. Of course, it can be argued that an individual who purchased the manuscript made all the corrections, which was a common practice in ancient times. But the extent of corrections in P66 and the fact that the paginator (a different scribe) made many of the corrections speaks against this (see description of P66 in chap. 2). It was more the exception than the rule in ancient times that a manuscript would be fully checked by a diorthotes. P66 has other markings of being professionally produced. The extant manuscript still shows the pinpricks in the corners of each leaf of the papyri; these served as a guide for left hand justification and right hand. The manuscript also exhibits a consistent set of marginal and interlinear correction signs. Another sign of professionally produced manuscript is the use of the diple (>) in the margin, which was used to signal a correction in the text and/or the need for a correction in the text. There are very few of these in the extant New Testament manuscripts. (P. W. Comfort 2008, 26)

The production and distribution of New Testament manuscripts were carried out at the congregation and individual Christian level in the early days of Christianity.

Moreover, this process did not negate the use of professional scribes. Just as Paul would not have used an inexperienced scribe to produce the book of Romans, congregations and wealthy Christians would have likely used professional scribes to make copies. Of course, there are exceptions to the rule and some congregations may not have had access to a professional scribe, so they would have to have chosen to use the best person available to them. Nevertheless, if a congregation had access to a semi-professional or professional scribe, it would have been a lack of good sense or practicality not to take advantage of such a person. Think of anything we want to have done in our Christian congregation today: would we not seek out a professional, if we had access to one as a member, be it plumbing, wiring, teaching, or computer technology? We naturally look to the most skilled person that we can find even if we have a clogged up a commode. Would we do any less if we were in the first century and had just received a letter from the apostle Paul, who was imprisoned hundreds of miles away in Rome?

CHAPTER 3 Books, Reading, and Writing; Literacy In Early Christianity

Before delving into the discussion, we should mention the severe difficulty of defining what literacy was in the ancient Roman Empire of the first three centuries of Christianity and just how literate was the populace.

Full Illiteracy: This one has *no* reading or writing *skills*, no math skills, and is incapable of signing his name for daily living and employment beyond fundamental manual labor. He would work as fruit and vegetable picking, handling materials or low-level tools, manual digging or building, farming, or working in large workshops that produced items such as dishes or pots, as well as household slaves.

Fragmentary Literacy: (inconsistent or incomplete in some areas) The *very basic ability* to understand spoken words, a *very basic grasp* of written words, *very basic math skills* (buying in the market place), and the ability to sign one's name for daily living and employment. He would work as a manual laborer in the market place not requiring math, a shop assistant that performs manual labor, or a soldier.

Fundamental Literacy: The *basic ability* to understand spoken words, an *elementary grasp* of written words, *basic* math skills and the ability to sign one's name and the *ability* to read and write simple words for daily living and employment, such as work as a craftsman, works in the marketplace, or soldier.

Functional Literacy: This one has the *competent ability* to understand spoken words, a *beginner-intermediate level grasp* of written words, and the ability to prepare *basic documents* for daily living and employment tasks that require reading skills beyond a basic level. He is a semiliterate writer who is untrained in writing but has the ability to read or write simple sentences and can take on some basic jobs, such as a copyist or scribe.

Proficient Literacy: This one is a *highly skilled* person, who can understand spoken words, and has an *intermediate-advanced level grasp* of written words. He has the *proficient ability* to prepare short texts for daily living and employment tasks that require reading skills at the *intermediate* level. He is a literate writer who is trained in writing and can take on jobs, such as a copyist or scribe, a tax collector or clerk.

Full Literacy: This one is a *highly skilled expert*, who can understand spoken words, an *advanced level grasp* of written words. He has the *professional ability* to prepare long texts for daily living and employment tasks that require reading skills at the *advanced* level. He is a fully literate writer who is professionally trained in writing and can take on jobs, such as a copyist or scribe, a tax collector, teacher, lawyer, or a clerk to high-ranking positions like Senators.

Rome was a complex society. Levels of literacy were fluid because of the conditions of the day being as culturally and ethnically diverse as it was. The Roman Empire from the first century to the fourth century was as culturally and ethnically diverse as New York City and its five boroughs: the Bronx, Brooklyn, Manhattan, Queens, and Staten Island. A person's literacy level to carry out different job functions and skills for daily living and employment would not be the same in Nazareth as would have been the case in Rome. The need or desire for literacy would not be as important in Nazareth as it would have been in Rome. As we will see, the need or desire for literacy was likely not as important to the pagan as it would have been to the Jew or the Christian.

Therefore, when we look at all of the evidence over the next two chapters, we will discover that literacy on all levels was more prominent than has long been held by historians, who have felt literacy in ancient Rome was no greater than 10-20 percent. It is clear that a *far greater proportion* of the population of the Roman Empire from the days of Jesus Christ to the time of Constantine the Great could make use of their skills in understanding the spoken word, grasping the written word, math skills, and writing. The Roman world was in this time that we speak of overflowing with documents, a range of literacies as we can see from above, as well as different literary genres: historical, religious, military, commercial, poetry, and so on. These were distinguished by the social location of those who possessed them, by the method in which they were produced, the material used to receive the writing, the publication, and circulation, as well as the languages, the kinds of text, and those who used them.

The city of Rome is founded in 753 B.C.E., some 750 years before Jesus was born. The Roman citizens had long believed that reading and writing strengthened them. It gave them confidence that their rulers were not going to take advantage of them. It is a given that as an empire grows, what is expected out of their subjects grows exponentially as well. When a state bureaucracy develops, the use of documents grows right alongside it and the people have no choice but to become *functionally literate*.[62]

Based on what you will learn over the next two chapters consider the accuracy of the following quote from Dr. Bart D. Ehrman, who is a

---

[62] Hopkins, K. (1991) 'Conquest by book', in Humphrey (1991) 11.

prominent scholar of early Christianity and the history of the Greek manuscripts of the New Testament.

> The best and most influential study of literacy in ancient times, by Columbia University professor William Harris, indicates that at the very best of times and places—for example, Athens at the height of the classical period in the fifth century B.C.E.— literacy rates were rarely higher than 10–15 percent of the population. To reverse the numbers, this means that under the best of conditions, 85–90 percent of the population could not read or write. In the first Christian century, throughout the Roman Empire, the literacy rates may well have been lower. (B. D. Ehrman, *Misquoting Jesus: The Story Behind Who Changed the Bible and Why* 2005, 37-38)

On this Larry Hurtado writes, "A few decades ago, it became fashionable in some scholarly circles, including NT/Christian Origins, to hold the view that in the Roman period there was an extremely low level of literacy, and that only elite levels of society had that skill. One still sees this view touted today (typically by those echoing what they believe to be authoritative pronouncements on the matter by others). But a number of studies show that such generalizations are simplistic, and that "literacy" was both more diverse and much more widely distributed than some earlier estimates. The earlier claims of an extremely low level of literacy resurfaced in some comments, so I take the time to draw attention to some previous postings on the subject. Likewise, the older (early 20th century) notion that early Christian circles were composed of slaves and unlearned nobodies has rightly been corrected by various studies. The pioneering study by Edwin Judge, *The Social Pattern of Christian Groups in the First Century* (1960), was followed by a number of works focused on the social description of early Christian groups." – *Larry Hurtado's Blog*[63]

Literacy in the First Century

Craig A. Evans writes, "In recent years, a number of scholars have suggested that Jesus could not read, and that in all likelihood none of his disciples could read either. They maintain this because of studies that have concluded that rates of literacy in the Roman Empire were quite low, and that Jesus and his earliest followers were probably not exceptions."[64] We

---

[63] Retrieved Tuesday, March 26, 2019 (Larry Hurtado's Blog Comments on the New Testament and Early Christianity (and related matters)

https://larryhurtado.wordpress.com/2018/11/01/literacies-in-the-roman-world/

[64] Craig A. Evans (2012-03-16). Jesus and His World: The Archaeological Evidence (Kindle Locations 1403-1406). Westminster John Knox Press. Kindle Edition.

will see this is not the case below but for now let it be said that we cannot take aggregate data and apply it to individuals. In other words, we cannot say that the literacy level in the Roman Empire of the first four centuries of our Common Era is less than ten percent; therefore, Jesus, the apostles and the New Testament authors were illiterate. This is especially true when we can extrapolate from the data that we have, that this is not the case. This would be like saying the average income for Columbus, Ohio is 52,000 dollars a year, so John Smith who lives in Columbus makes 52,000 dollars a year. You cannot apply that aggregate data to individuals unless you have direct information, such as tax records.

How can we, modern readers, know so much about letters from the ancient Roman Empire? We have two different sources that provide us some insight into the writer and his letters. Lucius or Marcus Annaeus Seneca, known as **Seneca the Elder** (54 B.C.E.-39 C.E.), was a Roman rhetorician[65] and writer, born of a wealthy equestrian family of Cordoba, Hispania. Seneca lived through the reigns of three significant emperors: Augustus, Tiberius, and Caligula. For our purpose here we are particularly interested in his letters, which were published; i.e., someone paid to have a scribe produce a copy of them. As was the case with many works of antiquity, the process was repeated over and over again throughout the centuries. Today, we have critical editions of them.

Our other source for insight into the development of the letter writing process is found in the letters of ordinary people, uncovered by archaeologists. These were never published, as they were simply discarded after they served their purpose. In many cases, in order to save costs, these writers would simply flip a letter over and use the other side for something else. Many such letters ended up in garbage dumps. However, some recipients of these letters valued them, so they stored them as though they were a treasure. Therefore, when archaeologists uncovered homes, these letters would be found within the ruins of the home.

In some cases, they were even buried with the deceased because they were so valued. Hundreds of thousands of letters have been discovered over the past century by archaeologists. These were the work of common folk, writing about everyday things. On the subjects of an empire learning a language so as not to be exploited by a powerful kingdom, Gregory Wolf writes,

> This is wonderfully illustrated by the Roman Empire by the personal archive of the Jewish woman named Babatha, found in the Cave of Letters on the shore of the Dead Sea and dating to

---

[65] A rhetorician is a speaker whose words are primarily intended to impress or persuade.

the early second century C.E.[66] Babatha's papers comprised thirty-five documents written in Greek, Nabatean, and Aramaic or a mixture of these languages, with occasional transliterated Latin terms for Roman institutions. The archive included documents relating ing to the sale of land, dates and probably also wine, various marriage contracts and probably details of a dowry, a bequest, a court summons, various notices of deposits and loans, a court summons and a deposition, petitions, and an extract from the minutes of the council of Petra relating to the guardianship of her son. Much of this was generated by private transactions-both commercial and disputes arising from her complicated family life. But it was the recourse to law, and to civic and provincial administration, that generated this mass of material, which she kept with her until her death in the disturbances arising from the Bar Kokhba war.[67]

Most of us have heard of Marcus Tullius Cicero, or simply Cicero (106 B.C.E.-43 B.C.E.), who was a Roman philosopher, politician, lawyer, orator, political theorist, consul, and constitutionalist. He came from a wealthy municipal family in Rome. In his everyday affairs, he penned letters in order to correspond with others. However, while Cicero was writing letters to one person, he knew that others would be reading them as well. Therefore, he took advantage of these opportunities to use writing to communicate points persuasively, using logic and reason, philosophical arguments, and the like. His letters grew from very short letters to far longer, intricate rhetorical letters.

We find yet another famous Roman named Seneca in the days of the apostle Paul. He was the second son of Seneca the Elder. Lucius Annaeus Seneca, or simply **Seneca the Younger** (c. 4 B.C.E.–65 C.E.), was a Roman Stoic philosopher, statesman, and dramatist, i.e., a very famous, skilled, and effective speaker. As for written works, Seneca is known for twelve philosophical essays, 124 letters to Lucilius Junior, nine tragedies, and an uncertain satire. Seneca was a representative of the Silver Age of Latin literature. In his letters to his friend Lucilius, dealing with moral issues, he delved into philosophical ideas, setting aside the simple and bare letters of the day for something far more complex.

The apostle Paul, as we have seen, used personal letters and letter carriers as a substitute until he could visit churches and key people. He produced through his scribe Tertius 433 verses, 7,111 words in the book of

---

[66] N. Lewis 1989.

[67] William A Johnson; Holt N Parker. Ancient Literacies: The Culture of Reading in Greece and Rome (Kindle Locations 655-659). Kindle Edition.

Romans, which would have taken two days to copy. Like the skilled rhetoricians before him, Paul knew that many others would be reading his letters. In fact, he exhorted them to do so. – Colossians 4:16.

We should note that the level of literacy in the first century is a somewhat subjective measurement, because of the limited available evidence, as well as one's interpretation of that evidence. Consider as an analogy the historian today, as compared to the historian during the first few centuries of Christianity. Today, we are capable of covering almost anything that goes on in life, from the most insignificant to the most noteworthy. We in the United States may watch live on television or a laptop as some firefighters in New Zealand rescue a puppy that had been trapped in a storm drain. Then again, we can observe a 9.0 earthquake as it hits Japan, causing the deaths of over 15,000 people.

What about the first few centuries of Jesus, the apostles, and the earliest Christians? The coverage of people, places, and events are not even remotely comparable. The coverage at that time was of the most prominent people, like Seneca the Elder, Cicero, Seneca the Younger, Mark Antony, and Augustus, i.e., the emperor of Rome, senators, generals, the wealthy, with very little press being given to the lower officials, let alone the lower class. We do not have much information on Pontius Pilate at all, but what we do have is an exception to the rule.

> History from antiquity, then, is recoverable but incomplete due to the limited extent and frequently tendentious nature of the sources. Ancient historiography, more than its modern counterpart, is to a greater degree approximate or provisional. A new discovery may alter previous perceptions. Until the discovery of Claudius's Letter to the Alexandrians, written on his accession in 41 but lost until modern times, that emperor's steely resolve could not have been guessed. In short, evidence from Greco-Roman antiquity is fragmentary, generally devoted to "important" people and events and its texts overtly "interpreted." (Barnett 2005, 13)

According to E. Randolf Richards, literacy in the first century was determined by being able to read, not write.[68] The need for writing today is far greater than antiquity. Richards offers an excellent analogy when he says, "I am right handed, so to pen a long paper with my left hand would be quite difficult, and not very legible. The man of antiquity would write

---

[68] (Richards, Paul And First-Century Letter Writing: Secretaries, Composition and Collection 2004, 28)

with the same difficulty because the need to write was so seldom."[69] This author finds this to be true of himself, now that we have entered an era of texting and typing. I have not written a paper by hand in many years. When I fill out a form or even sign my name, I struggle to write, because it is so seldom required. Many have argued that the lower class of antiquity was almost entirely illiterate. However, recent research shows that this was not the case,[70] as literacy was more of an everyday need than they had thought.[71]

Richard's definition of literacy is too simplistic because defining literacy among historians has been plagued by many different definitions. It is also relative to the person determining how the word should be defined. For some historians of the first three centuries of Christianity under the Roman Empire, literacy could refer to any ancient person who merely had the ability to write one's name. For another, it might be as Richard's suggested, one who can read but cannot write. Then, again, it could be a semiliterate writer who is untrained in writing but could prepare short documents, to a literate writer who has had experience in making lengthy documents and has an understanding of what he is writing, to the professional who is paid to write for others. The levels of literacy that was laid out at the beginning of this chapter cover the different levels of literacy in early Christianity.

In passing, I will mention something that few historians or textual scholars will address, the gift of languages. An extraordinary gift conveyed through the Holy Spirit to a number of disciples starting at Pentecost 33 C.E. that made it possible for them to speak or otherwise glorify God in a tongue in addition to their own. Therefore, the ability to be miraculously able to speak a foreign language in the Roman Empire would have been greatly appreciated. In conjunction with this, we must also remember that Christianity grew out of a melting pot of languages: Hebrew, Aramaic, Greek, Latin, Coptic, and Syriac (an Aramaic dialect). Thus, when we think about it, the first and second century Jewish Christian **in Palestine** may be quite familiar with Hebrew, Greek, and even Aramaic but be illiterate when it comes to Latin. On the other hand, the Gentile Christian may be very

---

[69] (Richards, Paul And First-Century Letter Writing: Secretaries, Composition and Collection 2004, 28)

[70] "Throughout the Hellenistic and Roman world the distinction prevailed in that there were educated people who were proficient readers and writers, less educated ones who could read but hardly write, some who were readers alone, some of them only able to read slowly or with difficulty and some who were illiterate."--Millard, Alan Reading and Writing in the Time of Jesus (Sheffield, Sheffield Academic Press, 2000), p. 154

[71] Exler, Form. P. 126 warns, "The papyri discovered in Egypt have shown that the art of writing was more widely, and more popularly, known in the past, than some scholars have been inclined to think." For example, see PZen. 6, 66, POxy. 113,294, 394, 528, 530, 531 and especially 3057.

familiar with Greek, somewhat familiar with Hebrew and a little familiar with Aramaic but possess the very basic ability to understand spoken words and have an elementary grasp of written words when it comes to Latin. Then, **in Rome**, the Gentile and Jewish Christian might be literate when it comes to Latin and also be quite familiar with Greek, and yet be wholly illiterate when it comes to Hebrew and Aramaic.

Even though Greek was very much used **in Egypt**, in time, the need to have a translation in the native language of the growing Egyptian Christian population would come. Coptic was a later form of the ancient Egyptian language. In the late first or early second century C.E., a Coptic alphabet was developed using somewhat modified Greek letters (majuscules and seven characters from the demotic,[72] representing Egyptian sounds the Greek language did not have). At least by the end of the second or the beginning of the third century (c. 200 C.E.), the first translation of parts of the New Testament had been produced for the Coptic natives of Egypt. Various Coptic dialects were used in Egypt, and in time, different Coptic versions were made. Therefore, In the Egyptian part of the Roman Empire, the Christian may be literate when it comes to Coptic but struggles with Greek. And whether the Egyptian Christian is Gentile or Jew, he may or may not have any working knowledge when it comes to Hebrew or Aramaic.

Syria was a region with the Mesopotamia to its East, with the Lebanon Mountains on the West, the Taurus Mountains to it's North, and Palestine and the Arabian Desert to its south. Syria played a very prominent role in the early growth of Christianity. The city of Antioch in Syria was the third largest city in the Roman Empire. Luke tells us of "those who were scattered because of the persecution that occurred in connection with Stephen [shortly after Pentecost, yet just before the conversion of Paul in 34 or 35 C.E.] made their way to Phoenicia and Cyprus and **Antioch**, speaking the word to no one except to Jews alone. But there were some of them, men of Cyprus and Cyrene, **who came to Antioch** [of Syria] and began speaking to the Greeks also, preaching the Lord Jesus." (Ac 11:19-20, bold mine) Because of the thriving interest of the Gospel manifested in Antioch, where many Greek-speaking people were becoming believers, the apostles in Jerusalem sent Barnabas, who then called Paul in from Tarsus to help. (Ac 11:21-26) Both Barnabas and Paul remained there for a year, teaching the people. Antioch became the center for the apostle Paul's missionary journeys.

---

[72] Demotic is a simplified form of Egyptian hieroglyphics. Hieroglyphics is a writing system that uses symbols or pictures to denote objects, concepts, or sounds.

Moreover, "the disciples were first called Christians in Antioch." (Ac 11:26) While the New Testament letters were written in Koine Greek, the common language of the Roman Empire, Latin being the official language, it was thought best to **translate the New Testament books into Syriac in mid-second century C.E.** as Christianity spread throughout the rest of Syria.

However, let us assume for the sake of discussion that literacy was very low among the lower class, and even relatively low among the upper class, who had the ability to pay for the service. What does this say about individual Christians throughout the Roman Empire? It is believed that more than 30–40 million people lived in the combined eastern and western Roman Empire (50–200 C.E.). Now, assume that statistically, the literacy rate is low in a specific area, or a particular city, like Rome (slave population). Does this mean that everyone is illiterate in that region or city? Do we equate the two? If we accept the belief that the lower class were likely to be illiterate, meaning they could not write, or struggled to write; what does this really mean for individuals or Christianity? Very little, because if there are 40-100 million people living throughout the Roman Empire and one million of them were Christian by 125-150 C.E., we are only referring to one or two percent of the population. There is no way to arrive at a specific statistical level of literacy for this small selection, in a time when history focused on the prominent. If a person from that period said anything about the lower class, this was only based on the sphere of whom he knew or what he had seen in his life, which would be very limited when compared to the whole. The last 20 years or so has seen many new directions in the field of literacy in the ancient world. Johnson and Parker offer the following.

> The moment seems right, therefore, to try to formulate more interesting, productive ways of talking about the conception and construction of 'literacies' in the ancient world—literacy not in the sense of whether 10 percent or 30 percent of people in the ancient world could read or write, but in the sense of text-oriented events embedded in particular sociocultural contexts. The volume in your hands [*ANCIENT LITERACIES*] was constructed as a forum in which selected leading scholars were challenged to rethink from the ground up how students of classical antiquity might best approach the question of literacy, and how that investigation might materially intersect with changes in the way that literacy is now viewed in other disciplines. The result is intentionally pluralistic: theoretical reflections, practical demonstrations, and combinations of the two share equal space in the effort to chart a new course. Readers will come away, with food for thought of many types: new ways of thinking about specific elements of literacy in antiquity, such

as the nature of personal libraries, or the place and function of bookshops in antiquity; new constructivist questions, such as what constitutes reading communities and how they fashion themselves; new takes on the public sphere, such how literacy intersects with commercialism, or with the use of public spaces, or with the construction of civic identity; new essentialist questions, such as what "book" and "reading" signify in antiquity, why literate cultures develop, or why literate cultures matter. (Johnson and Parker 2011, 3-4)

Books, Reading, and Writing; Literacy and Early Jewish Education

The priests of Israel (Num. 5:23) and leading persons, such as Moses (Ex. 24:4), Joshua (Josh. 24:26), Samuel (1 Sam 10:25), David (2 Sam. 11:14-15), and Jehu (2 Ki 10:1, 6), were capable of reading and writing. The Israelite people themselves generally could read and write, with few exceptions. (Judges 8:14; Isa. 10:19; 29:12) Even though Deuteronomy 6:8-9 is used figuratively, the command to write the words of the Law on the doorposts of their house and their gates implied that they were literate. Yes, it is true that even though Hebrew written material was fairly common, few Israelite inscriptions have been discovered. One reason for this is that the Israelites did not set up many monuments to admire their accomplishments. Thus, most of the writing, which would include the thirty-nine books of the Bible were primarily done with ink on papyrus or parchment. Most did not survive the damp soil of Palestine. Nevertheless, the Hebrew Old Testament Scriptures were preserved throughout the centuries by careful, meticulous copying and recopying.

During the first seven years of Christianity (29-36 C.E.), three and a half with Jesus' ministry and three and a half after his ascension, only Jewish people became disciples of Christ and formed the newly founded Christian congregation. In 36 C.E. the first gentile was baptized: Cornelius.[73] From that time forward Gentiles came into the Christian congregations. However, the church still consisted mostly of Jewish converts. What do we know of the Jewish family, as far as education? Within the nation of Israel, everyone was strongly encouraged to be literate. The texts of Deuteronomy 6:8-9 and 11:20 were figurative (not to be taken literally). However, we are to ascertain what was meant by the figurative language, and that meaning is what we take literally.

---

[73] Cornelius was a centurion, an army officer in charge of a unit of foot soldiers, i.e., in command of 100 soldiers of the Italian band.

Deuteronomy 6:8-9 Updated American Standard Version (UASV)

⁸ You shall bind them [God's Word] as a sign on your hand and they shall be as frontlets bands between your eyes.[74] ⁹ You shall write them on the doorposts of your house and on your gates.

Deuteronomy 11:20 Updated American Standard Version (UASV)

²⁰ You shall write them on the doorposts of your house and on your gates,

The command to bind God's Word "as a sign on your hand," denoted constant remembrance and attention. The command that the Word of God was "to be as frontlet bands between your eyes," denoted that the Law should be kept before their eyes always, so that wherever they looked, whatever was before them, they would see the law before them. Therefore, while figurative, these texts implied that Jewish children grew up being taught how to read and to write. The Gezer Calendar (ancient Hebrew writing), dated to the 10th-century B.C.E., is believed by some scholars to be a schoolboy's memory exercise.

The Jewish author Philo of Alexandria (20 B.C.E.–50 C. E.) a Hellenistic Jewish philosopher, whose first language was Greek, had this to say about Jewish parents and how they taught their Children the Law and how to read it. Philo stated, "All men guard their own customs, but this is especially true of the Jewish nation. Holding that the laws are oracles vouchsafed by God and having been trained [*paideuthentes*] in this doctrine from their earliest years, they carry the likenesses of the commandments enshrined in their souls." (Borgen 1997, 187) This certainly involved the ability to read and write at a competent level. Philo also wrote, "for parents, thinking but little of their own advantage, think the virtue and excellence of their children the perfection of their own happiness, for which reason it is that they are anxious that they should obey the injunctions which are laid upon them, and that they should be obedient to all just and beneficial commands; for a father will never teach his child anything which is inconsistent with virtue or with truth."[75] In the nation of Israel some 1,550 years before Philo, everyone was strongly encouraged to be literate. (Deut. 4:9; 6:7, 20, 21; 11:19-21; Ps 78:1-4) Not only the father to the children but also prophets, Levites, especially the priests, and other wise men served as teachers. Fathers taught their sons a trade, while mothers taught their daughters the domestic skills. Fathers also taught their children the geography of their land, as well as the rich history. As Philo

---

[74] I.e. on your forehead

[75] Charles Duke Yonge with Philo of Alexandria, *The Works of Philo: Complete and Unabridged* (Peabody, MA: Hendrickson, 1995), 590–591.

informs us of the Jewish people of his day, saying that it is the father, who is responsible for educating the children academically, philosophically, physically, as well as moral instruction and discipline.

Josephus (37-100 C.E.), the first-century Jewish historian, writes, "Our principle care of all is this, to educate our children [*paidotrophian*] well; and we think it to be the most necessary business of our whole life to observe the laws that have been given us, and to keep those rules of piety that have been delivered down to us." (Whiston 1987, Against Apion 1.60) Even allowing for an overemphasis for apologetic purposes; clearly, Jesus was carefully grounded in the Word of God (Hebrew Old Testament), as was true of other Jews of the time. Josephus also says, "but for our people, if anybody do but ask any one of them about our laws, he will more readily tell them all than he will tell his own name, and this in consequence of our having learned them immediately as soon as ever we became sensible of anything, and of our having them, as it were engraven on our souls. Our transgressors of them are but few; and it is impossible when any do offend, to escape punishment." (Whiston 1987, Against Apion 2.178) He also says: "[the Law] also commands us to bring those children up in learning [*grammata* paideuein] and to exercise them in the laws, and make them acquainted with the acts of their predecessors, in order to their imitation of them, and that they may be nourished up in the laws from their infancy, and might neither transgress them, nor yet have any pretense for their ignorance of them." (Whiston 1987, Against Apion 2.204) Again, this clearly involves at a minimum the ability to read and write at a competent level.

From the above, we find that the Jewish family education revolved around the study of the Mosaic Law. If their children were going to live by the Law, they needed to know what it says, as well as understand it. If they were going to know and understand the Law, this would require the ability to read it, and hopefully apply it. Emil Schurer writes: "All zeal for education in the family, the school and the synagogue aimed at making *the whole people a people of the law*. The common man too was to know what the law commanded, and not only to know but to do it. His whole life was to be ruled according to the norm of the law; obedience thereto was to become a fixed custom, and departure therefrom an inward impossibility. On the whole, this object was to a great degree attained." (Schurer 1890, Vol. 4, p. 89) Scott writes that "from at least the time of Ezra's reading of the law (Neh. 8), education was a public process; study of the law was the focus of Jewish society as a whole. It was a lifelong commitment to all men. It began with the very young. The Mishnah[76]

---

[76] The Mishnah was the primary body of Jewish civil and religious law, forming the first part of the Talmud.

requires that children be taught 'therein one year or two years before [they are of age], that they may become versed in the commandments.' Other sources set different ages for beginning formal studies, some as early as five years."[77] (Scott 1995, 257)

It may be that both Philo and Josephus are presenting their readers with an idyllic picture, and what they have to say could possibly refer primarily to wealthy Jewish families who could afford formal education. However, this would be shortsighted, for the Israelites had long been a people who valued the ability to read and write competently. In the apocryphal account of 4 Maccabees 18:10-19, a mother addresses her seven sons, who would be martyred, reminding them of their father's teaching. There is nothing in the account to suggest that they were from a wealthy family. Herein the mother referred to numerous historical characters throughout the Old Testament and quoted from numerous books – Isaiah 43.2; Psalm 34:19; Proverbs 3:18; Ezekiel 37:3; Deuteronomy 32:39.

Jesus would have received his education from three sources. As was made clear from the above, Joseph, Jesus' stepfather would have played a major role in his education. Paul said that young Timothy was trained in "the sacred writings" by his mother, Eunice, and his grandmother Lois. (2 Tim. 1:5; 3:15) Certainly, if Timothy received education in the law from his mother because his Father was a Greek (Acts 16:1), no doubt Jesus did as well after Joseph died.

Jesus would have also received education in the Scriptures from the attendant at the synagogue. In the first-century C.E., the synagogue was a place of instruction, not a place of sacrifices. The people carried out their sacrifices to God at the temple. The exercises within the synagogue covered such areas as praise, prayer, and recitation and reading of the Scriptures, in addition to expository preaching. – Mark 12:40; Luke 20:47

> Before any instruction in the holy laws and unwritten customs are taught... from their swaddling clothes by parents and teachers and educators to believe in God, the one Father, and Creator of the world. (Philo *Legatio ad Gaium* 115.)

The Mishnah tells us the age that this formal instruction would have begun, "At five years old one is fit for the scripture... at thirteen for the commandments." (Mishnah *Abot* 5.21.) Luke 4:20 tells of the time Jesus stood to read from the scroll of Isaiah in the synagogue in Nazareth, and once finished, "he rolled up the scroll and gave it back to the attendant." An attendant such as this one would have educated Jesus, starting at the age of five. As Jesus grew up in Nazareth, he "increased in wisdom and in

---

[77] Mishnah *Yoma* 8:4

stature and in favor with God and man." (Lu 2:52) Jesus and his half-brothers and sisters would have been known to the people of the city of Nazareth, which was nothing more than a village in Jesus' day. "As was his custom, [Jesus] went to the synagogue on the Sabbath day," each week. (Matt. 13:55, 56; Lu. 4:16) While Jesus would have been an exceptional student, unlike anything that the Nazareth synagogue would have ever seen, we must keep in mind that the disciples would have been going through similar experiences as they grew up in Galilee. Great emphasis was laid on the need for every Jew to have an accurate knowledge of the Law. Josephus wrote,

> for he [God] did not suffer the guilt of ignorance to go on without punishment, but demonstrated the law to be the best and the most necessary instruction of all others, permitting the people to leave off their other employments, and to assemble together for the hearing of the law, and learning it exactly, and this not once or twice, or oftener, but every week; which thing all the other legislators seem to have neglected. (Whiston 1987, Against Apion 2.175)

The high priest questioned Jesus about his disciples and his teaching. Jesus answered him, "I have spoken openly to the world. I have always taught in synagogues and in the temple, where all Jews come together. I have said nothing in secret." (John 18:19-20) We know that another source of knowledge and wisdom of Jesus came from the Father. Jesus said, "My teaching is not mine, but his who sent me," i.e., the Father. – John 7:16.

Mark 1:22 Updated American Standard Version (UASV)	Mark 1:27 Updated American Standard Version (UASV)
22 And they were **astounded**[78] at **his teaching**, for he taught them as **one who had authority**, and not as the scribes.	27 And they were all **astonished**,[79] so that they questioned among themselves, saying, "What is this? A new teaching **with authority**! ..."

At first, in the days of Ezra and Nehemiah, the priests served as scribes. (Ezra 7:1-6) The scribes referred to here in the Gospel of Mark are more

---

[78] **Astounded**: (Gr. *ekplēssō*) This is one who is extremely astounded or amazed, so much so that they lose their mental self-control, as they are overwhelmed emotionally.–Matt. 7:28; Mark 1:22; 7:37; Lu 2:48; 4:32; 9:43; Ac 13:12.

[79] **Astonished**: (Gr. *thambeō;* derivative of *thambos*) This is one who is experiencing astonishment, to be astounded, or amazed as a result of some sudden and unusual event, which can be in a positive or negative sense.–Mark 1:27; 10:32; Lu 4:36; 5:9; Acts 3:10.

than copyists of Scripture. They were professionally trained scholars, who were experts in the Mosaic Law. As was said above, a great emphasis was laid on the need for every Jew to have an accurate knowledge of the Law. Therefore, those who gave a great deal of their life and time to acquire an immense amount of knowledge were admired, becoming scholars, forming a group separate from the priests, creating a systematic study of the law, as well as its exposition, which became a professional occupation. By the time of Jesus, these scribes were experts in more than the Mosaic Law (entire Old Testament actually) as they became experts on the previous experts from centuries past, quoting them in addition to quoting Scripture. In other words, if there was any Scriptural decision to be made, these scribes quoted previous experts in the law, i.e., their comments on the law, as opposed to quoting applicable Scripture itself. The scribes were among the "teachers of the law," also referred to as "lawyers." (Lu 5:17; 11:45) The people were **astonished** and **amazed** at Jesus' **teaching** and **authority** because he did not quote previous teachers of the law but rather referred to Scripture alone as his authority, along with his exposition.

Jesus' Childhood Visits to Jerusalem

Only one event from Jesus' childhood is given to us, and it is found in the Gospel of Luke. It certainly adds weighty circumstantial evidence to the fact that Jesus could read and, therefore, was literate.

Luke 2:41-47 Updated American Standard Version (UASV)

[41] Now His parents went to Jerusalem every year at the Feast of the Passover. [42] And when he [Jesus] was twelve years old, they went up according to the custom of the feast. [43] And after the days were completed, while they were returning, the boy Jesus stayed behind in Jerusalem. And his parents did not know it, [44] but supposing him to be in the company, they went a day's journey; and they began looking for him among their relatives and acquaintances. [45] and when they did not find him, they returned to Jerusalem, looking for him. [46] Then, it occurred, after three days they found him in the temple, sitting in the midst of the teachers and **listening** to them and **questioning them.** [47] And all those listening to him were **amazed at his understanding** and his answers.

As we pointed out earlier in chapter 2, this was no 12-year-old boy's questions of curiosity. The Greek indicates that Jesus, at the age of twelve did not ask childlike questions, looking for answers, but was likely challenging the thinking of these Jewish religious leaders.

This incident is far more magnificent than one might first realize. Kittel's *Theological Dictionary of the New Testament* helps the reader to appreciate that the Greek word *eperotao* (to ask, to question, to demand of), for "questioning" was far more than the Greek word erotao (to ask, to request, to entreat), for a boy's inquisitiveness. *Eperotao* can refer to questioning, which one might hear in a judicial hearing, such as a scrutiny, inquiry, counter questioning, even the "probing and cunning questions of the Pharisees and Sadducees," for instance those we find at Mark 10:2 and 12:18-23.

The same dictionary continues: "In [the] face of this usage it may be asked whether . . . [Luke] 2:46 denotes, not so much the questioning curiosity of the boy, but rather His successful disputing. [Verse] 47 would fit in well with the latter view." Rotherham's translation of verse 47 presents it as a dramatic confrontation: "Now all who heard him were beside themselves, because of his understanding and his answers." Robertson's Word Pictures in the New Testament says that their constant amazement means, "they stood out of themselves as if their eyes were bulging out."

After returning to Jerusalem, and three days of searching, Joseph and Mary found young Jesus in the temple, questioning the Jewish religious leaders, at which "they were astounded." (Luke 2:48) Robertson said of this, "second aorist passive indicative of an old Greek word [*ekplesso*]), to strike out, drive out by a blow. Joseph and Mary 'were struck out' by what they saw and heard. Even they had not fully realized the power in this wonderful boy."[80] Thus, at twelve years old, Jesus, only a boy, is already evidencing that he is a great teacher and defender of truth. BDAG says, "to cause to be filled with amazement to the point of being overwhelmed, amaze, astound, overwhelm (literally, Strike out of one's senses).[81]

Some 18 years later Jesus again confronted the Pharisees with these types of interrogative questions, so much so that not "anyone [of them] dare from that day on to ask him any more questions." (Matthew 22:41-46) The Sadducees fared no better when Jesus responded to them on the subject of the resurrection: "And no one dared to ask him any more questions." (Luke 20:27-40) The scribes were silenced just the same after they got into an exchange with Jesus: "And from then on no one dared ask him any more questions." (Mark 12:28-34) Clearly, this insight into Jesus' life and ministry provide us with evidence that he had the ability to read very well and likely write. There is the fact that Jesus was also divine. However, he was also fully human, and he grew, progressing in wisdom, because of his studies in the Scriptures.

---

[80] A.T. Robertson, Word Pictures in the New Testament (Nashville, TN: Broadman Press, 1933), Lk 2:48.

[81] William Arndt, Frederick W. Danker and Walter Bauer, A Greek-English Lexicon of the New Testament and Other Early Christian Literature, 3rd ed. (Chicago: University of Chicago Press, 2000), 308.

Luke 2:40, 51-52 Updated American standard Version (UASV)

40 And the child continued growing and became strong, **being filled with wisdom.** And the favor of God was upon him. 51 And he went down with them and came to Nazareth, and he continued in subjection to them; and his mother treasured all these things in her heart. 52 And Jesus kept **increasing in wisdom** and stature, and in favor with God and men.

Jesus was often called "Rabbi," which was used in a real or genuine sense as "teacher." (Mark 9:5; 11:21; 14:45; John 1:38, 49 etc.) We find "*Rabbo(u)ni*" (Mark 10:51; John 20:16) as well as its Greek equivalents, "schoolmaster" or "instructor" (*epistata*; Luke 5:5; 8:24, 45; 9:33, 49; 17:13) or "teacher" (*didaskalos*; Matt. 8:19; 9:11; 12:38; Mark 4:38; 5:35; 9:17; 10:17, 20; 12:14, 19, 32; Luke 19:39; John 1:38; 3:2). Jesus used these same terms for himself, as did his disciples, even his adversaries, and those with no affiliation.

Another inference that Jesus was literate comes from his constant reference to reading Scripture, when confronted by the Jewish religious leaders: law students, Pharisees, Scribes and the Sadducees. Jesus said, "**Have you not read** what David did when he was hungry, and those who were with him ... Or **have you not read in the Law** how on the Sabbath the priests in the temple profane the Sabbath and are guiltless? (Matt. 12:3, 5; reference to 1 Sam 21:6 and Num 28:9) Again, Jesus responded, "**Have you not read** that he who created them from the beginning made them male and female." (Matt. 19:3; a paraphrase of Gen 1:27) Jesus said to them, "Yes; **have you never read**, "'Out of the mouth of infants and nursing babies you have prepared praise'?" (Matt. 21:16; quoting Psa. 8:2) Jesus said to them, "**Have you never read in the Scriptures**: "'The stone that the builders rejected has become the cornerstone; this was the Lord's doing, and it is marvelous in our eyes'? (Matt. 21:42; Reference to Isaiah 28:16) Jesus said to him, "**What is written in the Law? How do you read it?**" (Lu. 10:26) Many of these references or Scripture quotations were asked in such a way to his opponents; there is little doubt Jesus himself had read them. When Jesus asked in an interrogative way, "have you not read," it was taken for granted that he had read them. Jesus referred to or quoted over 120 Scriptures in the dialogue that we have in the Gospels.

The data that have been surveyed are more easily explained in reference to a literate Jesus, a Jesus who could read the Hebrew Scriptures, could paraphrase and interpret them in Aramaic and could do so in a manner that indicated his familiarity with current interpretive tendencies in both popular circles (as in the synagogues) and in professional, even elite circles (as seen in debates with scribes, ruling priests and elders). Of course, to conclude that Jesus was literate is not necessarily to conclude that

Jesus had received formal scribal training. The data do not suggest this. Jesus' innovative, experiential approach to Scripture and to Jewish faith seems to suggest the contrary.[82]

How did Jesus gain such wisdom? Jesus, although divine, was not born with this exceptional wisdom that he demonstrated at the age of twelve and kept increasing. It was acquired. (Deut. 17:18-19) This extraordinary wisdom was no exception to the norm, not even for the Son of God himself. (Luke 2:52) Jesus' knowledge was acquired by his studying the Hebrew Old Testament, enabling him to challenge the thinking of the Jewish religious leaders with his questions at the age of twelve. Therefore, Jesus had to be very familiar with the Hebrew Old Testament, as well as the skill of reasoning from the Scriptures.

Books, Reading, and Writing; the Literacy Level of the Apostle Peter and John

Acts 4:13 Updated American Standard Version (UASV)	Acts 4:13 New American Standard Bible (NASB)
[13] Now when they saw the boldness of Peter and John, and perceived that **they were uneducated**[83] and untrained men, they were astonished, and they recognized that they had been with Jesus.	[13] Now as they observed the confidence of Peter and John and understood that **they were uneducated** and untrained men, they were amazed, and *began* to recognize them as having been with Jesus.

How are we to understand the statement that Peter and John **were uneducated**? (ESV, NASB, HCSB, LEB, UASV, and others) [*unlettered* (YLT) or *unlearned* (ASV)] This did not necessarily mean that they could not read and write, as the letters that were penned by these apostles (or their secretaries) testify that they could. What this means is that they were not educated in higher learning of the Hebrew schools, such as studying under someone like Gamaliel, as was the case with Paul (Ac 5:34-39; 22:3).[84] The Greek words literally read καταλαβομενοι [having perceived] οτι [that] ανθρωποι [men] αγραμματοι [unlettered] εισιν [they are] και [and]

---

[82] (Evans, Jesus and His World: The Archaeological Evidence 2012)

[83] Or *unlettered* (YLT) that is, not educated in the rabbinic schools; not meaning illiterate.

[84] Gamaliel was a Pharisee and a leading authority in the Sanhedrin, as well as a teacher of the law, of which Acts says, Paul was "educated at the feet of Gamaliel according to the strict manner of the law of our fathers." (Ac 22:3)

ιδιωται [untrained]. This means that the disciples were not educated in rabbinic schools. It did not mean that they were illiterate. In other words, they lacked scribal training. In addition, ιδιωται [untrained], simply means that in comparison to professionally trained scribes of their day, they were not specialists, i.e., were not trained or expert in the scribal duties. This hardly constitutes the idea that they were illiterate.

It was the same reason that the Jewish religious leaders were surprised by the extensive knowledge that Jesus had. They said of him, "How is it that this man has learning when he has never studied?" (John 7:15) This is our best Scriptural evidence that Jesus could read. Let us break it down to what the religious leaders were really saying of Jesus. They asked πως [how] ουτος [this one] γραμματα [letters/writings] οιδεν [has known] μη [not] μεμαθηκως [have learned]. First, this is a reference to the fact that Jesus did not study at the Hebrew schools, i.e., scribal training. In other words, 'how does this one [Jesus] have knowledge of letters/writings, when he has not studied at the Hebrew schools. This question means more than Jesus' ability to read because as we saw in the above, Jewish children were taught to read.

Another example: Luke 4:16-30 says that Jesus "came to Nazareth, where he had been brought up. And as was his custom, he went to the synagogue on the Sabbath day, and he stood up to read. And the scroll of the prophet Isaiah was given to him. He unrolled the scroll and found" (Lu 4:16-17) Jesus was able to take the scroll of Isaiah and read what is now known as Isaiah 61:1-2. While the parallel account in Mark 6:1-6 does not refer to Jesus reading this text, scholars have long known that the gospel writers shared the events through their separate viewpoints, i.e., they drew attention to what stood out to them, and what served their purpose for writing their Gospel accounts.

Within the Roman Empire from the first to the fourth century, we find public writings in and throughout all of the cities. It encompasses inscriptions, which are "dedications, lists of names, imperial decrees, statements or reminders of law, quotations of famous men and even rather pedestrian things, such as directions. Many gravestones and tombs are inscribed with more than the name of the deceased; some have lengthy, even poetic obituaries; others have threats and curses against grave robbers (literate ones, evidently!). The impression one gains is that everybody was expected to be able to read; otherwise, what was the point of all of these expensive inscriptions, incised on stone?"[85] This impression does not end with inscriptions, because archaeology can extrapolate that between the fourth and sixth centuries C.E., millions upon millions of documents came out of Oxyrhynchus, just one city, based on the more than 1.5 million

---

[85] (Evans, Jesus and His World: The Archaeological Evidence 2012)

documents found in their garbage dumps. Of these, five hundred thousand have been recovered.

The **Library of Celsus** (45-ca. 120 C.E.) is an ancient Roman building in Ephesus (completed in 135 C.E.) which contained some 12,000 scrolls. The library was also built as a monumental tomb for Celsus. He is buried in a stone coffin beneath the library. The **Ancient Library of Alexandria**, Egypt (third-century to 30 B.C.E.), was one of the largest and most important libraries of the ancient world. Most of the books were kept as papyrus scrolls. King Ptolemy II Philadelphus (309–246 B.C.E.) is believed to have set 500,000 scrolls as a goal for the library. Apparently, by the first century C.E., the library contained one million scrolls. The **Library of Pergamum** (Asia Minor) was one of the most significant libraries in the ancient world. It is said to have housed roughly 200,000 volumes. Historical records say that the library had a large central reading room. We have not even mentioned Rome, Athens, Corinth, Antioch (Syria), and the rest. The Mediterranean world from Alexander the Great (356-323 B.C.E.) to Constantine the Great (272-337 C.E.), some 700 years, saw hundreds of major libraries, as well as thousands of moderate to minor ones, with hundreds of millions of documents being written and read. Certainly, this does not suggest illiteracy, but literacy.

Some point out that "Celsus,[86] the first writer against Christianity, makes it a matter of mockery, that labourers, shoemakers, farmers, the most uninformed and clownish of men, should be zealous preachers of the Gospel."[87] Paul explained it this way: "For consider your calling, brothers: not many of you were wise according to worldly standards, not many were powerful, not many were of noble birth. But God chose what is foolish in the world to shame the wise; God chose what is weak in the world to shame the strong." (1 Cor. 1:26-27) It seems that these so-called illiterate Christians were able to grow from 120 in Jerusalem about 33 C.E., to some one million by 125 C.E., a mere 92 years later. This growth in the Christian population all came about because they effectively evangelized, using the Septuagint (Greek Old Testament). They were so effective with the Septuagint that the Jews abandoned it and went back to the Hebrew Old Testament.

In any case, Celsus was an enemy of Christianity. Also, as was stated above, what Celsus observed was only within the sphere of his personal experiences. How many Christians could he have known out of almost a

---

[86] This Celsus was a second-century Greek philosopher and opponent of early Christianity, who should not be confused with the previously mentioned Celsus, Roman Senator Tiberius Julius Celsus Polemaeanus.

[87] The History of the Christian Religion and Church, During the Three First Centuries, by Augustus Neander; translated from the German by Henry John Rose, 1848, p. 41

million at the time of his writing? Moreover, although not highly educated in schools, it **need not** be assumed that most or all of the early Christians were entirely illiterate, but rather a good number of them could read and write (with difficulty). Many had a *very basic* ability to understand spoken words, a *very basic* grasp of written words, *very basic* math skills (buying in the market place), and the ability to sign one's name for daily living and employment.

Let us return to Peter and John. We will assume for the sake of argument that literacy was between five and ten percent, with most readers being men. We will accept that Peter and John were entirely illiterate in the sense the modern historian believes it to be true (even though they likely were not). The time of the statement in Acts about the two apostles' being **"uneducated"** (i.e., unlettered) was about 33 C.E.[88] Peter would not pen his first letter for about 30 more years. Throughout those 30 years, Peter progressed spiritually, maturing into the position of being one of the leaders of the entire first-century Christian congregation. A few years later, Peter and John were viewed as developing and growing into their new position, as leaders in the Jerusalem congregation; as Paul said of them, "James and Cephas and John, who seemed to be pillars" of the Christian community. John, on the other hand, did not pen his books until about 60 years after Acts 4:13. Are we to assume that he too had not grown in 60 years? Could education in the first century have become more accessible?

The Birth of Koine Greek

After the conquests of Alexander the Great and the extension of Macedonian rule in the fourth-century B.C.E., a transferal of people from Greece proper to the small Greek communities in the Middle East took place. Throughout what became known as the Hellenistic period, the Attic dialect, spoken by the educated classes as well as by the traders and many settlers, became the language common to all the Middle East. From about 300 B.C.E. to about 500 C.E. was the age of Koine, or common Greek, a combination of different Greek dialects of which Attic was the most significant. Koine soon became the universal language. It had a tremendous advantage over the other languages of this period, in that it was almost universally used. "Koine" means the "common" language, or dialect common to all. The Greek vocabulary of the Old Testament translation, the Septuagint, was the Koine of Alexandria, Egypt, from 280 to 150 B.C.E. Everett Ferguson writes,

> Literacy became more general, and education spread. Both abstract thought and practical intelligence were enhanced in a

---

[88] B.C.E. means "before the Common Era," which is more accurate than B.C. ("before Christ"). C.E. denotes "Common Era," often called A.D., for *anno Domini,* meaning "in the year of our Lord."

greater proportion of the population. This change coincided with the spread of Greek language and ideas, so that the level and extent of communication and intelligibility became significant. (Ferguson 2003, 14)

Education was voluntary, but elementary schools at least were widespread. The indications, especially on the evidence of the papyri, are that the literacy rate of Hellenistic and early Roman times was rather high, probably higher than at any period prior to modern times. Girls as well as boys were often included in the elementary schools, and although education for girls was rarer than for boys, it could be obtained. The key for everyone was to get what you could on your own. (Ferguson 2003, 111)

By the time we enter the first-century C.E., the era of Jesus and the apostles, Koine Greek had become the international language of the Roman Empire. The Bible itself bears witness to this; e.g. when Jesus was executed by the Roman Pontius Pilate, the inscription above his head was in Aramaic, the language of the Jews, in Latin, the official language of Rome. It was also in Greek, which was the language spoken on the streets of Alexandria to Jerusalem, to Athens, to Rome and the rest of the Empire. (John 19:19, 20; Acts 6:1) Acts 9:29 informs us that Paul was preaching in Jerusalem to Greek-speaking Jews. As we know, Koine, a well-developed tongue by the first-century C.E., would be the tool that would facilitate the publishing of the 27 New Testament books.

Books, Reading, and Writing; Archaeological Evidence for Literacy In Early Christianity

Archaeologists have discovered hundreds of thousands of examples of graffiti on the outsides of buildings throughout the ancient Roman world, over 11,000 in Pompeii alone.

Graffiti and Literacy in Early Christianity

Pompeii was a prosperous, populace (15,000), economically diverse ancient Roman city near modern Naples in the Campania region of Italy. Over 11,000 graffiti samples, etched into the plaster or painted on the walls, in both public and private places, have been uncovered in the excavations of Pompeii. Archaeologists have been studying and recording graffiti in Pompeii since the 1800s.

Mount Vesuvius blew a column of gas, magma, and debris for thirty-six hours that literally darkened the sky as though it were night, which caused a dreadful rain of ash and lapilli (small lava rock fragments ejected from a volcano). It only took two days until Pompeii and an enormous area of rural area were covered with a thick layer, with the average depth of about eight feet [2.5 m]. The earth continued to be shaken by violent tremors that released into the air a huge cloud of poisonous gases. These gases were invisible but deadly, which covered the city, bringing death. As Pompeii was being buried, the small Roman town Herculaneum vanished instantly, being preserved more or less intact. "Lava flowed down on Herculaneum, submerging that town under a mass of mud and volcanic debris to a depth that reached twenty-two meters [72 feet] near the shore." (Dell'Orto 1990, 131)

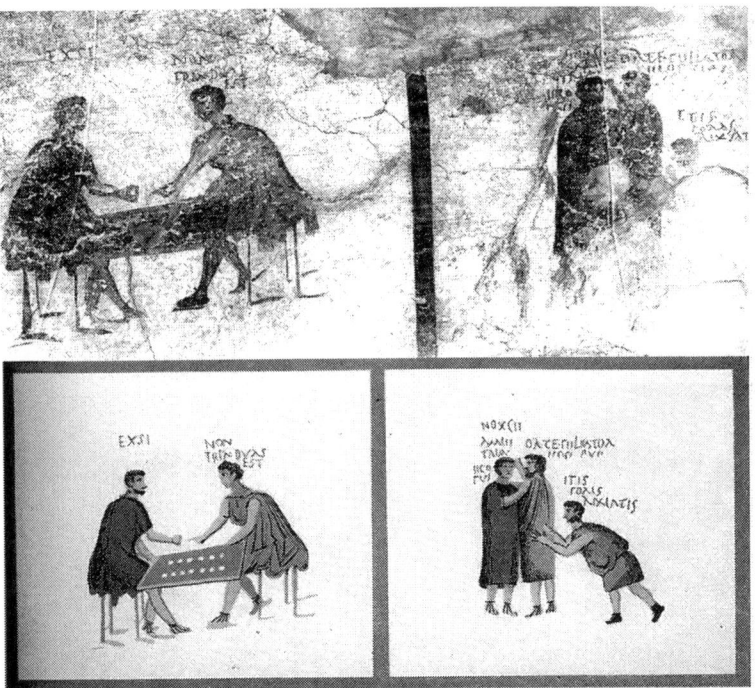

CIL IV, 03494 National Archaeological Museum of Naples (inv. N. 111482), Scenes of osteria, Pompeian fresco (50 x 205 cm) from the Caupona of Salvius (VI, 14, 35-36) with "comics."

It is these buried cities that have helped us to understand the ancient Roman world better and specifically it's Graffiti that has enabled us to understand its literary level better. The Graffiti of the ancient Roman world was **writing** in charcoal, scratched with a stylus or stick, painted with a brush, **or drawings** scribbled, scratched, or painted with a brush on a wall or other surface in a public place. In the ancient world of the first-century Roman Empire, graffiti was a valued form expression, which was even interactive, and should not be confused with the modern-day criminal defacement we now see in most of our modern cities.

CIL IV, 10237 A graffito from Pompeii that shows musicians, the emperor, and a fight between a murmillō and a secūtor.

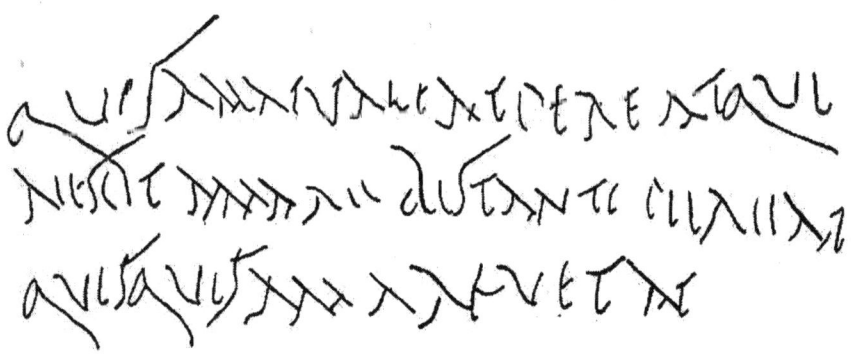

C.I.L. IV 4091
QVIS AMAT VALEAT PEREAT QVI
NESCIT AMARE BIS TANTI PEREAT
QVISQVIS AMARE VETAT

CIL IV, 4091 "Whoever loves, let him flourish, let him perish who knows not love, let him perish twice over whoever forbids love"

Some scholars as we have already seen from above and others not mentioned herein have attempted to downplay the importance of the texts of the Greek New Testament within early Christianity. Instead, they argue that the oral gospel played a far more important, dominant role. This is largely supported by the long-held belief that the vast majority of those in the ancient Roman world was unable to read and write. Many scholars throughout the twentieth century have argued that the low literacy level is evidence that the early Christians did not place a significant value of the texts of the New Testament. On this Alan Millard, professor of Hebrew and ancient Semitic languages, writes, "Another authority stated, 'there was a gap of several decades between the public ministry of Jesus and the writing down of his words by the authors of the Gospels. During this time what was known about Jesus was handed on orally.'" The Jesus Seminar, fifty critical Biblical scholars and one-hundred laymen founded in 1985 by Robert Funk, even argue that Jesus' early disciples "were technically illiterate." (Millard 2000, 185)

From the last forty to fifty years, the evidence supports that people of all sorts knew how to read and write in the first century. The Hebrew, Aramaic, and Greek languages were common at all levels of society during Jesus' life and ministry and the apostle's lifetime. The argument that the Gospels came out of an utterly illiterate society is a false narrative because the evidence tells another story entirely, as reading and writing would be quite common throughout the Roman Empire. In almost every circumstance there would be people who could write something that someone tells them, be it for their personal use, or the benefit of another.

C.I.L. IV 5092
AMORIS IGNES SI SENTIRES MVLIO
MAGI PROPERARES VT VIDERIS VENEREM
DILIGO IVVENEM (PVERVM) VENVSTVM ROGO PVNGE IAMVS
BIBISTI IAMVS PRENDE LORA ET EXCVTE
POMPEIOS DEFER VBI DVLCIS EST AMOR
MEVS ES

CIL IV, 5092 Graffiti from Pompeii, in verse. The writer, burned by the flames of love, incites the mule driver to stop drinking and goad the mules to get to Pompeii first, where a handsome boy, whose writer is in love, awaits him, and where love is sweet.

For example, consider the commonness of the graffiti in Pompeii and throughout the Roman Empire. The elites that argue for orality do not include this kind of evidence into the discussion, which they should because it would detract from their theme of literacy impacting the production, publication, and distribution of a written text. Think about graffiti by its very nature cannot be derived from the wealthy, prominent members of Roman society. Who would argue that such memorable writers as Vergil (or Virgil), Horace, Catullus, Propertius, Tibullus, and Ovid were found scribbling on the side of some public building? On this, Kristina Milnor writes, "The corpus of Pompeian wall writings, moreover, has been seen as a window onto the language of everyday life in the ancient Roman world, one of our few opportunities to read words written by ordinary people performing an activity (writing graffiti) that we in the modern day do not associate with the cultural elite."[89]

As Milnor rightly points out, the graffiti is not by the hands of elite writers but rather common everyday people. She makes the acute observation that the prominent Latin poets of the day had mixed feelings and concerns about the production of their book that they knew would be read and reread, which meant being copied and copied. They knew this also meant that human error would creep into the work and copyist may even take liberties. Moreover, these published authors knew that they also faced public criticism, while the authors of the graffiti knew their work was an autograph and never had to face any production, publication, and distribution issues. The author of a graffito simply concerned himself with the **technical** aspects of his written work: its properties and techniques as seen from a literary and language perspective. In many cases, the Latin poet's work may become known throughout the entire empire, while the graffito author is simply a local phenomenon.

We need to view graffiti in the light of all written works that had an impact on the ancient Roman culture of the day. Some might mistakenly believe that graffiti was at the bottom of the written record spectrum. However, we might place the graffiti above the daily writings of advertisements for rental properties, shopping lists, or signs throughout the city offering public information to the passerby. We might even place the graffiti on the same level as the local newspaper or rather something like the tabloid magazine of the first century C.E., with writers showing much interest in the classics, who dabbled in poetry and mythology, as well as local gossip, with a mixture of advertisements. While it is true that the messages were likely more impactful on the urban level, let's not think the elites were any less impacted by the graffiti than the elites of today and TMZ. The readers were incidental in nature, happening upon the graffiti,

[89] William A. Johnson; Holt N. Parker, *Ancient Literacies: The Culture of Reading in Greece and Rome* (Oxford: Oxford University Press, 2011), 291.

not seeking it out like a published book. However, the workers of the elites likely communicated these things to their employers or masters if the subject or context was relevant, and there is nothing to say that when a wealthy person walked the streets through the shops, they never paused to read the graffiti. The general conclusion being "It seems clear that a significant percentage of wall writers and readers were literate in Greek, although the common practice of transliteration suggests that there may have been more speakers than writers/readers."[90]

While we have focused on the public places of Pompeii and the Roman empire as a whole, graffiti can also be found in the catacombs and on various early Christian monuments. Throughout the Roman Empire of the first three centuries of Christianity, graffiti could have been in the millions engraved into or painted on walls, floors and engraved on tombstones. Craig A. Evans informs us that Israel was not exempt from graffiti, stating, "There are many examples in Israel too, though not nearly as 'colourful' as those preserved on the scorched walls of Pompeii and Herculaneum. At the very least these graffiti and inscriptions attest to a crude literacy that reached all levels of society." Evans sites Rock Inscriptions and Graffiti Project (3 vols, SBLRBS 28, 29, 31; Atlanta: Scholars Press, 1992-4), "Stone and his colleagues catalogued some 8,500 inscriptions and graffiti found in southern Israel: the Judean desert, the desert of the Negev and Sinai. The inscriptions are in several languages, including Hebrew, Aramaic, Greek, Latin, Nabatean, Armenian, Georgian, Egyptian hieroglyphs and others. Not many date to late antiquity, because, unlike the graffiti and inscriptions of Pompeii and Herculaneum, the graffiti and inscriptions in the deserts of Israel were exposed to the eroding elements."[91] The graffiti help us to illustrate literacy and the literary sources of the life of the early Christians.

Figure 1 CIL IV, 8364 Pompeyan inscription Translation: "I subscribe to your dear Prima in every place a cordial greeting, I beg of you, my mistress, to love me."

---

[90] William A. Johnson; Holt N. Parker, *Ancient Literacies: The Culture of Reading in Greece and Rome* (Oxford: Oxford University Press, 2011), 295.

[91] Craig A. Evans, *Jesus and His World: The Archaeological Evidence* (Westminster: John Knox Press, 2012), Section 3317, KDP.

Public Writing

Theodotus Inscription to Greek-Speaking Jews: The inscription reads: "Theodotus son of Vettenus, priest and synagogue-president, son of a synagogue-president and grandson of a synagogue-president, has built the synagogue for the reading of the Law and the teaching of the Commandments, and (he has built) the hostelry and the chambers and the cisterns of water in order to provide lodgings for those from abroad who need them—(the synagogue) which his fathers and the elders and Simonides had founded." (*Biblical Archaeology,* by G. Ernest Wright, 1962, p. 240)

The text was carved on a limestone slab measuring 72 cm (28 in.) in length and 42 cm (17 in.) in width. It was discovered early in the 20th century on the hill of Ophel in Jerusalem. The inscription, written in Greek, refers to a priest, Theodotus. It has been dated to shortly before the destruction of Jerusalem in 70 C.E. It is evidence that there were Greek-speaking Jews in Jerusalem in the first century C.E. (Ac 6:1) Some believe that the writing is referring to "the synagogue of the Freedmen (as it was called)," The inscription also references that Theodotus, as well as his father Vettenus and his grandfather, had the title *archisynagogos* (**leader of a synagogue,** local ruler of the community),[92] a title that used a number of times in the Greek New Testament. (Mark 5:22, 35-36, 38; Lu 8:49; 13:14; Ac 13:15; 18:8, 17, etc.).

---

[92] James Swanson, *Dictionary of Biblical Languages with Semantic Domains: Greek (New Testament)* (Oak Harbor: Logos Research Systems, Inc., 1997).

There has been a countless number of archaeological finds that seem to suggest that many within the Roman Empire could read. Literally, throughout the Roman Empire, we find literally hundreds if not thousands of public inscriptions like the Theodotus Inscription shown above. These inscriptions range from a list of names, general public information, imperial decrees, laws and regulations, quotations from famous people, as well as directions, or distances from one place to another. In addition, even in the graveyards and the tombs, we find far more inscribed on the gravestones then merely the names of the deceased. On these tombstones, we find graffiti as mentioned above but also an inscription on the stone itself, such as threats and curses against any suspecting grave robbers who might happen upon their burial site. Indeed, it seems that they believed that the lowest criminal elements of the day could read. The impression from all of this public writing is that the public as a whole could read; otherwise, what is the point of spending all of the time and money so that a mere 5-10 percent of 100 million people could read it.

Literacy and the Literature from Egyptian Garbage Heaps

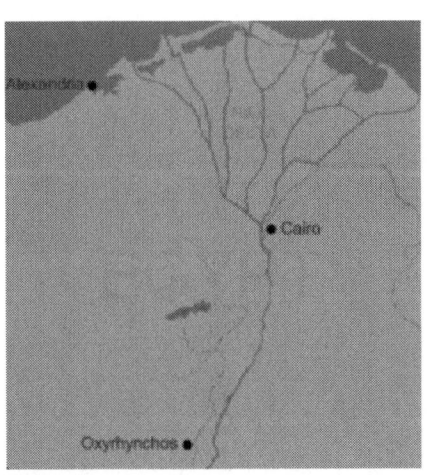

Beginning in 1778 and continuing to the end of the 19th century, many papyrus texts were accidentally discovered in Egypt that dated from 300 B.C.E. to 500 C.E., almost 500 million documents in all. About 130 years ago, there began a systematic search. At that time, a continuous flow of ancient texts was being found by the native fellahin, and the Egypt Exploration Society, a British non-profit organization, founded in 1882, realized that they needed to send out an expedition team before it was too late. They sent two Oxford scholars, Bernard P. Grenfell and Arthur S. Hunt, who received permission to search the area south of the farming region in the Faiyūm district. Grenfell chose a site called Behnesa because of its ancient Greek name, Oxyrhynchus. A search of the graveyards and the ruined houses produced nothing. The only place left to search was the town's garbage dumps, which were some 30 feet [9 m] high. It seems to Grenfell and Hunt that all was lost but they decided to try.

Grenfell (left) and Hunt (right) in about 1896

In January of 1897, a trial trench (excavation or depression in the ground) was dug, and it only took a few hours before ancient papyrus materials were found. These included letters, contracts, and official documents. The sand had blown over them, covering them, and for nearly 2,000 years, the dry climate had served as a protection for them.

Illustrates excavations at Oxyrhynchus

It took only a mere three months to pull out and recover almost two tons of papyri from Oxyrhynchus. They shipped twenty-five large cases back to England. Over the next ten years, these two courageous scholars returned each and every winter, to grow their collection. They discovered ancient classical writing, along with royal ordinances and contracts mixed in with business accounts private letters, shipping lists, as well as fragments of many New Testament manuscripts.

Of what benefit were all these documents? Foremost, the bulk of these documents were written by ordinary people in Koine (common) Greek of the day. Many of the words that would be used in the marketplace, not by the elites appeared in the Greek New Testament Scriptures, which woke scholars up to the fact that Biblical Greek was not some special Greek, but instead, it was the ordinary language of the common people, the man on the street. Thus, by comparing how the words had been used in these papyri, a clearer understanding of Biblical Greek emerged. As of the time of this writing, less than ten percent of these papyri have been published and studied. Most of the papyri were found in the top 10 feet 93 m] of the garbage heap because the other 20 feet [6 m] had been ruined by water from a nearby canal. If we look at it simply, this would mean that the 500 thousand documents found could have been two million in total. Then, we must ponder just how many documents must have come through Oxyrhynchus that were never discarded in the dumps.

We have almost a half million papyrus documents (likely there were millions more that did not survive) in garbage dumps in the dry sands of Oxyrhynchus, Egypt. This is but one city in the entirety of the Roman Empire. Are we to believe that Oxyrhynchus is the exception, and some of the biggest cities, such as Rome, Corinth, Athens, Pergamum, Ephesus, Smyrna, Antioch, Jerusalem, Alexandria, and Carthage, which numbered anywhere from one hundred thousand to over a million in their population, did not have equal or greater writings discarded in their dumps? Then we should consider the temples and the libraries that boasted of tens of thousands of books. Reportedly, by the first century C.E., the Alexandrian library housed one million scrolls. In fact, Mark Antony took 200,000 scrolls from the library at Pergamum to replenish the Alexandrian library for Cleopatra. Because of moisture damage and they're being written on perishable material, we cannot discover the documents of these centers of education as we have in the dry sands of Egypt. Yet, should we for a moment believe that their garbage dumps saw any fewer books that were discovered at Oxyrhynchus, Egypt?

Clearly, the tremendous amount of document discoveries begs for widespread literacy not low levels. We are not trying to overturn the apple cart here. The common consensus of the historians is that in the Roman Empire of the first three centuries of Christianity were 5-10 percent literate and they were male. We **are not** trying to suggest that widespread means the 80-90 percent literacy but instead at least 40-50 percent, if not more. We think of the immense production of the twenty-seven New Testament books of the first century and the Apostolic Fathers in the late first and early second centuries, as well as the Apologists from near the middle of the second century through its end. Then, we consider the publication of these books, the copying of these books, as well as their circulation, and we conclude that the use of these books in the early Christian Church are apparent. They, along with all else that has been discussed in this chapter give us clear visible proof of some level literacy within Christianity, but it cannot offer us the exact extent. We would argue the percentage be broken down instead of trying to suggest a one size fits all.

Full Illiteracy (20%): This one has no reading or writing skills, no math skills, and is incapable of signing his name for daily living and employment beyond fundamental manual labor. He would work as fruit and vegetable picking, handling materials or low-level tools, manual digging or building, farming, or working in large workshops that produced items such as dishes or pots, as well as household slaves.

Fragmentary Literacy (40): (inconsistent or incomplete in some areas) The very basic ability to understand spoken words, a very basic grasp of written words, very basic math skills (buying in the market place), and the ability to sign one's name for daily living and employment. He would work as a manual laborer in the market place not requiring math, a shop assistant that performs manual labor, or a soldier.

Fundamental Literacy (20): The basic ability to understand spoken words, an elementary grasp of written words, basic math skills and the ability to sign one's name and the ability to read and write simple words for daily living and employment, such as work as a craftsman, works in the marketplace, or soldier.

Functional Literacy (15%): This one has the competent ability to understand spoken words, a beginner-intermediate level grasp of written words, and the ability to prepare basic documents for daily living and employment tasks that require reading skills beyond a basic level. He is a semiliterate writer who is untrained in writing but has the ability to read or write simple sentences and can take on some basic jobs, such as a copyist or scribe.

Proficient Literacy (3%): This one is a highly skilled person, who can understand spoken words, and has an intermediate-advanced level grasp of written words. He has the proficient ability to prepare short texts for daily living and employment tasks that require reading skills at the intermediate level. He is a literate writer who is trained in writing and can take on jobs, such as a copyist or scribe, a tax collector or clerk.

Full Literacy (2%): This one is a highly skilled expert, who can understand spoken words, an advanced level grasp of written words. He has the professional ability to prepare long texts for daily living and employment tasks that require reading skills at the advanced level. He is a fully literate writer who is professionally trained in writing and can take on jobs, such as a copyist or scribe, a tax collector, teacher, lawyer, or a clerk to high-ranking positions like Senators.

CHAPTER 4 The Reading Culture of Early Christianity

There is evidence of universality in the early orthodox Christian manuscripts. While the elite of the Roman society preferred the roll or scroll for their pagan literature, the Christian preferred the codex book form. This is even the case with the roll or scroll being preferred for apocryphal apostate Christian literature as opposed to the codex. Except for P[22] (John 15:25–16:2, 21–32), all of the third/fourth-century canonical gospel manuscripts were papyrus codices. Going back to the second/third centuries, we also find that the Gospel codices were given some special status, as they were all produced in standard sizes that were smaller than the other canonical NT books. The gospels were 11.5–14 cm in width and height at least 3 cm higher than width, while other NT books were 12–14 cm in width and height not quite twice that. Even so, while the other NT books might have been a little taller, they all were easily carried. (Hill and Kruger 2012, 38) The codex came to be used toward the end of the first century, and the Christians were commonly using it after the first century.[93] The evidence for such a conclusion comes from our earliest Christian manuscripts that are still in existence, which were produced in codex form. The manuscripts include the Old Testament that was used by the Christians and the New Testament texts, as well as the Apostolic Fathers, the Apologists, and other early Church Fathers.

Another piece of evidence of universality in the early orthodox Christian manuscripts was the *nomina sacra* (Lat. "sacred names"), which were contractions and abbreviations of several frequently occurring divine names or titles in the early texts, the Greek counterparts of God, Lord, Jesus, Christ, Son, Spirit, David, Cross, Mother, Father, Israel, Savior, Man, Jerusalem, and Heaven. (Metzger 1981, 36-37) Early on there was universality with the four divine names or titles God, Jesus, Christ, and Lord, to which were later added the other sacred names above. Even how the sacred names were to be contracted in the manuscripts was standardized and universal. It was decided early that regardless of whether sacred names were used in a sacred or mundane way, they were to be contracted. For example, whether the Greek *kurios* (Lord) was used in reference to the Son Jesus (sacred) as opposed to the master of a household (mundane/non-sacred), it was to be contracted. Another example of whether the Greek *pater* (Father/father) was used in reference to the Father

---

[93] T. C. Skeat, *Zeitschrift für Papyrus und Epigraphic* 102 (1994): 263–68.

(sacred) or a father in some narrative or parable (mundane/non-sacred), it was to be contracted. For example, in P[66] (c. 200 C.E.),[94] *kurios* ("Lord") is contracted through the entire manuscript whether it was sacred or mundane in its use. We have the same situation with *pneuma* (spirit) in P[75] (c. 175-225 C.E.),[95] even when it is a reference to an unclean spirit. This is evidence of a universal, systematic approach to the Christian canonical books, which shows a concern for the accuracy of the content and the handiness, convenience, and portability of the New Testament books in the latter half of the second-century C.E.[96]

The Reading Culture of Early Christianity

Textual scholar Larry Hurtado (Hill and Kruger 2012, 49) borrows an approach from William A. Johnson in his book *Readers and Reading Culture in the High Roman Empire: A Study of Elite Communities*, and I would like to take the liberty of borrowing this concept as well. Johnson, under the heading, CONTEXTUALIZING READING COMMUNITIES, writes, "The more proper goal, as I [Johnson] have argued, is to understand the particular reading cultures that obtained in antiquity, rather than to try to answer decontextualized questions that assume in 'reading' a clarity and simplicity it manifestly does not have." (Johnson 2012 (Reprint), 14)

---

[94] CONTENTS: John 1:1–6:11; 6:35–14:26, 29–30; 15:2–26; 16:2–4, 6–7; 16:10–20:20, 22–23; 20:25–21:9, 12, 17.

[95] CONTENTS: Luke 3:18–22; 3:33–4:2; 4:34–5:10; 5:37–6:4; 6:10–7:32, 35–39, 41–43; 7:46–9:2; 9:4–17:15; 17:19–18:18; 22:4–24:53; John 1:1–11:45, 48–57; 12:3–13:1, 8–10; 14:8–29; 15:7–8.

[96] What we have learned here and in the whole of THE TEXT OF THE NEW TESTAMENT undermine what secular scholars such as Walter Bauer, Robert A. Kraft, and agnostic Bart D. Ehrman maintain. These argue that **Gnosticism** (a false philosophy, speculation, and pagan mysticism of apostate Christianity), **Montanism** (a heresy based on the teachings of the charismatic prophet Montanus), and **Marcionism** (condemned as a Christian heresy that rejected the Old Testament) were just alternative forms of Christianity, just as organized and fast-growing if not faster. They have maintained, moreover, that the form of Christianity in Rome prevailed in the fourth century and became the standard, causing these groups and others to be seen as apostate forms of Christianity. This is not the case. First, the early evidence is that these groups were only tiny apostate offshoots of true Christianity, who broke away, abandoning the truth. Second, they were busy arguing amongst themselves over doctrine, as opposed to making disciples. Third, the apocryphal non-canonical Gospel of Thomas, the Gospel of Mary, the Gospel of Peter, the so-called Egerton Gospel, and the Gospel of Judas were composed in the second century C.E. by no apostle or anyone associating directly with Jesus, not to mention that they all indicate that they were private manuscripts, having no earmarks that they were meant to be universal. Finally, if these heresies and their apocryphal writings were just as far-reaching as Orthodox Christianity, why are there no citations of them in the second/third century apostolic fathers? Only the Gospel of Thomas has two early third-century citations. If they were as impactful as the canonical gospels, they should have been cited as much. The early papyri do not support Walter Bauer, Robert A. Kraft, and Bart D. Ehrman's in their views of early Christianity.

Johnson focuses his reading culture on "'the reading of Greek literary prose texts by the educated elite during the early empire (first and second centuries AD)'" (Hill and Kruger 2012, 49), just one of many surrounding reading cultures of the time. We are going to focus our attention on the reading culture of early Christianity, namely, the first three centuries. Just as the manuscript evidence above gave us proof of a universal approach of early Christianity to the publication of their canonical books, showing concern for the accuracy of the content, this will be an extension of that.

What made Johnson's work so appetizing for Hurtado is the Roman elite reading culture and how he demonstrated that their approach was actually designed to keep out anyone who could not handle the difficulty with which their reading community functioned. The Roman literary world had long had word separation within their texts, but the elite reading culture of the Roman world in the second and third centuries returned to *scriptio continua* (Lat. for "continuous script"), a style of writing without spaces or other marks between the words and sentences. This choice of writing style over others that were current and common, with spaces between words and sentences as well as punctuation, diacritical marks that indicate how words are to be pronounced, and distinguished letter case, is evidence that they were putting up roadblocks to keep the uneducated out of their elite reading culture.

This is even further evidenced when we consider that they ignored the codex and stayed with the rolls or scrolls that were held horizontally, with the text being read vertically. The text was in "columns ranging from 4.5 to 7.0 centimetres in width, about 15–25 letters per line, left and right justification, and about 15–25 centimetres in height, with about 1.5–2.5 centimetres spacing between columns. The letters were carefully written, calligraphic in better quality manuscripts, but with no spacing between words, little or no punctuation, and no demarcation of larger sense-units. The strict right-hand justification was achieved by 'wrapping' lines (to use a computer term), ending each line either with a given word or a syllable, and continuing with the next word or syllable on the next line, the column 'organized as a tight phalanx of clear, distinct letters, each marching one after the other to form an impression of continuous flow, the letters forming a solid, narrow rectangle of written text, alternating with narrower bands of white space'." (Hill and Kruger 2012, 50)

Another feature of this elite reading culture was the fact that they cared deeply about the elegant and beautiful or artistic handwriting that was pleasing to the eyes, but not as reader-friendly as the rounded, unadorned writing in the Christian texts. Indeed, the elite reading culture cared about the accuracy of the content in their documents as well, but it took a backseat to visually stimulating handwriting. The reader had the task of bringing to life this text with no sense breaks or punctuation.

The early codex manuscripts present us a picture of early Christianity that was a book-buying, book-reading, and book-publishing culture unlike no other, as they turned to the book form, i.e., the codex, finding it handy, convenient, and portable. Matthew, Mark, Luke, John, Paul, Peter, James, and Jude were moved along by the Holy Spirit, penning their books. The writings were then delivered and distributed by a trusted traveling companion, who then read it aloud to the Christian congregation(s).

Paul in his final greeting to the Ephesians writes, "So that you also may know how I am and what I am doing, Tychicus the beloved brother and faithful minister in the Lord will tell you everything. I have sent him to you for this very purpose, that you may know how we are, and that he may encourage your hearts." (Eph. 6:21-22, ESV) Paul tells the Christians in Colossae, "Tychicus will tell you all about my activities. He is a beloved brother and faithful minister and fellow servant in the Lord. I have sent him to you for this very purpose, that you may know how we are and that he may encourage your hearts." (Col. 4:7-8, ESV) The first Christians were encouraged to read the Scriptures during their religious services and to discuss them. (1 Cor. 14:26; Eph. 5:18-19; Col. 3:16; 1 Tim. 4:13; See Matt. 24:15; Mark 13:14; Rev. 1:3)

The members of these early Christian congregations were from a wide-ranging spectrum; the poor, slaves, freedman (emancipated from slavery), male and female, old and young, children, workers, business owners, landowners, and even some from the wealthy segment of society. Generally, the powerful political leaders of the day and the very wealthy were missing from these Christian meetings. The apostle Paul exhorted Timothy, "devote yourself to the **public reading** of Scripture, to exhortation, to teaching." (1 Tim 4:13, UASV) Writing about 155 C.E., Justin Martyr says of the weekly Christian meetings, "And on the day called Sunday, all who live in cities or in the country gather together to one place, and the memoirs of the apostles or the writings of the prophets are read, as long as time permits; then, when the reader has ceased, the president verbally instructs, and exhorts to the imitation of these good things.[97]

Gamble says that Justin Martyr's words suggest what was typical in mid-second century weekly Christian meetings in Asia Minor and Rome. Scholars agree that the reading of Scripture at Christian meetings, offering an exposition of what had been read, was common and likely universal in

---

[97] Justin Martyr, "The First Apology of Justin," in *The Apostolic Fathers with Justin Martyr and Irenaeus*, ed. Alexander Roberts, James Donaldson, and A. Cleveland Coxe, vol. 1, The Ante-Nicene Fathers (Buffalo, NY: Christian Literature Company, 1885), 186.

Justin's day, the practice originating with the first-century Christians. (Gamble 1995, 151-152) By the end of the first century, it is likely that every Christian community in the then-known world had as many of the New Testament books as were available (excluding the Gospel of John, his three epistles, and the book of Revelation, since they were written between 95-98 C.E.). Also, they would have had Old Testament books as well. These congregations would have had several readers who were responsible for the congregation's library. Further, it is highly likely that many Christians themselves could read. In addition, it is likely that these assigned readers were also serving as scribes. In some cases, these readers/scribes would likely have had the same training as the Jewish Sopherim (scribes), meaning that they possessed excellent reading, copying, translating, and interpreting skills. It might even have been that these were Jewish converts to Christianity, very familiar with the synagogue practice of copying manuscripts, studying the texts, and reading and interpreting the texts. As Comfort points out, 'the relationship between scribes and readers is found in the subscription to 1 Peter and to 2 Peter in P[72], wherein both places, it says, "Peace to the one having written [i.e., the scribe] and to the one having read [i.e., the lector].' As such, the scribe of P[72] was asking for a blessing of God's peace on the scribe [presumably himself] and on the lector. As such, the scribe knew that the publication of 1 Peter and 2 Peter was dependent on the twofold process—the copying of the text and the oral reading of it."[98]

When we look at the evidence for the first three centuries of Christianity, we find that most early Christians were from a lower social stratum, a minority from the middle level, and a minute few from the upper levels of society. (Hill and Kruger 2012, 55) It would seem that the early Christian manuscripts were prepared for the early Christian reading culture. We have already spoken at length about the book form of the codex, as opposed to the roll or scroll with its continuous text. Unlike the elite reading culture that Johnson surveyed, the Christian reading culture was not aiming for what was pleasing to the eyes, i.e., elegant handwriting. The highest priority was creating a text that was accurate in content and reader-friendly. While the elite reading culture during this same period was creating texts designed to keep the uneducated out (too overwhelming for the average reader), the Christian texts were prepared in such a way that they placed fewer demands on the reader (more Christians could reach out to be readers), so as to bring this to a more diverse audience. If we are to understand fully early Christianity, the early reading culture, and their view of their text, we need to look to the early papyri and scribal activity, the

---

[98] Philip Comfort, *Encountering the Manuscripts: An Introduction to New Testament Paleography & Textual Criticism* (Nashville, TN: Broadman & Holman, 2005), 52.

patristic quotations, and any early attitudes that have been expressed about textual transmission.

Literacy in the Roman Empire and the Early Church

The question of reading, writing, and literacy levels in the Roman Empire and the early Church is not as settled or decided as secular scholarship might like us to believe. We can start by noting that there is a difference between what we deem literate today, and what the situation was in the Roman Empire and the first three centuries of the Church. Being literate today means having the ability to read and write, while literacy in the Roman Empire mainly applied to those who could read. The ability to write was not necessarily assumed.[99] Secular sources suggest that the literacy level in the Greco-Roman world was rarely if ever more than twenty percent. Scholars argue that the average was possibly not much more than ten percent in the Roman Empire. They point out that it varied within different regions, which however would be true for any period. They further argue that in the western province's literacy never rose above five percent.[100] Some Bible scholars are unfamiliar with the reading culture of early Christianity.

In many cases, the scholars fail to mention the overabundance of evidence for a literate culture between 50 B.C.E. and 325 C.E. What is more; there is considerable evidence that the early Christians' literacy rates were higher than those of the Roman Empire in general. Bible scholar Christopher D. Stanley offers us the commonly accepted misconception about the literacy level among the early Christians:

> Literacy levels were low in antiquity, access to books was limited, and most non-Jews had little or no prior knowledge of the Jewish Scriptures. Of course, Gentile Christians who had been Jewish sympathizers (Luke's "God-fearers") would have been exposed to the Jewish Scriptures, but we have no reason to think that their literacy levels differed appreciably from their contemporaries.[101]

In the Greco-Roman world, education was voluntary. Nevertheless, we do know that elementary schools were widespread. The archaeological evidence, especially the papyri, actually point to a literacy rate in the

---

[99] See Eric A. Havelock, The Literate Revolution in Greece and its Cultural Consequences (Princeton, N.J.: Princeton University Press, 1982), 38-59.

[100] William V. Harris, *Ancient literacy* (Harvard University Press, 1989) 328.

[101] Christopher D. Stanley, *Arguing with Scripture: The Rhetoric of Quotations in the Letters of Paul* (London; New York: T&T Clark, 2004), 3.

Hellenistic-Roman world that was higher than at any other time outside modern history. We have already spoken at length on the literacy level of early Christianity in the previous chapter and will briefly look at more evidence here in this chapter.

THE DAILY NEWSPAPER OF ROME

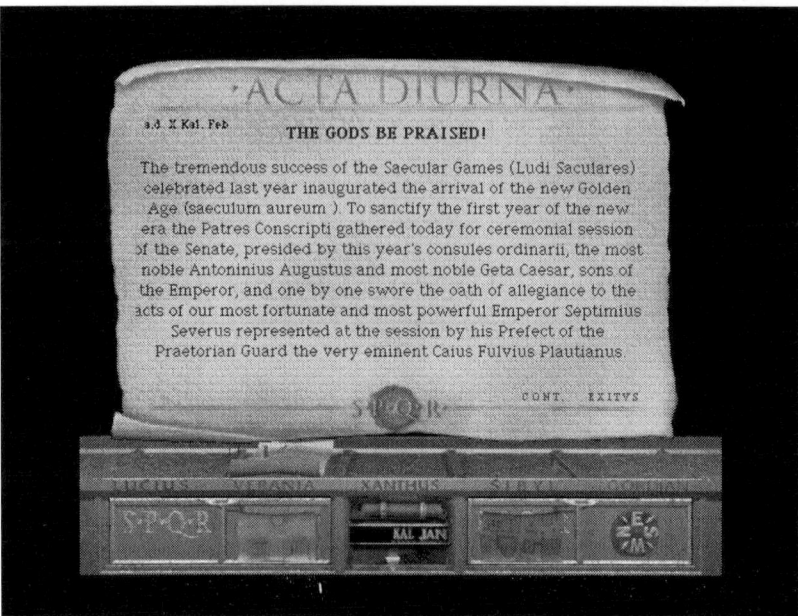

From the days of Gaius Octavius, who became the first emperor of Rome (thereafter known as Caesar Augustus), to almost two centuries after the execution of Christ (59 B.C.E. to 222 C.E.), the Roman Empire published and distributed a regular news publication for the city of Rome. The Latin phrase *Acta Diurna* (Daily Acts/Events or Daily Public Records) were the official notices from Rome, a sort of Daily Roman Times. Much of the news out of the city of Rome was also published broadly across the Empire as well.[102] Acta Diurna introduced the expression "publicare et propagare," meaning, "Make public and propagate." The expression was placed at the end of the news release, which was to both Roman citizens and non-citizens. There was a daily *papyrus* newspaper, which informed all who could read of the daily events. It was distributed throughout Rome, in such places as the public bathhouses,[103] as well as message boards.

---

[102] Propertius 2.7.17–18; Pliny the Elder, *Naturalis historia* 35.2.11; *Epigrams* 7.17; *Epigrams* 5.5; *Tristia* 4.9.20-25; *Tristia* 4.10.130.

[103] The largest of these was the Baths of Diocletian, which could hold up to 3,000 bathers.

Pliny the Elder (23 C.E. – 79 C.E.) was a Roman author, naturalist, and natural philosopher, as well as a naval and army commander. Pliny informs us that there were different grades of papyrus, such as the low-grade Saitic paper, so called from the city of that name in Lower Egypt, as well as the taeniotic paper, possibly from Alexandria.[104] These low-grade papyruses were likely used for the public notices, which would also explain why we have never discovered a single piece of the Acta Diurna (Daily Events). This Daily Newspaper of Rome covered such important information as royal or senatorial decrees and events, military and political news, deaths, crimes, trials, as well as economic insights. It also offered social information like wedding and divorces, births, festivals, astrology, human-interest stories, and even gossip. On this, Brian J. Wright writes,

> The Latin term *Acta* in its broadest sense means 'the things that have been done,'[105] or more simply, 'events'. Without any additional qualifiers, these events could – and did – include public and private activities; secular and sacred matters; government and civilian affairs. With additional qualifiers, these events had a narrower and even more specialized meaning. The *Acta Militaria* refers to published military events,[106] the *Acta Senatus* indicates published senatorial events,[107] and the *Acta Triumphorum*

---

[104] Pliny, *Natural History*, book 13, ch, 23

[105] John Percy Vyvian Dacre and Andrew William Lintott, 'Acta', in *The Oxford Classical Dictionary*, 4th ed., ed. Simon Hornblower and Antony Spawforth (Oxford: UP, 2012), 10.

[106] The first-century papyrus PSI 13.1307 is one example. For further details, see J. F. Gilliam, 'Notes on PSI 1307 and 1308', Classical Philology 47.1 (1952), 29-31. Cf. Sergio Daris, 'Osservazioni AD alcuni papyri di carattere militare', *Aegyptus* 38 (1958), 151-58, esp. 157-58; Sergio Daris, 'Note di lessico e di onomastica militare', *Aegyptus* 44 (1964), 47-51. For other examples from inscriptions and ancient authors see M. Léon Renier, *Inscriptions Romaines de l'Algérie* (Paris: Imprimerie Impériale, 1855); J. F. Gilliam, 'Some Military Papyri from Dura', in *Yale Classical Studies: Volume 11*, ed. Harry M. Hubbell (New Haven, CT: Yale University Press, 1950), 171-252, esp. 209–252.

[107] The bulletin of daily news was almost exclusively a private affair before Julius Caesar made it regular and official in 59 BC. Although private publications continued, he ordered that these occasionally published *Acta* were to be published daily for mass consumption under the authority of the government from the court reporters' notes (e.g. Seneca the Younger *Apocolocyntosis* 9). After Julius Caesar's death, a custom arose that future emperors (and their magistrates every January) were to swear to keep and respect all previous *Acta Senatus* from their predecessors (e.g. Dio Cassius 47.48; cf. 37.20); with a few exceptions (e.g. Dio Cassius 56.33). For inscriptional evidence of how emperors dealt with the *acta* of their predecessors, see Benjamin Wesley Kicks, 'The Process of Imperial Decision-Making from Augustus to Trajan' (Ph.D. dissertation, Rutgers, 2011), 86-91, the case study regarding the *Epistula Domitiani ad Falerienses*. For additional details and texts, see, among others, William Smith, William Wayte, and G. E. Marindin, eds., *A Dictionary of Greek and Roman Antiquities* (London: John Murray, 1890); Harry Thurston Peck, ed., *Harper's Dictionary of Classical Literature and Antiquities* (New York: Cooper Square, 1965), 14-15.

denotes the published triumphs of emperors.[108] The main qualifier for the purposes of this study is diurna, which simply means 'daily'. Thus, the Acta Diurna represents published 'daily events'.[109] Though there are no authentic fragments of these specific kinds of acta,[110] and thus no physical features to discuss, there are ample references to them in ancient authors (again, by various nomenclature). Both Tacitus and Suetonius used these Acta as sources for information about the Empire's earlier emperors when they were writing their histories of Rome.[111] (Wright 2016)[112]

Moreover, it should be noted that the Roman *Acta Diurna* (Daily Acts/Events or Daily Public Records) was not the only newspaper of its kind during this period of 59 B.C.E. to about 222 C.E. Around 225 C.E., we find a Roman official ordering several mayors in the Hermopolite region of Egypt to post copies of his letter 'in well-known places so that all may be aware of his pronouncements' (P. Oxy. 2705). When we consider these things on face value, they indicate that notices were being written so that the populace could be updated about current affairs by reading them, not having them read to them.

We can conclude from these facts that reading, writing, and the dissemination of information was far more extensive than has long been held, with a much higher basic literacy level, which then adds to our understanding of the writing, publication, and distribution of the Greek New Testament letters that were read in the Christian congregations throughout the Roman Empire (Col. 4:46; 1 Thess. 5:27; 1 Tim. 4:13; Jam. 1:1; Rev. 1:3). Evidence indicates a far higher level of basic literacy

---

[108] *Pliny*, Naturalis historia. *37.6.*

[109] Too much emphasis should not be placed on the word 'daily' since it is possible that it could mean 'everyday' events, as in 'current events.'

[110] I say 'authentic' here because some forgeries have been published. For example, eleven fragments of the *Acta Diurna* were published in 1615 by Pighius, and defended by Dodwell. Though the fragments were exposed as a fifteenth century forgery (by Wesseling, Ernesti et al.), some scholars still attempted to defend their authenticity at least as far as 1844; with Lieberkühn. For more details and background to this story, see Wilhelm Sigismund Teuffel, *A History of Roman Literature: Volume One, The Republican Period*, trans. Wilhelm Wagner (London: George Bell and Sons, 1873), 381. Cf. Hermann L. G. Heinze, ' *De Spuriis Actorum Diurnorum Fragmentis Undecim: Fasciculus Prior'* (Ph.D. dissertation, University of Greifswald, 1860), 11-24; Andrew Lintott, 'Acta Antiquissima: A Week in the History of the Roman *Republic,'* Papers of the British School at Rome *54 (1986), 213-28.*

[111] A. W. Mosley, 'Historical Reporting in the Ancient World', *NTS* 12.1 (1965), 10-26.

[112] COMING FALL 2017

Brian J. Wright, *Communal Reading in the Time of Jesus: A Window into Early Christian Reading Practices* (Minneapolis: Fortress Press, 2017).

throughout the Roman Empire than thought, as well as Christians who originated primarily as Jewish converts who prided themselves on their ability to read and write, coupled with a message that they were commanded to evangelize to the whole inhabited earth (Matt. 24:14; 28:19-20; Ac 1:8). As a result, it is no exaggeration to say that Christians were able to take over the Roman power that had a military unlike any other up to that time, by growing the faith in a pagan world. They went from 120 disciples at Pentecost in 33 C.E. to over one million disciples about a century later.

Jewish education under this same period was significantly different as to the content, though in some respects they had stages similar to Greco-Roman education. The primary objective of Jewish education was knowledge of the Hebrew Scriptures. The parents were the first and primary educators of their Jewish children, especially their earlier elementary education in reading, writing, and understanding the Torah (2 Tim 1:5; 3:14-15). We read briefly of young Jesus as he grew up in Nazareth. He would have received his education from three sources: Joseph, Jesus' stepfather, would have played a major role in his education. Paul said that young Timothy was trained in "the sacred writings" by his mother, Eunice, and his grandmother Lois (2 Tim. 1:5; 3:15). Certainly, if Timothy received education in the Scriptures from his mother though his Father was a Greek (Acts 16:1), no doubt Jesus did as well from Joseph during his childhood. Jesus would have also received education in the Scriptures from the attendant at the synagogue, which was a place of instruction.

We know that another source of knowledge and wisdom for Jesus was the divine Father. Jesus said, "My teaching is not mine, but his who sent me," i.e., the Father (John 7:16, UASV). Mark 1:22 reads, "And they were **astounded at his teaching**, for he taught them as **one who had authority**, and not as the scribes" (UASV).

The third century Rabbi Judah b. Tema outlines the stages of Jewish education. "At five years old *one is fit* for the Scripture, at ten years for Mishnah, at thirteen for the commandments, at fifteen for Talmud, at eighteen for marriage, at twenty for retribution (a vocation)."[113] Again, the home was the primary place of Jewish education in reading, writing, and the memorization of the Hebrew Scriptures. In the first century, there were a number of primary schools in Jerusalem, but it was not until the second century C.E. that they grew more numerous outside of Jerusalem. Children began their studies as early as age 4-5 in primary school **Beth Sefer** ("house

---

[113] Robert Henry Charles, ed., *Pseudepigrapha of the Old Testament*, vol. 2 (Oxford: Clarendon Press, 1913), 710.

of reading"). Both boys and girls could attend the class in the synagogue, or in an adjoining room. (Ferguson 2003, 112)

First-century Jewish historian Josephus (30-100 C.E.) said of the Jewish life, "Our principle care of all is this, to educate our children well."[114] In speaking of what the Mosaic Law commands, he wrote, "It also commands us **to bring those children up in learning** and to exercise them in the laws, and make them acquainted with the acts of their predecessors, in order to their imitation of them, and that they may be nourished up in the laws from their infancy, and might neither transgress them, nor yet have any pretense for their ignorance of them."[115] We have even more texts, especially from the later Rabbis, which make similar statements. If we take these comments at face value, it is evidence of a reading culture among the Jews that is surely higher than that of the Roman Empire, which was certainly higher than the secular sources claim.

Five hundred years from now, what if we were to ask the historian, "how well could the Amish in America read and write?" It would be difficult to be accurate because they teach themselves. It is 2017, and they have one-room county schoolhouses with chalkboards, which remind us of the pioneer days in America, or some Laura Ingalls Wilder novels. The historian might find slate chalkboards and tablets that are blank, so they could only guess at the level of the reading and writing. Would it surprise anyone that this highly religious community, who value the ability to read their religious books, very similar to the first-century Jewish community, can speak two to three languages (Dutch or German and English), as well as read and write well?

When we see signs of a reading environment, it suggests a populace with at least a basic reading level. In the first-century Roman Empire, there were hundreds of public inscriptions of dedications, imperial decrees, lists of names, laws, and regulation, and even directions. Even the gravestones of the time were meant to do more than mark the name of the person. Some had lines of poetry; others had threats and curses for any who even thought of robbing the graves. The painstaking time taken to publish these things indicates the expectation that the public is able to read them, even lowly grave robbers.

We have almost a half million papyrus documents (likely there were millions more that did not survive) in garbage dumps in the dry sands of Oxyrhynchus, Egypt. This is but one city in the entirety of the Roman

---

[114] Flavius Josephus and William Whiston, *The Works of Josephus: Complete and Unabridged* (Peabody: Hendrickson, 1987).

[115] Flavius Josephus and William Whiston, *The Works of Josephus: Complete and Unabridged* (Peabody: Hendrickson, 1987).

Empire. Are we to believe that Oxyrhynchus is the exception, and some of the biggest cities, such as Rome, Corinth, Athens, Pergamum, Ephesus, Smyrna, Antioch, Jerusalem, Alexandria, and Carthage, which numbered anywhere from one hundred thousand to over a million in their population, did not have equal or greater writings discarded in their dumps? Then we should consider the temples and the libraries that boasted of tens of thousands of books. Reportedly, by the first century C.E., the Alexandrian library housed one million scrolls. In fact, Mark Antony took 200,000 scrolls from the library at Pergamum to replenish the Alexandrian library for Cleopatra. Because of moisture damage and they're being written on perishable material, we cannot discover the documents of these centers of education as we have in the dry sands of Egypt. Yet, should we for a moment believe that their garbage dumps saw any fewer books than were discovered at Oxyrhynchus, Egypt?

We have such great quantities of written material as to suggest a much higher literacy level than most are willing to accept. Only ten percent of the Oxyrhynchus papyri have been investigated, but they offer insight that indicates a more literate society, not less. Many men and women who wrote had scribes pen their words, indicating that they were literate by what they said, while their signatures at the end of letters show only that some of them had poor penmanship. We should not judge their literacy level by the limitations of their penmanship. We must remember, in that period, that it was reading that dictated one's level of literacy.

We also have the Vindolanda Writing Tablets. "The writing tablets are perhaps Vindolanda's greatest discovery and have been previously voted by experts and the public alike as 'Britain's Top Treasure.' Delicate, wafer-thin slivers of wood covered in spidery ink writing, the tablets were found in the oxygen-free deposits on and around the floors of the deeply buried early wooden forts at Vindolanda and are the oldest surviving handwritten documents in Britain. Like postcards from the past, the tablets allow a rare insight into the real lives of people living and working at Vindolanda near Hadrian's Wall nearly 2000 years ago. They provide a fascinating and compelling insight into private and military lives from a very different time but are hauntingly familiar, covering matters from birthdays through to underpants! Have we changed that much in two millennia?"[116]

The Vindolanda Writing Tablets, like the papyri in the dry sands of Oxyrhynchus, offer us insights into the literacy of the Roman officers who we would expect to be literate but also indicate the literacy of the low-ranking soldiers, wives, friends, and servants. The handwriting of these

---

[116] Vindolanda Writing Tablets - Roman Vindolanda and Roman .., https://www.vindolanda.com/roman-vindolanda/writing-tablets (accessed March 23, 2017).

tablets ranges from writing that is barely legible, to the professional hand. We have to ask ourselves the same question: if these common soldiers had some basic writing skills, some even to the document hand level, and even a few at the professional hand, what are we to think of the literacy level of the Roman Empire?[117] Must we keep disputing the obvious? If the evidence suggests, as it does, a far higher literacy level than a mere 5-10 percent throughout the Roman Empire, what are we to expect from the Christian community that grew out of the Jewish populace that so valued reading, writing, and memorization, that was commissioned with evangelizing the entire inhabited earth?

---

[117] (Bowman 1998, 82-99)

CHAPTER 5 The Early Christian's View of the Integrity of the Greek New Testament Books

Paul was the author of fourteen letters within the Greek New Testament.[118] Paul's earliest letters were 1 Thessalonians (50 C.E.), 2 Thessalonians (51 C.E.), Galatians (50-52 C.E.), 1&2 Corinthians (55 C.E.), Romans (56 C.E.), Ephesians, Philippians, Colossians, Philemon (60-61 C.E.), Hebrews (61 C.E.), 1 Timothy, and Titus (61-64 C.E.). 2 Timothy was penned last, about 65 C.E. This means that the apostle Peter could have been aware of at least thirteen out of fourteen Pauline letters at the time of his penning 2 Peter in 64 C.E., in which he writes,

2 Peter 3:15-16 Updated American Standard Version (UASV)

[15] and regard the patience of our Lord as salvation; just as also **our beloved brother Paul**, according to the wisdom given him, wrote to you, [16] as also **in all his letters**, speaking in them of these things, in which are some things hard to understand, which the untaught and unstable distort, as they do also **the rest of the Scriptures**, to their own destruction. [bold is mine]

Notice that Peter speaks of Paul's letters, referring to them as a collection. Thus, Peter is our earliest reference to Paul's letters that were gathered together as a collection. Peter also states that the letters were viewed as being on equal footing with the Hebrew Scriptures when he says that "the untaught and unstable distort" Paul's letters as they do "the rest of the Scriptures." Günther Zuntz was certain that there was a full collection of Pauline letters by 100 C.E. (Zuntz 1953, 271-272) In 65 C.E.[119] Peter

---

[118] This author accepts that Paul is the author of the book of Hebrews. For further information see the CPH Blog article, Who Authored the Book of Hebrews: A Defense for Pauline Authorship

https://christianpublishinghouse.co/2016/11/02/who-authored-the-book-of-hebrews-a-defense-for-pauline-authorship/

[119] 2 Peter generally is wrongly dated to about 100-125 C.E. (e.g. J. N. D. Kelly, A *Commentary on the Epistles of Peter and of Jude: Introduction and Commentary*; J. D. Mayor, the *Epistle of St. Jude and the Epistle of Second Peter*; D. J. Harrington, Jude and 2 Peter). Other Bible scholars date 2 Peter to 80-90 C.E. (e.g., R. Bauckham *Jude, 2 Peter*; B. Reicke, *The Epistle of James, Peter and Jude*). We should begin with a date of about 64 C.E. for 2 Peter. Then, the Greek makes it apparent that the author is a contemporary of the apostle Paul because it suggests that Paul is speaking to the churches at the time of this writing. The Greek ἐν πάσαις ἐπιστολαῖς λαλῶν ("*in all letters [he] speaking*") strongly implies such. The author of the document says that he is "Simon Peter, a bond-servant and apostle of Jesus

could say of Paul, "in all his letters," and his readers would know who Paul was and of Paul's many letters. Also, his readers would have accepted the idea that Paul's letters were equal to the Hebrew Scriptures, which indicates that they were being collected among the churches.

1 Timothy 5:18 Updated American Standard Version (UASV)

¹⁸ For **the Scripture says**, "You shall not muzzle the ox while he is threshing," and "The laborer is worthy of his wages." [bold is mine]

Notice that Paul says, "the Scripture says" (λέγει γὰρ ἡ γραφή), just before he quotes from two different Scriptures. The first half of the quote, "You shall not muzzle the ox while he is threshing," is from Deuteronomy 25:4. The Second half, "The laborer is worthy of his wages." seems to be from Luke 10:7. Here Paul is doing exactly what Peter did in the above at 2 Peter 3:16, placing the Gospel of Luke on par with the Hebrew Scriptures.

Some have tried to dismiss 1 Timothy 5:18 by saying that Paul was just quoting oral tradition, but that can hardly be the case when he says, "**the Scripture says**," which requires a written source and it happens that we have such a source: The Gospel of Luke. Luke was written about 56-58 C.E. in Caesarea, and First Timothy was written about 61-64 C.E. in Macedonia. Then, there is the fact that Luke was a faithful traveling companion and co-worker of the apostle Paul. Luke was one of Paul's closest traveling companions from about 49 C.E. until the time of Paul's martyrdom. The Gospel of Luke was written just after the two of them returned from Paul's third missionary journey, while Paul was imprisoned for two years at Caesarea, after which Paul was transferred to Rome in about 58 C.E. Other "scholars believe Luke wrote his Gospel and the book of Acts while in Rome with Paul during the apostle's first Roman imprisonment. Apparently, Luke remained nearby or with Paul also during the apostle's second Roman imprisonment. Shortly before his martyrdom, Paul wrote that 'only Luke is

---

Christ" (2 Pet. 1:1, NASB). He refers to this as "the second letter I am writing to you" (2 Pet. 3:1, NASB). The author clearly states that he was an eyewitness to the transfiguration of Jesus Christ, at which only Peter, James, and John were present (Matt. 17:1-13; Mark 9:1-13; Lu 9:28–36; See 2 Pet. 1:16-21). The author mentions that Jesus foretold his death, "knowing that the laying aside of my *earthly* dwelling is imminent, as also our Lord Jesus Christ has made clear to me" (2 Pet. 1:14; John 21:18, 19.). The argument that the style is different from 1 Peter is moot because the subject and the purpose in writing were different. The implication of the phrases "in all *his* letters" and "the rest of the Scriptures" is that many of Paul's letters (thirteen of them) were viewed as "Scripture" by the first-century Christian congregation and should not be "twisted" or "distorted." In addition, Second Peter was regarded as canonical by a number of authorities prior to the Third Council of Carthage (i.e., Irenaeus of Asia Minor c. 180 C.E., Origen of Alexandria c. 230 C.E., Eusebius of Palestine c. 320 C.E., Cyril of Jerusalem c. 348 C.E., Athanasius of Alexandria c. 367 C.E., Epiphanius of Palestine c. 368 C.E., Gregory Nazianzus of Asia Minor c. 370 C.E., Philaster of Italy c. 383 C.E., Jerome of Italy c. 394 C.E., and Augustine of N. Africa c. 397 C.E.).

with me' (2 Tim. 4:11)."[120] Either way, Luke was a very close co-worker with Paul for almost twenty years. In fact, Luke's writing shows evidence of Paul's influence (Lu 22:19-20; 1 Cor. 11:23-25). We must remember that Luke was a first-rate historian, as well as being inspired. He says that he "investigated everything carefully from the beginning, to write it out" (Lu 1:3). Regardless, the apostle Paul had access to Luke's Gospel for many years before penning 1 Timothy, where it appears that he made a direct quote from what we know now as Luke 10:7, referring to it as Scripture.

The use of the well-known phrase, "**it is written**," further confirms the authority of the New Testament books. We understand that when this phrase is used, it is a reference to the Scriptures of God, the inspired Word of God. It should be noted that the gospel writers themselves use the phrase "**it is written**" some forty times when referring to the inspired Hebrew Scriptures.

The *Epistle of Barnabas* dates after the destruction of the Second Temple in 70 C.E., but it dates before the Bar Kochba Revolt of 132 C.E. At Barn 4:14, we read, "let us be on guard lest we should be found to be, as **it is written**, 'many called, but few chosen.'"[121] Immediately after using the phrase "it is written," Barnabas quotes Jesus' words found in Matthew 22:14, "For many are called, but few are chosen."

The *Letter of Polycarp to the Philippians* dates to about 110 C.E. Poly 12:1 reads, "For I am convinced that you are all well trained in the sacred Scriptures and that nothing is hidden from you (something not granted to me). Only, as it is said in these Scriptures, 'be angry but do not sin,' and 'do not let the sun set on your anger.' Blessed is the one who remembers this, which I believe to be the case with you."[122] The first phrase "be angry but do not sin" is a quotation from Ephesians 4:26, where Paul is quoting Psalm 4:5. However, the latter part of the quote, "do not let the sun set on your anger" is Paul's words alone. It is clear here that Polycarp is referring to both the Psalm and the book of Ephesians when he writes, "it is said in these Scriptures."

Clement of Rome (c. 30-100 C.E.) penned two books: we focus on the second, *An Ancient Christian Sermon* (2 Clement), which dates to about 98-100 C.E. II Clement 2:4 reads, "And another Scripture says, 'I have not

---

[120] T. R. McNeal, "Luke," ed. Chad Brand et al., *Holman Illustrated Bible Dictionary* (Nashville, TN: Holman Bible Publishers, 2003), 1056–1057.

[121] Michael William Holmes, *The Apostolic Fathers: Greek Texts and English Translations*, Third ed. (Grand Rapids, MI: Baker Books, 2007), 373.

[122] Ibid., 294.

come to call the righteous, but sinners.'"[123] Here Clement is quoting Mark 2:17 or Matt. 9:13, which is likely the earliest quotation of a New Testament passage as Scripture. In the Gospel of Mark and Matthew, Jesus is quoted as saying, "I came not to call the righteous, but sinners" (ESV). II Clement 14:2 reads, "But if we do not do the will of the Lord, we will belong to those of whom the Scripture says, 'My house has become a robbers' den'" which is a quote from Matthew 21:13, Mark 11:17, and Luke 19:46, where Jesus himself is quoting Jeremiah 7:11 after cleansing the temple of greedy merchants.

Indeed, we can garner from this brief look at early Christianity's view of Scriptures that the New Testament books were placed on the same footing as the Hebrew Scriptures quite early, starting with the words of Peter about the apostle Paul's letters. Again, Justin Martyr tells us that at the early Christian meetings "the memoirs of the apostles or the writings of the prophets are read, as long as time permits; then, when the reader has ceased, the president verbally instructs and exhorts to the imitation of these good things" (1 Apology 67).[124] Ignatius of Antioch (c. 35-108 C.E.), Theophilus of Antioch (d. 182 C.E.), and Tertullian (c. 155-240 C.E.) also spoke of the Prophets, the Law, and the Gospels as equally authoritative.

The Early Christian View of the Integrity of the Greek New Testament Originals

If the early Christians' view of the New Testament books were on the same footing as the Hebrew Scriptures, then we would see them guarding the integrity of the New Testament in the same way the Old Testament authors and the scribes in ancient Israel guarded the Hebrew Old Testament.

Deuteronomy 4:2 Updated American Standard Version (UASV)	Deuteronomy 12:32 Updated American Standard Version (UASV)
2 You shall **not add to** the word which I am commanding you, **nor take away** from it, that you may keep the commandments of Jehovah your God which I command you.	32 "Everything that I command you, you shall be careful to do; you shall **not add to** nor **take away from** it.

---

[123] Ibid., 141.

[124] Justin Martyr, "The First Apology of Justin," in *The Apostolic Fathers with Justin Martyr and Irenaeus*, ed. Alexander Roberts, James Donaldson, and A. Cleveland Coxe, vol. 1, The Ante-Nicene Fathers (Buffalo, NY: Christian Literature Company, 1885), 186.

There certainly were severe consequences, even death to some, if scribes or copyists were to add to or take away from God's Word, disregarding these warnings. Eugene H. Merrill observes, "There is a principle of canonization here as well in that nothing is to be added to or subtracted from the word. This testifies to the fact that God himself is the originator of the covenant text and only he is capable of determining its content and extent."[125]

Proverbs 30:6 Updated American Standard Version (UASV)

⁶ **Do not add to** his words,
   lest he reprove you and you be found a liar.

This is an ongoing command about God's words given to the Israelites in Deuteronomy 4:2 and 12:32. There is no need to add to or take away from God's Word, for it is sufficient. Duane A. Garrett tells us that "Verse 6 is an injunction against adding to God's words similar to the injunctions found in Deut. 12:32 and Rev 22:18. It is noteworthy that this text does not warn the reader not to reject or take away from divine revelation; it is more concerned that no one supplements it. This is therefore not a warning to the unbelieving interpreter but rather to the believer. The temptation is to improve on the text if not by actually adding new material then by interpreting it in ways that make more of a passage's teaching than is really there. It is what Paul called "going beyond what is written" (1 Cor. 4:6).[126]

The attitude of the Jewish people and their Hebrew Scriptures can be summed up in the words of Josephus, the first-century (37 – c.100 C.E.) Jewish historian, who wrote, "We have given practical proof of our reverence for our own Scriptures. For, although such long ages have now passed, no one has ventured either to add, or to remove, or to alter a syllable; and it is an instinct with every Jew, from the day of his birth, to regard them as the decrees of God, to abide by them, and, if need be, cheerfully to die for them."[127] The longstanding view of the Jews toward the Hebrew Scriptures is very important, especially in view of what the apostle Paul wrote to the Roman Christian congregation. The apostle says, the Jews "were entrusted with the sayings[128] of God" (Rom. 3:1-2).

---

[125] Eugene H. Merrill, *Deuteronomy*, vol. 4, The New American Commentary (Nashville: Broadman & Holman Publishers, 1994), 229.

[126] Duane A. Garrett, *Proverbs, Ecclesiastes, Song of Songs*, vol. 14, The New American Commentary (Nashville: Broadman & Holman Publishers, 1993), 237.

[127] Josephus, *The Life/Against Apion*, vol. 1, LCL, ed. by H. St. J. Thackeray (Cambridge, MA: Harvard University Press, 1976), pp. 177–181.

[128] **Sayings:** (Gr. *logia, on* [only in the plural]) A saying or message, usually short, especially divine, gathered into a collection–Acts 7:38; Romans 3:2; Hebrews 5:12; 1 Peter 4:11.

Galatians 3:15 Updated American Standard Version (UASV)

¹⁵ Brothers, I speak according to man:[129] even though it is only a man's covenant, yet when it has been ratified, **no one sets it aside or adds conditions to it.**

The letter from Paul to Galatians was penned about **50-52 C.E.** Here Paul's words in dealing with the covenant to Abraham and his descendants echo the words from the Law of Moses at Deuteronomy 4:2, when he says, "no one sets it aside or adds conditions to it," i.e., "not add to… nor take away." The covenant word of God was not to be altered.

Revelation 22:18-19 Updated American Standard Version (UASV)

¹⁸ I testify to everyone who hears the words of the prophecy of this book: if anyone **adds to them,** God will add to him the plagues which are written in this book; ¹⁹ and if anyone **takes away from** the words of the book of this prophecy, God will take away his part from the tree of life and out of the holy city, which are written in this book.

The letter from John to the seven congregations was penned about 95 C.E. Kistemaker and Hendriksen write, "The solemn warning not to add to or detract from the words of this book is common in ancient literature. For instance, Moses warns the Israelites not to add to or subtract from the decrees and laws God gave them (Deut. 4:2; 12:32). This formula was attached to documents much the same as copyright laws protect modern manuscripts. In addition, curses were added in the form of a conditional sentence, 'If anyone adds or takes away anything from this book, a curse will rest upon him.' Paul wrote a similar condemnation when he told the Galatians that if anyone preached a gospel which was not the gospel of Christ, 'let him be eternally condemned' (Gal. 1:6–8). Now Jesus pronounces a curse on anyone who distorts his message."[130]

The Didache (The Teaching of the Twelve Apostles) dates to about 100 C.E. At 4:13, it reads, "You must not forsake the Lord's commandments, but must guard what you have received, neither adding nor subtracting anything."[131] This author is drawing on the command in Deuteronomy 4:2 and 12:32.[132] The point here is that while the author makes use of "the Lord" (i.e., Jehovah, that is, the Father) in Deut. 4:2, 12:32, he is actually

---

[129] Or *in terms of human relations;* or *according to a human perspective;* or *using a human illustration*

[130] Simon J. Kistemaker and William Hendriksen, *Exposition of the Book of Revelation,* vol. 20, New Testament Commentary (Grand Rapids: Baker Book House, 1953–2001), 594.

[131] Michael William Holmes, *The Apostolic Fathers: Greek Texts and English Translations,* Third ed. (Grand Rapids, MI: Baker Books, 2007), 351.

[132] (LXX 13:1.)

referring to Jesus' teaching found in the Gospels. Therefore, the Gospels and more specifically Jesus' teaching are equal to the Hebrew Scriptures.

Papias of Hierapolis about 135 C.E. records what he had to tell about the details surrounding the personal life and ministry of each of the apostles. Papias 3:3-4 says, "I will not hesitate to set down ... everything I carefully learned then from the elders and carefully remembered, guaranteeing their truth. For unlike most people I did not enjoy those who have a great deal to say, but those who teach the truth. Nor did I enjoy those who recall someone else's commandments, but those who remember the commandments given by the Lord to the faith and proceeding from the truth itself. And if by chance someone who had been a follower of the elders should come my way, I inquired about the words of the elders— what Andrew or Peter said, or Philip, or Thomas or James, or John or Matthew or any other of the Lord's disciples."[133]

Papias says of Mark's Gospel: "Mark, having become Peter's interpreter, wrote down accurately everything he remembered." Further confirming the Gospel's accuracy, Papias continues: "Consequently Mark did nothing wrong in writing down some things as he remembered them, for he **made it his one concern not to omit anything** which he heard **or to make any false statement in** them."[134] This is a clear reference to Deuteronomy 4:2 while referencing Mark's Gospel, again showing that Christians viewed the New Testament books as being equal to the Hebrew Scriptures. Papias offers testimony that Matthew initially penned his Gospel in the Hebrew language. Papias says, "So Matthew composed the oracles in the Hebrew language, and each person interpreted them as best he could."[135] As the overseer of Hierapolis in Asia Minor, Papias was in a position to enquire and carefully learn from the elders throughout the church at the time, establishing the authenticity and divine inspiration of the New Testament. Sadly, though, only scanty fragments of the writings of Papias survived.

The *Epistle of Barnabas,* dated about 130 C.E., declares, "You shall guard what you have received, **neither adding nor subtracting** anything" (Barn 19:11).[136] Here again, Barnabas is drawing on Deuteronomy 4:2 as he expresses his concern about the Word of God, as he speaks about "the way

---

[133] Michael William Holmes, *The Apostolic Fathers: Greek Texts and English Translations*, Third ed. (Grand Rapids, MI: Baker Books, 2007), 735.

[134] Ibid, 739-40.

[135] Ibid, 741.

[136] Ibid, 437.

of light" in chapter 19 of his letter, making multiple references to New Testament teachings and principles.

Dionysius of Corinth wrote in about 170 C.E. about those who had dared to alter his own writings. He writes, "For I wrote letters when the brethren requested me to write. And these letters the apostles of the devil have filled with tares [false information], **taking away some things and adding others**, for whom a woe is in store. It is not wonderful, then, if some have attempted to adulterate the Lord's writings when they have formed designs against those which are not such."[137] Here Dionysius is referring to Deuteronomy 4:2 and 12:32, noting the curse or a woe that is in store for altering his own writings, and all the more so for daring to alter the Scriptures themselves. The reference to adulterating "the Lord's writings" is a reference to the New Testament writings – "A probable, though not exclusive, reference to Marcion, for he was by no means the only one of that age that interpolated and mutilated the works of the apostles to fit his theories. Apostolic works—true and false—circulated in great numbers, and were made the basis for the speculations and moral requirements of many of the heretical schools of the second century."[138]

If there were no big concern over the integrity of the New Testament originals, we would not see early church leaders showing such concern. The principle of not adding nor taking away found in Deuteronomy 4:2 and 12:32 can be applied to just one word, or even a single number in the case of Irenaeus in about 180 C.E., who complained about the number 666 found in Revelation 13:18 that had been changed to 616. Irenaeus wrote, "Such, then, being the state of the case, and this number being found **in all the most approved and ancient copies** [of the Apocalypse], and those men who saw John face to face bearing their testimony [to it]; while reason also leads us to conclude that the number of the name of the beast, [if reckoned] according to the Greek mode of calculation by [the value of] the letters contained in it, will amount to six hundred and sixty and six."[139] The passage ἐν πᾶσι τοῖς σπουδαίοις καὶ ἀρχαίοις ἀντιγράφοις ("in all the most

---

[137] Dionysius of Corinth, "Fragments from a Letter to the Roman Church," in *Fathers of the Third and Fourth Centuries: The Twelve Patriarchs, Excerpts and Epistles, the Clementina, Apocrypha, Decretals, Memoirs of Edessa and Syriac Documents, Remains of the First Ages*, ed. Alexander Roberts, James Donaldson, and A. Cleveland Coxe, trans. B. P. Pratten, vol. 8, The Ante-Nicene Fathers (Buffalo, NY: Christian Literature Company, 1886), 765.

[138] Philip Schaff and Henry Wace, eds., *Eusebius: Church History, Life of Constantine the Great, and Oration in Praise of Constantine*, vol. 1, A Select Library of the Nicene and Post-Nicene Fathers of the Christian Church, Second Series (New York: Christian Literature Company, 1890).

[139] Irenaeus of Lyons, "Irenæus Against Heresies," in *The Apostolic Fathers with Justin Martyr and Irenaeus*, ed. Alexander Roberts, James Donaldson, and A. Cleveland Coxe, vol. 1, The Ante-Nicene Fathers (Buffalo, NY: Christian Literature Company, 1885), 558.

approved and ancient copies") shows that by then the autographs of the New Testament were not available, with various readings creeping into the manuscripts of the canonical books.

Irenaeus went on to let those guilty of willfully adding to or taking away from the Scriptures know that there will be severe punishment. He wrote, "Now, as regards those who have done this in simplicity, and without evil intent, we are at liberty to assume that pardon will be granted them by God. But as for those who, for the sake of vainglory, lay it down for certain that names containing the spurious number are to be accepted, and affirm that this name, hit upon by themselves, is that of him who is to come; such persons shall not come forth without loss, because they have led into error both themselves and those who confided in them. Now, in the first place, it is loss to wander from the truth, and to imagine that as being the case which is not; then again, as there shall be no light punishment [inflicted] **upon him who either <u>adds</u> or <u>subtracts</u> anything from the Scripture.**"[140] Here Irenaeus is referring to John's warning in Revelation 22:18.

Again, the *Letter of Polycarp to the Philippians,* dating to about 110 C.E., reads at 7:1, "For everyone who does not confess that Jesus Christ has come in the flesh is antichrist [cf. 1 John 4:2-3]; and whoever does not acknowledge the testimony of the cross is of the devil [cf. 1 John 3:8]; and **whoever twists the sayings of the Lord** to suit his own sinful desires and claims that there is neither resurrection nor judgment—well, that person is the first-born of Satan."[141] Of course, "the sayings of the Lord" come from the Gospels. Therefore, Polycarp was declaring a warning to anyone who would alter the Gospels. Some would argue that Polycarp was referring to oral traditions when he used the term "the sayings of the Lord" (τὰ λόγια τοῦ κυρίου), but this simply is not the case, since in the next verse he refers to these "sayings" (κυρίου) again and then quotes Matthew 6:13 and 26:41, where we find Matthew recording Jesus' sayings.

We could cite much more quotations from early church leaders about their concern for the integrity of the New Testament originals being preserved. However, we can see from our limited look at early Christianity's view of the Scriptures that the New Testament books were placed on the same footing as the Hebrew Scriptures from the very beginning. When we look at the first three centuries of Christianity, we find

---

[140] Irenaeus of Lyons, "Irenæus Against Heresies," in *The Apostolic Fathers with Justin Martyr and Irenaeus,* ed. Alexander Roberts, James Donaldson, and A. Cleveland Coxe, vol. 1, The Ante-Nicene Fathers (Buffalo, NY: Christian Literature Company, 1885), 559.

[141] Michael William Holmes, *The Apostolic Fathers: Greek Texts and English Translations,* Third ed. (Grand Rapids, MI: Baker Books, 2007), 289.

that the manuscripts were prepared for the reading culture of Christians, who placed the highest priority on disseminating a text that was accurate in content and reader-friendly. The Christian texts were prepared in such a way as to place the least demand on the reader, in order to bring the Scriptures to a more diverse audience.

Clearly, both Paul and Peter showed concern for their writings, as well as equating NT books other than their own with the Hebrew Scriptures in authority. Early on, the church leaders were very concerned about preserving the integrity of the original, down to the individual words. The papyri of the first three centuries after Christ **provides evidence** that most scribes (copyists) also cared about preserving the integrity of their exemplars and did not seek to change or alter the wording. On the other hand, we would be misleading others and ourselves if we were to deny that a small minority of the copyists did freely choose to make alterations—as Colwell said for example, that the scribe of P[45] worked "without any intention of exactly reproducing his source. He writes with great freedom, harmonizing, smoothing out, substituting almost whimsically." However, the scribe who worked on P[75] was a "disciplined scribe who writes with the intention of being careful and accurate." Then again, Colwell said that P[66] reflects "a scribe working with the intention of making a good copy, falling into careless errors, ... but also under the control of some other person, or second standard, ... It shows the supervision of a foreman, or a scribe turned proofreader."[142]

Generally speaking, the early scribes were very concerned about the accuracy of their copying, but while some were more successful than others, every one of them—due to human imperfection—made some transcriptional errors at times which were **unintentional** (Matt. 27:11; Mark 6:51; 10:40; Rom. 5:1; Eph. 1:15; 1 Thess. 2:7; Heb. 12:15). We can also attribute human imperfection to **intentional changes,** *purposeful* scribal alterations, such as *conflation* (Luke 24:53; John 1:34; Rom. 3:32), *interpolation* (Mark 9:29; Lu 23:19, 34; Rom. 8:1; 1 Cor. 15:51), and attempts to clarify the meaning of a text (1 Cor. 3:3) or to enhance a doctrinal position (1 John 5:7).

We can say that **on the whole,** the early church leaders valued the integrity of the original and the scribes valued the integrity of the exemplars which they were copying. In fact, the high value placed on the integrity of the original ironically led to some erroneous changes because scribes were prone at times to correct what they believed to be mistakes within the sacred text. Many modern textual scholars will tell their readers that the early copying period was "'free,' 'wild,' 'in a state of flux,' 'chaotic,' 'a

---

[142] Ernest Colwell, "Method in Evaluating Scribal Habits: A Study of P45, P66, P75," in *Studies in Methodology in Textual Criticism of the New Testament,* New Testament Tools and Studies 9 (Leiden: Brill, 1969), 114–21.

turbid textual morass." (Hill and Kruger 2012, 10) The truth was actually the opposite. The church leaders valued the originals above all else, and the scribes saw their exemplars as master copies of those originals and reverentially feared to make any mistakes.

The goal of textual scholarship since the days of Erasmus in the sixteenth century has been to get back to the original, preserving the exact wording of the original twenty-seven New Testament books penned by Matthew, Mark, Luke, John, James, Jude, Peter, and Paul. However, this has not always proved to be the case with recent scholarship. Philip W. Comfort has been one of the leading outspoken proponents of the traditional goal of reconstructing the exact wording of the originals, and I quote the following observation by Comfort at length:

> The time gap between the autographs and the earliest extant copies is quite close—no more than 100 years for most of the books of the New Testament. Thus, we are in a good position to recover most of the original wording of the Greek New Testament. Such optimism was held by the well-known textual critics of the nineteenth century—most notably, Samuel Tregelles, B. F. Westcott, and F. J. A. Hort, who, although acknowledging that we may never recover all of the original text of the New Testament books with absolute certainty, believed that the careful work of textual criticism could bring us extremely close. In the twentieth century, two eminent textual critics, Bruce Metzger and Kurt Aland, affirmed this same purpose, and were instrumental in the production of the two critical editions of the Greek New Testament that are widely used today.
>
> Tregelles, Hort, Metzger, and Aland, as well as Constantine von Tischendorf, the nineteenth-century scholar who famously discovered Codex Sinaiticus, all provided histories of the transmission of the New Testament text and methodologies for recovering the original wording. Their views of textual criticism were derived from their actual experience of working with manuscripts and doing textual criticism in preparing critical editions of the Greek New Testament. Successive generations of scholars, working with ever-increasing quantities of manuscripts (especially earlier ones) and refining their methodologies, have continued with the task of recovering the original wording of the Greek New Testament.
>
> By contrast, a certain number of textual critics in recent years have abandoned the notion that the original wording of the Greek New Testament can ever be recovered. Let us take, for example, Bart Ehrman (author of *The Orthodox Corruption of Scripture*) and David Parker (author of *The Living Text of the Gospels*). Having analyzed their positions, J. K. Elliott writes, "Both [men] emphasize the living and

therefore changing text of the New Testament and the needlessness and inappropriateness of trying to establish one immutable original text. The changeable text in all its variety is what we textual critics should be displaying" (1999, 17). Elliott then speaks for himself on the matter: "Despite my own published work in trying to prove the originality of the text in selected areas of textual variation, ... I agree that the task of trying to establish the original words of the original authors with 100% certainty is impossible. More dominant in text critics' thinking now is the need to plot the changes in the history of the text" (1999, 18).

Not one textual critic could or would ever say that any of the critical editions of the Greek New Testament replicates the original wording with 100 percent accuracy. But an accurate reconstruction has to be the goal of those who practice textual criticism as classically defined. To veer from this is to stray from the essential task of textual criticism. It is an illuminating exercise "to plot the changes in the history of the text," but this assumes a known starting point. And what can that starting point be if not the original text? In analyzing Ehrman's book, *The Orthodox Corruption of Scripture*, Silva notes this same paradox: "Although this book is appealed to in support of blurring the notion of an original text, there is hardly a page in that book that does not in fact mention such a text or assume its accessibility .... Ehrman's book is unimaginable unless he can identify an initial form of the text that can be differentiated from a later alteration" (2002, 149). In short, one cannot speak about the text being corrupted if there is not an original text to be corrupted.

I am not against reconstructing the history of the text. In fact, I devoted many years to studying all the early Greek New Testament manuscripts (those dated before A.D. 300) and compiling a fresh edition of them in The Text of the Earliest New Testament Greek Manuscripts (coedited with David Barrett). This work provides a representative sampling of New Testament books that were actually read by Christians in the earliest centuries of the church. But whatever historical insights we may gain by studying the varying manuscript traditions as texts unto themselves, this is no reason to abandon the goal of producing the best critical edition possible, one that most likely replicates the original wording. Thus, I echo Silva's comments entirely, when he says: "I would like to affirm—not only with Hort, but with practically all students of ancient documents—that the recovery of the original text (i.e., the text in its initial form, prior to the alterations produced in the copying process) remains the primary task of textual criticism" (2002, 149).[143]

---

[143] Philip Comfort, NEW TESTAMENT TEXT AND TRANSLATUION COMMENTARY: Commentary on the variant readings of the ancient New Testament manuscripts and how they relate to the major English translations (Carol Stream, ILL: Tyndale House Publishers, Inc., 2008), Page xi.

The author of this work would echo the words of Silva and Comfort, in that the primary task of a textual scholar is the process of attempting to ascertain the original wording of the original text that was published by Matthew, Mark, Luke, John, James, Jude, Peter, and Paul. Even if we acknowledge that we can never say with absolute certainty that we have established the original wording one hundred percent, this should always be the goal. Imagine any other field in life, the certainty of a successful heart transplant by a surgeon, the certainty of astronauts going to the moon and back, or just the certainty that our automobile will get us to our destination, and the like. Do we want a heart surgeon who aims for eighty-percent certainty in a successful operation on us? Most objective textual scholars would agree that between the 1881 Westcott and Hort text and the Nestle-Aland/United Bible Societies Greek text, we are in the very high nineties, if not ninety-nine percent mirror-like reflection of the original wording of the twenty-seven New Testament books. Of course, the ongoing objective is to reach one hundred percent even if it is not achievable.

TEXTUAL CRITICISM is the process of the textual scholar attempting to ascertain the original wording of the original text.

CHAPTER 6 The Early Christian Copyists

Today there are about two billion people who call themselves Christians, who own or are aware of the Bible. Most are unaware of just how that book came down to them, yet many if not most would acknowledge that it is inspired by God and free of errors and contradictions. In this chapter, we will take a brief look at how the early Christians went about the work of making copies of what would become known as New Testament books, books that they felt were Scripture, just like the inspired Hebrew Scriptures. Such background cannot only build confidence that we have been carrying the very Word of God, but it also allows us to 'be prepared to make a defense to anyone who asks you for a reason for the hope that is in you.' (1 Pet 3:15) One might say that the 128 New Testament papyrus manuscripts that are known today are hardly a notable amount.[144] When we consider that the ancients wrote on perishable materials, we understand why relatively few manuscripts have been preserved to our day.

Further, early Christianity suffered much persecution. Both emperors Nero (64 C.E.) and Domitian (95 C.E.) persecuted Christians, but this likely did not greatly affect the survival of manuscripts. However, other Roman Emperors throughout the second and third centuries C.E. persecuted Christians on an empire-wide scale, which did significantly affect manuscript survival.

---

[144] First, there are close to one million papyrus fragments in various libraries throughout the world that have not yet been published. Since only about one percent of all papyri have been published (about 10,000), there is a very high degree of probability that some of the remainders will be NT fragments. The last NT papyrus to be published was papyrus 127 or P127, a fifth-century fragment of Acts discovered in 2009. Therefore, when we speak of how many have survived, we can understand that the question is not that easy to answer.

NT scholars use the term "extant" to describe MSS that have survived. It means that some have survived and are known to exist. With that definition, you might think that 127 is the number. However, there is a slight problem with that, too. Some fragments, such as P64 and P67, were later determined to belong to the same manuscript. This happens a few times for NT MSS, but mostly for minuscules (of which we now have extant about 2900). However, most scholars do not wrestle with such details. Therefore, 128 is the answer you are looking for.

As for dates, the papyri range in date from early second century C.E. to early seventh century C.E. I have worked up a chart of all NT MSS through the 8th century: as much as 43% of all the verses of the NT are attested by the end of the third century in the extant papyri.-- Dr. Daniel B. Wallace of The Center for the Study of New Testament Manuscripts.

Many scholars tend to speak disapprovingly of the work of the early Christian copyists. First, they maintain that copyists were not concerned with the importance of accurately copying the manuscripts, resulting in many mistakes. Second, they claim that most of the copyists were untrained in the practice of making copies, resulting in more copyist errors. Third, they say that the copyists were freely taking liberties by freely changing words, clauses, even whole sentences, omitting and inserting to improve the account, and at times to strengthen orthodoxy. However, as we have seen and will see shortly, this observation is not the case. We do not claim the early copyists were error-free, or that they were inspired. However, professional and semi-professional scribes copied many of the early New Testament manuscripts, with most being done by copyists who at a minimum had experience making documents.[145] Nevertheless, there undoubtedly were copyists with no training at all, who did copy some manuscripts.

Therefore, some of the early Christian copyists, because they were untrained in the task of making copies, did make errors. However, were these errors noteworthy? No. Again, what we can say is that the vast majority of the Greek text is not affected by variants at all. Of the **small amount** of the text that is affected by variants, the vast majority of these are minor slips of the pen, such as misspelling words. Also, they are minor intentional changes, e.g., using a synonym in place of the word in the text, or using a pronoun for a noun, and spelling the same word different ways. With these insignificant mishaps, we are sure what the original reading is in these places. Of our **small amount**, a minor number of variants are difficult in establishing the original reading. Lastly, there are very rare variants where we would say that we are uncertain as to the original reading. However, these latter two categories affect no doctrine; moreover, variant readings can be placed in a footnote, giving the reader access to the original using either the main text or the footnote.

Excursion on How Our Bible Manuscripts Survived the Elements

One may wonder why more Old and New Testament manuscripts have not survived. Really, the better question would be how come so many of our Bible manuscripts survived in comparison to secular ancient

---

[145] C. H. Roberts wrote, "In the second century, locally produced texts such as the scrap of *The Shepherd* [of Hermas] on the back of a document from the Fayum or the Baden Exodus-Deuteronomy might be carefully collated and corrected; the numerous duplications and omissions of the first hand of the Chester Beatty Numbers-Deuteronomy codex were put right by the corrector. This scrupulous reproduction of the text may be a legacy from Judaism and reminds us that no more in this period than in any other does quality of book production go hand in hand with quality of text." (C. H. Roberts, Manuscript, Society, and Belief in Early Christian Egypt 1979, 22)

manuscripts? The primary materials used to receive writing in ancient times were perishable papyrus and parchment. It must be remembered that the Christians suffered intense persecution during intervals in the first 300 years from Pentecost 33 C.E. With this persecution from the Roman Empire came many orders to destroy Christian texts. In addition, these texts were not stored in such a way as to secure their preservation; they were actively used by the Christians in the congregation and were subject to wear and tear. Furthermore, moisture is the enemy of papyrus, and it causes them to disintegrate over time. This is why, as we will discover, the papyrus manuscripts that have survived have come from the dry sands of Egypt. Moreover, it seems not to have entered the minds of the early Christians to preserve their documents, because their solution to the loss of manuscripts was just to make more copies. Fortunately, the process of making copies transitioned to the more durable animal skins, which would last much longer. Those that have survived, especially from the fourth century C.E. and earlier, are the path to restoring the original Greek New Testament.[146]

Both papyrus and parchment jeopardized the survival of the Bible because they were perishable materials. Papyrus, the weakest of the two, can tear and discolor. Because of moist climates, a sheet of papyrus can decay to the point where it is nothing more than a handful of dust. We must remember papyrus is a plant and when the scroll has been stored, it can grow mold and it can rot from dampness. It can even be eaten by starving rodents or also insects, especially white ants (i.e., termites) when it has been buried. When some of the manuscripts were first discovered early on, they were exposed to excessive light and humidity, which hastened their deterioration.

While parchment is far more durable than papyrus, it will also perish in time if mishandled or exposed to the elements (temperature, humidity, and light) over time.[147] Parchment is made from animal skin, so it too is also a victim of insects. Hence, when it comes to ancient records, Everyday Writing in the Graeco-Roman East states, "survival is the exception rather than the rule." (R. S. Bagnall 2009, 140) Think about it for a moment; the Bible and its special revelation could have died from decay in the elements.

The Mosaic Law commanded every future king, "And when he sits on the throne of his kingdom, he shall write for himself in a book a copy of this law, approved by the Levitical priests." (Deuteronomy 17:18)

---

[146] Cf. J. H. Greenlee, *Introduction to New Testament Textual Criticism* (Peabody: Hendrickson, 1995), 11.

[147] For example, the official signed copy of the U.S. Declaration of Independence was written on parchment. Now, less than 250 years later, it has faded to the point of being barely legible.

Moreover, the professional copyist of the Hebrew Old Testament made so many manuscripts, by the time of Jesus and the apostles, throughout all of Israel and even into distant Macedonia, there were many copies of the Scriptures in the synagogues (Luke 4:16, 17; Acts 17:11) How did our Hebrew Old Testament and Greek New Testament survive the elements to the point where there are far more of them than any other ancient document. For example, there are 5,830+ New Testament manuscripts in the original Greek alone.

New Testament scholar Philip W. Comfort writes, "Jews were known to put scrolls containing Scripture in pitchers or jars in order to preserve them. The Dead Sea scrolls found in jars in the Qumran caves are a celebrated example of this. The Beatty Papyri were very likely a part of a Christian library, which was hidden in jars to be preserved from confiscation during the Diocletian persecution."[148] Christianity were initially made up Jewish Christians only for the first seven years (29-36 C.E.), with Cornelius being the first Gentile baptized in 36 C.E. Much of early Christianity (33-350 C.E.) was made up of Jewish Christians, who evidently carried over the tradition of putting "scrolls containing Scripture in pitchers or jars in order to preserve them." It is for this reason that some of our earliest Bible manuscripts have been discovered in unusually dry regions, in clay jars and even dark closets and caves.

Manuscripts Saved from Egyptian Garbage Heaps

Beginning in 1778 and continuing to the end of the 19th century, many papyrus texts were accidentally discovered in Egypt that dated from 300 B.C.E. to 500 C.E., almost 500 million documents in all. About 130 years ago, there began a systematic search. At that time, a continuous flow of ancient texts was being found by the native fellahin, and the Egypt Exploration Society, a British non-profit organization, founded in 1882, realized that they needed to send out an expedition team before it was too late. They sent two Oxford scholars, Bernard P. Grenfell and Arthur S. Hunt, who received permission to search the area south of the farming region in the Faiyūm district. Grenfell chose a site called Behnesa because of its ancient Greek name, Oxyrhynchus. A search of the graveyards and the ruined houses produced nothing. The only place left to search was the town's garbage dumps, which were some 30 feet [9 m] high. It seems to Grenfell and Hunt that all was lost but they decided to try.

In January of 1897, a trial trench (excavation or depression in the ground) was dug, and it only took a few hours before ancient papyrus materials were found. These included letters, contracts, and official

---

[148] Philip Wesley Comfort and David P. Barrett, *The Text of the Earliest New Testament Greek Manuscripts* (Wheaton, IL: Tyndale House, 2001), 158.

documents. The sand had blown over them, covering them, and for nearly 2,000 years, the dry climate had served as a protection for them.

It took only a mere three months to pull out and recover almost two tons of papyri from Oxyrhynchus. They shipped twenty-five large cases back to England. Over the next ten years, these two courageous scholars returned each and every winter, to grow their collection. They discovered ancient classical writing, along with royal ordinances and contracts mixed in with business accounts private letters, shipping lists, as well as fragments of many New Testament manuscripts.

Of what benefit were all these documents? Foremost, the bulk of these documents were written by ordinary people in Koine (common) Greek of the day. Many of the words that would be used in the marketplace, not by the elites appeared in the Greek New Testament Scriptures, which woke scholars up to the fact that Biblical Greek was not some special Greek, but instead, it was the ordinary language of the common people, the man on the street. Thus, by comparing how the words had been used in these papyri, a clearer understanding of Biblical Greek emerged. As of the time of this writing, less than ten percent of these papyri have been published and studied. Most of the papyri were found in the top 10 feet 93 m] of the garbage heap because the other 20 feet [6 m] had been ruined by water from a nearby canal. If we look at it simply, this would mean that the 500 thousand documents found could have been two million in total. Then, we must ponder just how many documents must have come through Oxyrhynchus that were never discarded in the dumps. We have almost a half million papyrus documents (likely there were millions more that did not survive) in garbage dumps in the dry sands of Oxyrhynchus, Egypt.

The end result is that the New Testament has been preserved in over 5,836 complete or fragmented Greek manuscripts, as well as some 10,000 Latin manuscripts and 9,300 manuscripts in various other ancient languages, which include Syriac, Slavic, Gothic, Ethiopic, Coptic and Armenian. Some of these are well over 2,000 years old. End of excursion.

Public Reading Indicates the Importance of New Testament Books

Public reading is yet another important inference that the first-century Christian congregation valued the books that were being produced by the New Testament authors Matthew, Mark, Luke, John, Paul, Peter, James, and Jude.

Matthew 24:15 New American Standard Bible (NASB)

[15] "Therefore when you see the abomination of desolation which was spoken of through Daniel the prophet, standing in the holy place (let the reader understand),

This parenthetical "let the reader understand" is a reference to a public reader within the congregations.

1 Timothy 4:13 New American Standard Bible (NASB)

¹³ Until I come, give attention to the *public* reading *of Scripture*, to exhortation and teaching.

Only the privileged owned scrolls of the Holy Scriptures. Most Christians in the first century gained access to God's Word, as Paul explains here in his first letter to Timothy, by "the public reading of Scripture." Public reading was a major part of Christian meetings, a traditional practice of the Jews from the time of Moses, and one which was carried over to the Christian congregation. – Acts 13:15; 15:21; 2 Corinthians 3:15.

Revelation 1:3 New American Standard Bible (NASB)

³ Blessed is he who reads and those who hear the words of the prophecy, and heed the things which are written in it; for the time is near.

This reference to "he who reads and those who hear" is to the public reader and his audience in each of the seven mentioned congregations. Another factor is how the writers of the Christian Greek Scriptures viewed their own published works.

2 Peter 3:16 New American Standard Bible (NASB)

¹⁶ as also in all *his* letters, speaking in them of these things, in which are some things hard to understand, which the untaught and unstable distort, **as *they do* also the rest of the Scriptures,** to their own destruction. (Bold added.)

Here, about 64 C.E., we have the apostle Peter, who has just canonized Paul's letters, grouping them together as a collection. This is evidence of their being viewed as having authority. At 2 Timothy 3:16 and 2 Peter 1:20, the apostles Paul and Peter respectively appear to be referring to both the Hebrew Old Testament and the Greek Christian writings as [Greek *graphe*] "Scripture." Note that Peter is comparing Paul's letters to "*the rest of the Scriptures.*" What exactly does that mean?

Both Jesus and the writers of the Christian Greek Scriptures often used the Greek word *graphe* in their references to Moses' writings and the prophets, viewing them as having authority from God, being inspired. Many times, Jesus designates these Old Testament books as a whole as *graphe*, i.e., "Scripture." (Matthew 21:42; 22:29; Mark 14:49; John 5:39; Acts 17:11; 18:24, 28) At other times, the singular for "Scripture" was used when quoting a specific text to make a point, referring to it as a part of the whole of writings encompassing our 39 books of the Hebrew Old Testament. (Rom. 9:17; Gal. 3:8) Still, at other times *graphe* is used in a single text reference, such as Jesus' reference when dealing with the Jewish religious leaders: "Have you not read this [*graphe*] Scripture: 'The stone that the builders rejected has become the cornerstone.'" (Mark 12:10) Jesus' use of *graphe* in such an authoritative way only strengthens the point that immediately the writings of the New Testament authors were viewed as *graphe*, namely, Scripture.

From an Oral Gospel to the Written Record

Jesus had commanded his disciples to, "Go therefore and make disciples of all nations, baptizing them in the name of the Father and of the Son and of the Holy Spirit, teaching them to observe all that I have commanded you. And behold, I am with you always, to the end of the age." (Matt 28:19-20, ESV) How then was this gospel (good news) to be made known?

> During the forty-day period between Jesus' resurrection and his ascension, Jesus instructed his disciples in the teaching of the gospel. Accordingly, he prepared them for the tremendous task that awaited them on and after Pentecost.[149]

There were only ten days after Jesus ascension to Pentecost, when "they were all filled with the Holy Spirit." Jesus put it this way, in his words, it being only "a few days." This time would have been filled with the process of replacing Judas Iscariot, prayer, and the established gospel message, which would be the official oral message until it was deemed necessary to have a written gospel some 10 to 15 years later. The gospel message was quite simple: 'Christ died for our sins, was buried, and he was resurrected on the third day according to Scripture.' – 1 Corinthians 15:1-8

1 Corinthians 15:1-2 New American Standard Bible (NASB)

15 Now I make known to you, brethren, the gospel which I preached to you, which also you received, in which also you stand, 2 by which also you are saved, if you hold fast the word which I preached to you, unless you believed in vain.

By the time of the destruction of Jerusalem by General Titus of Rome (70 C.E.), all of the books of the Greek New Testament had been written, except for those penned by the apostle John. The Gospel of Matthew was penned first, published between 45 and 50 C.E. The Gospel of Luke was written about 56-58 C.E. and the Gospel of Mark between 60 to 65 C.E. Matthew, Mark, and Luke are known as the Synoptic Gospels, as they are similar in content, while John chose to convey other information, perhaps because he wrote his gospel to the second generation of Christians in about

---

[149] Simon J. Kistemaker and William Hendriksen, vol. 17, New Testament Commentary: Exposition of the Acts of the Apostles, New Testament Commentary (Grand Rapids: Baker Book House, 1953-2001), 47-48.

98 C.E. Luke informs us of just how the very first Christians received the gospel message. Very few translations make explicit the exact process.

Luke 1:1-4 Updated American Standard Version (UASV)[150]

[1] Inasmuch as many have undertaken to compile a narrative of the things that have been fulfilled among us, [2] just as they were handed down to us by those who from the beginning were eyewitnesses and servants of the word, [3] It also seemed good to me, since I have carefully investigated everything from the very first, to write an orderly account for you, most excellent Theophilus, [4] so that you may know the certainty concerning the things about which you were **taught** orally [Gr., *katechethes*].

Acts 18:24-25 Updated American Standard Version (UASV)

[24] Now a Jew named Apollos, an Alexandrian by birth, came to Ephesus. He was an eloquent man, competent in the Scriptures. [25] This man had been **orally** [*katechethes*] **instructed** in the way of the Lord, and being fervent in spirit, he spoke and taught accurately the things concerning Jesus, knowing only the baptism of John.

Galatians 6:6 Updated American Standard Version (UASV)

The one who is **orally** [*katechethes*] **taught** the word must share all good things with the one who teaches.

We can see clearly from the above that both Theophilus and Apollos received the initial gospel message, just as all Christians did in the early years, and even after the written gospels were available, the gospel of Jesus was taught by oral instruction (*katechethes*). In time, it was deemed that there was a need for a written record, which is the reason Luke gives for his Gospel. This was not to discount what Theophilus had been orally taught, but rather to give credence to that oral message that he had already received. Of course, the New Testament was not limited to these gospels.

The publishing of these New Testament books in written form would have come about in the following stages:

(1) the inspired author probably would have used a well-trusted, skilled Christian scribe to take down what he was inspired to convey, *some believe* by shorthand;[151]

---

[150] The Updated American Standard Version (UASV) is under production by Christian Publishing House. It is by permission that we use these next few verses before it is published, as their rendering better conveys the original Greek.

[151] "I Tertius, who wrote this letter, greet you in the Lord." (Rom. 16:22) "By Silvanus, a faithful brother as I regard him, I have written briefly to you, exhorting and declaring that this is the true grace of God. Stand firm in it." (1 Pet. 5:12)

(2) The scribe would then make a rough draft *if it had been taken* by shorthand. If shorthand had not been used, this first copy would have been the rough draft;

(3) this draft would then be read by both the scribe and author, making corrections because the copyist, though professional or at least skillful at making documents, was not inspired;

(4) thereafter, the scribe would make what is known as the autograph, original, or initial text, to be signed by the author,

(5) which would then be used as the official exemplar to make other copies.

Both Tertius and Silvanus were very likely skilled Christian scribes, who assisted the writers of the New Testament. (Rom. 16:22; 1 Pet. 5:12) It is unlikely that Paul personally wrote any of his letters that were of great length. It is clear that Peter used the trained Silvanus to pen his first letter, and likely, the second letter was possibly the result of Jude's penman skills, as it is very similar in style to the letter by Jude. This may explain the differences in style between First and Second Peter. We should emphasize that *it is not possible* that the inspired author would give some latitude to his skilled Christian scribe to serve as a coauthor regarding word choices, as some have suggested.

Papyrus or Parchment?

The Hebrew Old Testament that would have been available to the early Christians was written on the processed hide of animals after the hair was removed, and the hide was smoothed out with a pumice stone.[152] Leather scrolls were sent to Alexandria, Egypt in about 280 B.C.E., to make what we now know as the Greek Septuagint.[153] Most of the Dead Sea scrolls that were discovered between 1947 and 1956 are made of leather, and it is almost certain that the scroll of Isaiah that Jesus read from in the synagogue was as well. Luke 4:17 says, "And the scroll of the prophet Isaiah was given to him. He unrolled the scroll and found the place where it was written."

The Dead Sea Scroll of Isaiah (1QIsa) dates to the end of the second century B.C.E., written on 17 sheets of parchment, one of the seven Dead Sea Scrolls that were first recovered by Bedouin shepherds in 1947. The

---

[152] A very light porous rock formed from solidified lava, used in solid form as an abrasive and in powdered form as a polish.

[153] A Greek translation of the Hebrew Bible started in about 280 and completed about 150 B.C.E. to meet the needs of Greek-speaking Jews outside Palestine.

Nash Papyrus is a collection of four papyrus fragments acquired in Egypt in 1898 by W. L. Nash, dating to about 150 B.C.E. It contains parts of the Ten Commandments from Exodus chapter 20, along with some verses from Deuteronomy chapters 5 and 6. It is by far one of the oldest Hebrew manuscript fragments.

Both leather and papyrus were used before the first-century Christians. Vellum is a high-quality parchment made from calfskin, kidskin, or lambskin. After the skin was removed, it would be soaked in limewater, after which the hair would be scraped off, the skin then being scraped and dried, and rubbed afterward with chalk and pumice stone, creating an exceptionally smooth writing material. During the first three hundred years of Christianity, the secular world viewed parchment as being inferior to papyrus, it being relegated to notebooks, rough drafts, and other non-literary purposes.

A couple of myths should be dispelled before continuing. It is often remarked that papyrus is not a durable material. Both papyrus and parchment are durable under normal circumstances. This is not negating the fact that parchment is more durable than papyrus. Another often-repeated thought is that papyrus was fragile and brittle, making it an unlikely candidate to be used for a codex, which would have to be folded in half. Another issue that should be sidelined is whether it was more expensive to produce papyrus or parchment. Presently there is no data to aid in that evaluation. We know that papyrus was used for all of the Christian codex manuscripts up to the fourth century, at which time we find the two great parchment codices, the Sinaiticus and Vaticanus manuscripts. Parchment of good quality has been called "the finest writing material ever devised by man." (Roberts and Skeat, The Birth of the Codex 1987, 8) Why then did parchment take so long to replace papyrus? This may be answered by R. Reed, in *Ancient Skins, Parchments, and Leathers:*

> It is perhaps the extraordinary high durability of the product, produced by so simple a method, which has prevented most people from suspecting that many subtle points are involved.... The essence of the parchment process, which subjects the system of pelt to the simultaneous action of stretching and drying, is to bring about peculiar changes quite different from those applying when making leather. These are (1) reorganization of the dermal fibre network by stretching, and (2) permanently setting this new and highly stretched form of fibre network by drying the pelt fluid to a hard, glue-like consistency. In other words, the pelt fibres are fixed in a stretched condition so that they cannot revert to their original relaxed state. (Reed 1973, 119-20)

Where the medieval parchment makers were greatly superior to their modern counterparts was in the control and modification of the ground substance in the pelt, before the latter was stretched and dried …. The major point, however, which modern parchment manufacturers have not appreciated, is what might be termed the integral or collective nature of the parchment process. The bases of many different effects need to be provided for simultaneously, in one and the same operation. The properties required in the final parchment must be catered for at the wet pelt stage, for due to the peculiar nature of the parchment process, once the system has been dried, and after-treatments to modify the material produced are greatly restricted. (Reed 1973, 124)

This method, which follows those used in medieval times for making parchment of the highest quality, is preferable for it allows the grain surface of the drying pelt to be "slicked" and freed from residual fine hairs while stretching upon the frame. At the same time, any process for cleaning and smoothing the flesh side, or for controlling the thickness of the final parchment may be undertaken by working the flesh side with sharp knives which are semi-lunar in form…. To carry out such manual operations on wet stretched pelt demands great skill, speed of working, and concentrated physical effort. (Reed 1973, 138-9)

Enough has been said to suggest that behind the apparently simple instructions contained in the early medieval recipes there is a wealth of complex process detail which we are still far from understanding. Hence it remains true that parchment-making is perhaps more of an art than a science. (Reed 1973, 172)

The Christian's Use of the Codex

Going back to the first-century once again, let us take a moment to deal with the invention of the codex. Was it the first-century Christians who invented the codex, or at least put it on the stage of the world scene?

The writing tablet of ancient times was made from two flat pieces of wood, held together by a thong hinge, which looks something like our modern book. It had its limits because of the impracticality of fastening more than a few such tablets together. The center of the tablet pages was slightly hollowed, to receive a wax coating. A stylus was the standard instrument used to write on these waxed tablets. The stylus was made of metal, ivory, or bone, and was sharpened to a point on one side while having a rounded knob on the other for erasing, and making corrections.

This was the oldest form of writing for the Greeks, who borrowed it from the Hittites. History and evidence credit the Romans with replacing the wooden tablet with the parchment notebook. The apostle Paul is the only Greek writer of the first-century C.E. to mention the parchment notebook.

2 Timothy 4:13 New American Standard Bible (NASB)

[13] When you come bring the cloak which I left at Troas with Carpus, and the books, especially the parchments. [Gr., *membranai*, parchment notebooks]

However, it should be recognized that the parchment notebook was not used for literature in the first two centuries before the Christian era (B.C.E.); this was done with the roll or scroll. Even though the codex was commonly used for books, the first indication that it was going to displace the roll came toward the end of the first century C.E. (Roberts and Skeat, The Birth of the Codex 1987, 24) Thus, again, the Jews of the late first century C.E. and thereafter used scrolls, while the Christians used codices. However, many of the first Christians were Jewish and likely read their Old Testament from a scroll. Before becoming a Christian, the apostle Paul was a Pharisee and would have used scrolls. However, at least until about the end of the first century C.E. Christians used scrolls primarily.

Only a handful of manuscripts of the New Testament that are still in existence were written on scrolls (P[13], P[18], and P[98]). However, these were written on the backs of other writings, so they were not composed in the scroll form. P[22] was written on a roll, and we await more research there, as it is a peculiarity among the group of papyri. All other New Testament manuscripts were written on codices. As there is evidence that the second-century Christians were trying to set themselves apart from the Jews, so they likely made the transition in part because they wished to be different. We say in part because it is quite evident that the first Christians grouped their writings together, the Gospels and Paul's letters. The codex afforded them the means of doing this, while a scroll of the gospels would have been far too long and bulky, and finding a portion of desired text would have been difficult at best. For example, P[46] dating to about 150 C.E., contained ten of Paul's letters. P[45] dates to about 225 C.E. and originally contained all four Gospels and the book of Acts. In the end, it can be said that the Christians adopted the codex (1) to be different from the Jews, (2) to have the Gospels and the Apostle Paul's letters all in one book, and (3) because of the ease of being able to find a portion of text, and this made the spread of the good news much more convenient.

We do learn a good deal from the New Testament. The apostle Peter writes, "… just as our beloved brother Paul also wrote to you according to the wisdom given him, as he does in all his letters when he speaks in them of these matters ...." (2 Pet 3:15-16, about 64 C.E.) This shows how early Paul's letters were grouped together. The apostle John wrote, "Though I have much to write to you, I would rather not use paper and ink. Instead, I hope to come to you and talk face to face so that our joy may be complete." (2 John 12, about 98 C.E.) We see from this that John used papyrus in writing to a sister congregation. The Greek word *chartou* means "papyrus," "a sheet of paper." The apostle Paul wrote Timothy and asked him, "when you come, bring the cloak that I left with Carpus at Troas, also the books [likely scrolls of OT books], and, above all, the parchments [codices]." (2 Tim 4:13, about 65 C.E) While it is thought by most scholars that Paul was talking about two different items here, it is quite possible that he was referring to only one, which is Skeat's position. Let us look at the verse again:

When you come bring ... the books, especially the parchments.

When you come, bring ... the books, that is my parchment notebooks.

If the second version above is correct, Paul hoped to obtain some of his notebooks, possible rough drafts that he had left behind. The Old Testament books could have been located right where he was, but he would have been highly interested in unpublished works that he wanted to get out before his execution. Of course, this latter thought is the formation of judgments based on incomplete or inconclusive information. However, one thing is sure, that either Paul was asking for codices in complete book form or notebook form. This indicates that Paul was the first to have his books collected into codex form, and we can conclude that the Christians were using the codex at the end of the first century.

The Trustworthiness of Early Copyists

Throughout much of the twentieth century, it was common to form three conclusions about the earliest copyists and their work:

(1) The first three centuries saw copyists who were semiliterate and unskilled in the work of making copies.

(2) Copyists in these early centuries felt as though the end was nigh, so they took liberties with the text in an attempt to strengthen orthodoxy.

(3) In the early centuries, manuscripts could be described as "free," "wild," "in a state of flux," "chaotic," "a turbid textual morass," i.e., a "free text" (so the Alands).

The first in the above would undoubtedly lead to many unintentional changes while the second would escalate intentional changes. J. Harold Greenlee had this to say:

> In the very early period, the NT writings were more nearly "private" writings than the classics . . . the classics were commonly, although not always, copied by professional scribes, the NT books were probably usually copied in the early period by **Christians who were not professionally trained** for the task, and **no corrector** was employed to check the copyist's work against his exemplar (the MS from which the copy was made) .... It appears that a copyist sometimes even took liberty to add or change minor details in the narrative books on the basis of personal knowledge, alternative tradition, or a parallel account in another book of the Bible .... At the same time, the importance of these factors in affecting the purity of the NT text must not be exaggerated. The NT books doubtless came to be considered as "literature" soon after they began to be circulated, with attention to the precise wording required when copies were made.[154]

Greenlee had not changed his position 14 years later when he wrote the following:

> The New Testament, on the other hand, was probably copied during the earliest period mostly by ordinary Christians **who were not professional scribes** but who wanted a copy of the New Testament book or books for themselves or for other Christians.[155]

The Alands in their *Text of the New Testament* saw the New Testament books as not being canonical, i.e., not viewed as Scripture in the first few centuries, so the books were subject to changes. They wrote, "not only every church but each individual Christian felt 'a direct relationship to God.' Well into the second century Christians still regarded themselves as possessing inspiration equal to that of the New Testament writings which they read in their worship service." Earlier they wrote, "That was all the more true of the early period when the text had not attained canonical status, especially in the early period when Christians considered themselves filled with the Spirit." They claimed that "until the beginning of the fourth

---

[154] J. Harold Greenlee, Introduction to New Testament Textual Criticism (Revised Edition, 1995), 51–52.

[155] J. Harold Greenlee, The Text of the New Testament: From Manuscript to Modern Edition (2008), 37.

century the text of the New Testament developed freely." (Aland and Aland, The Text of the New Testament 1995, 295, 69)

Generally, once an established concept is set within the world of textual scholars, it is not easily displaced. During the start of the 20th century (1900–1930), there was a handful of papyri discovered that obviously represented the work of a copyist who had no training. It is during this time that Sir Frederic Kenyon, director and principal librarian of the British Museum for many years, said,

> The early Christians, a poor, scattered, often **illiterate** body, looking for the return of the Lord at no distant date, **were not likely to care** sedulously for minute accuracy of transcription or to preserve their books religiously for the benefit of posterity.[156]

The first papyri discovered (P[45], P[46], P[66]) showed this to be the case. However, as more papyri became known, especially after the discovery of P[75], it proved to be just the opposite, prompting Sir Frederic Kenyon to write,

> We must be content to know that the general authenticity of the New Testament text has been remarkably supported by the modern discoveries which have so greatly reduced the interval between the original autographs and our earliest extant manuscripts, and that the differences of reading, interesting as they are, do not affect the fundamental doctrines of the Christian faith.[157]

Even though many textual scholars were crediting the Alands' *The Text of the New Testament* with their description of the text as "free," that was not the entire position of the Alands. True, they spoke of the different text styles such as the "normal," "free" "strict" and the "paraphrastic." However, like Kenyon, they saw a need based on the evidence, which suggested a rethinking of how the evidence should be described:

> Our research on the early papyri has yielded unexpected results that require a change in the traditional views of the early text. We have inherited from the past generation the view that the early text was a "free" text, and the discovery of the Chester Beatty papyri seemed to confirm this view. When P[45] and P[46] were joined by P[66] sharing the same characteristics, this position seemed to be definitely established. P[75] appeared in contrast to be a loner with its "strict" text anticipating Codex Vaticanus. Meanwhile the other witnesses of the early period had been

---

[156] F. Kenyon, Our Bible and the Ancient Manuscripts (1895), 157.

[157] F. Kenyon, Our Bible and the Ancient Manuscripts (1962), 249.

ignored. It is their collations which have changed the picture so completely.[158]

While we have said this previously, it bears repeating once again that *some* of the earliest manuscripts we now have indicate that a professional scribe copied them.[159] *Many* of the other papyri confirm that a semi-professional hand copied them, while *most* of these early papyri give evidence of being produced by a copyist who was literate and experienced. Therefore, either literate or semi-professional copyist did the vast majority of our early papyri, with some being done by professionals. As it happened, the few poorly copied manuscripts became known first, establishing a precedent that was difficult for some to discard when the enormous amount of evidence came forth that showed just the opposite.

Distribution of Papyri by Century and Type					
DATE	ALEX	WEST	CAES	BYZ	Hand
150	P^{52} P^{90} P^{104}	0	0	0	0
200	P^{32} P^{46} $P^{4/64/67}$ P^{66} P^{77} 0189	0	0	0	0
250	P^1 P^5 P^9 P^{12} P^{15} P^{20} P^{22} P^{23} P^{27} P^{28} P^{29} P^{30} P^{39} P^{40} P^{45} P^{47} P^{49} P^{53} P^{65} P^{70} P^{75} P^{80} P^{87} 0220	0	0	P^{48} P^{69}	1

---

[158] (Aland and Aland, The Text of the New Testament 1995, 93-5)

[159] Some may argue that we can only be confident that we have good manuscripts of an "early" form of the text but not necessarily of the originally published text. This hypothesis cannot be disproven. However, I think it is highly doubtful for four reasons: (1) The intervening time between the publication date of various New Testament books (from AD 60–90) and the date of several of our extant manuscripts (from AD 100–200) is narrow, thereby giving us manuscripts that are probably only three to five "manuscript generations" removed from the originally published texts. (2) We have no knowledge that any of these manuscripts go back to an early "form" that postdates the original publications. (3) We are certain that there was no major Alexandrian recension in the second century. (4) Text critics have been able to detect any other other second-century textual aberrations, such as the D-text, which was probably created near the end of the second century, not the beginning. Thus, it stands to reason that these "reliable" manuscripts are excellent copies of the authorized published texts." (P. Comfort, Encountering the Manuscripts: An Introduction to New Testament Paleography and Textual Criticism 2005, 269)

300	P13 P16 P18 P37 P72 P78 P115 O162	0	0	P38 0171	1
Acts	14	0	0	0	4

Also, as we noted earlier, textual scholars such as Comfort[160] and others believe that the very early Alexandrian manuscripts that we now possess are a reflection of what would have been found throughout the whole of the Greco-Roman Empire from about 85–275 C.E. So these early papyri can play a major role in our establishing the original readings.

However, Epp asks, "If Westcott-Hort did not utilize papyri in constructing their NT text, and if our own modern critical texts, in fact, are not significantly different from that of Westcott-Hort, then why are the papyri important after all?"[161] From there, Epp goes on to strongly advise that the papyri should play an essential role in three areas: (1) "to isolate the earliest discernable text-types, (2) assisting "to trace out the very early history of the NT text," and, (3) "Finally, the papyri can aid in refining the canons of criticism—the principles by which we judge variant readings—for they open to us a window for viewing the earliest stages of textual transmission, providing instances of how scribes worked in their copying of manuscripts."[162] We should add that the early papyri have changed decisions of textual scholars and committees so that they have not retained the readings of Westcott and Hort at times.

To offer just one example, both Metzger and Comfort inform us that it was the external evidence of the papyri that resulted in the change in the NU text, adopting the reading that was also in the Textus Receptus, as opposed to what was in the Westcott and Hort text.

Matthew 26:20 (WH)	Matthew 26:20 (TRNU)
[20] μετα των δωδεκα μαθητων	[20] μετα των δωδεκα
With the twelve disciples	With the twelve

Metzger writes, "As is the case in 20:17,[163] the reading μαθηταί after οἱ δώδεκα is doubtful. In the present verse [26:20] the weight of the external

---

[160] Philip W. Comfort, The Quest for the Original Text of the New Testament (Eugene, Oregon: Wipf and Stock Publishers, 1992).

[161] The New Testament Papyrus Manuscripts in Historical Perspective, in To Touch the Text: Biblical and Related Studies in Honour of Joseph A. Fitzmyer, S. J. (ed. Maurya P. Horgan and Paul J. Kobelski; New York: Crossroad, 1989), 285 (there italicized) repr. in Epp, Perspectives, 338.

[162] Ibid., 288

[163] 20:17 τοὺς δώδεκα [μαθητάς] {C}

evidence seems to favor the shorter reading." (B. M. Metzger, A Textual Commentary on the Greek New Testament 1994, 53) Comfort in his *New Testament Text and Translation* writes, "Even though both P[37] and P[45] are listed as 'vid,' it is certain that both did not include the word μαθητων because line spacing would not accommodate it. P[37] has the typical abbreviation for 'twelve,' as ῑβ; and P[45] has it written out as [δω]δεκα. P[64+67] is less certain, but line lengths of the manuscript suggest that it reads ῑβ (see *Texts of Earliest MSS*, 69)." Comfort more explicitly explains what Metzger hinted at; "The testimony of the papyri (with B and D) created a change in the NU text. Prior to NA26, the NU text included the word μαθητων ("disciples"). But the early evidence shows that this must have been a later addition." Comfort continues, "Such an addition is not necessary in light of the fact that Jesus' closest followers were often designated by the gospel writers as simply "the twelve." (P. W. Comfort 2008, 77)

Again, many textual scholars before 1961 believed that the early copyists of the New Testament papyri were among the untrained in making documents (P[45], P[46], P[47]; P[66] and P[72] in 2 Peter and Jude), and that the papyri were texts in flux.[164] It was not until the discovery of P[75] and other papyri that textual scholars began to think differently. Nevertheless, the attitude of the 1930s through the 1950s is explained well by Kurt and Barbara Aland:

> Of special importance are the early papyri, i.e., of the period of the third/fourth century. As we have said, these have an inherent significance for the New Testament textual studies because they witness to a situation before the text was channeled into major text types in the fourth century. Our research on the early papyri has yielded unexpected results that require a change in the traditional views of the early text. We have inherited from the past generation the view that the early text was a "free"

Although copyists often add the word μαθηταίto the more primitive expression οἱ δώδεκα (see Tischendorf's note *in loc.* and 26.20 below), a majority of the Committee judged that the present passage was assimilated to the text of Mark (10:32) or Luke (18:31). In order to represent both possibilities it was decided to employ square brackets. (B. M. Metzger, A Textual Commentary on the Greek New Testament 1994, 42)

On 20:17, Comfort writes, "Either reading could be original because they both have good support and because the gospel writers alternated between the nomenclature 'the twelve disciples' and 'the twelve.'" (P. W. Comfort 2008, 60)

[164] Kurt and Barbara Aland write, "By the 1930s the number of known papyri had grown to more than forty without any of them arousing any special attention, despite the fact that many of them were of a quite early date. (Aland and Aland, The Text of the New Testament 1995, 84)

text,[165] and the discovery of the Chester Beatty papyri seemed to confirm this view. When P[45] and P[46] were joined by P[66] sharing the same characteristics, this position seemed to be definitely established. (Aland and Aland, The Text of the New Testament 1995, 93)

Before P[75], scholars were under the impression that scribes must have used manuscripts of untrained copyists to make a recension (critical revision, i.e., revised text); and this, according to scholars prior to 1961, was how Codex Vaticanus (B) came about. In 1940, Kenyon inferred the following:

> During the second and third centuries, a great variety of readings came into existence throughout the Christian world. In some quarters, considerable license was shown in dealing with the sacred text; in others, more respect was shown to the tradition. In Egypt, this variety of texts existed, as elsewhere; but Egypt (and especially Alexandria) was a country of strong scholarship and with a knowledge of textual criticism. Here, therefore, a relatively faithful tradition was preserved. About the beginning of the fourth century, a scholar may well have set himself to compare the best accessible representatives of this tradition, and so have produced a text of which B is an early descendant.[166]

While Kenyon was correct about the manuscripts coming up out of Egypt being a reasonably pure text, he was certainly mistaken when he suggested that Codex Vaticanus was the result of a critical revision by early scribes. P[75] put this theory to rest. Agreement between P[75] and codex B is 92% in John and 94% in Luke. However, Porter has it at about 85% agreement. Zuntz, on the other hand, went a little further than Kenyon did. Kenyon believed that the critical text had been made in the early part of the fourth century, leading to Codex Vaticanus. Zuntz believed similarly but felt that the recension began back in the mid-second-century and was a process that ran up into the fourth-century. Zuntz wrote:

> The Alexander correctors strove, in ever repeated efforts, to keep the text current in their sphere free from the many faults

---

[165] Early manuscripts (from before the fourth century) are classified by the Alands as "strict," "normal," or "free." The "normal" text "transmitted the original text with the limited amount of variation." Then, there is the "free" text, "characterized by a greater degree of variation than the 'normal' text." Finally, there was the "strict" text, "which reproduced the text of its exemplar with greater fidelity (although still with certain characteristic liberties), exhibiting far less variation than the 'normal' text." (Aland 1987, 93)

[166] F. Kenyon, "Hesychius and the Text of the New Testament," in *Memorial Lagrange* (1940), 250.

that had infected it in the previous period and which tended to crop up again even after they had been obelized [i.e., marked as spurious]. These labours must time and again have been checked by persecutions and the confiscation of Christian books, and counteracted by the continuing currency of manuscripts of the older type. Nonetheless they resulted in the emergence of a type of text (as distinct from a definite edition) which served as a norm for the correctors in provincial Egyptian scriptoria. The final result was the survival of a text far superior to that of the second century, even though the revisers, being fallible human beings, rejected some of its own correct readings and introduced some faults of their own.[167]

P75, as we can see from the above, influenced the thinking of Kurt Aland. While he said, "We have inherited from the past generation the view that the early text was a 'free' text," he was one of those saying that very thing. However, as he would later say, "Our research on the early papyri has yielded unexpected results that require a change in the traditional views of the early text." P75 greatly affected the Alands: "P75 shows such a close affinity with the Codex Vaticanus that the supposition of a recension of the text at Alexandria, in the fourth century, can no longer be held."[168] Gordon Fee clearly states that there was no Alexandrian recension prior to P75 (175-225 C.E.) and the time of Codex Vaticanus (350 C.E.), as he commented that P75 and Vaticanus "seem to represent a 'relatively pure' form of preservation of a 'relatively pure' line of descent from the original text."[169] For many decades now, New Testament textual scholarship has been aware that P75 is an extremely accurate copy. Of the copyist behind P75, Colwell said, "his impulse to improve style is for the most part defeated by the obligation to make an exact copy."[170] Colwell went on to comment on the work of that scribe:

> In P75 the text that is produced can be explained in all its variants as the result of a single force, namely the disciplined scribe who writes with the intention of being careful and accurate. There is no evidence of revision of his work by anyone

[167] G. Zuntz, *The Text of the Epistles* (1953), 271–272.

[168] Kurt Aland, "The Significance of the Papyri for New Testament Research" in *The Bible in Modern Scholarship* (1965), 336.

[169] Gordon Fee, "P75, P66, and Origen: The Myth of Early Textual Recension in Alexandria" in *New Dimensions in New Testament Study* (1974), 19–43.

[170] Ernest C. Colwell, "Method in Evaluating Scribal Habits: A Study of P45, P66, P75," in *Studies in Methodology in Textual Criticism of the New Testament,* New Testament Tools and Studies 9 (Leiden: Brill, 1969), 121.

else, or in fact of any real revision, or check.... The control had been drilled into the scribe before he started writing.[171]

We do not want to leave the reader with the impression that P[75] is perfect, as it is not. On this Comfort says,

> The scribe had to make several corrections (116 in Luke and John), but there was no attempt 'to revise the text by a second exemplar, and indeed no systematic correction at all.'[172] The scribe of P[75] shows a clear tendency to make grammatical and stylistic improvements in keeping with the Alexandrian scriptorial tradition, and the scribe had a tendency to shorten his text, particularly by dropping pronouns. However, his omissions of text hardly ever extend beyond a word or two, probably because he copied letter by letter and syllable by syllable.[173]

As the early Nestle Greek text moved from edition to edition, the influence of the New Testament papyri increased. It was the son of Eberhard Nestle, Erwin, who added a full critical apparatus in the thirteenth edition of the 1927 Nestle Edition. It was not until 1950 that Kurt Aland began to work on the text that would eventually become known as the Nestle-Aland text. He would begin to add even more evidence from papyri to the critical apparatus of the twenty-first edition. At Erwin Nestle's request, he looked over and lengthened the critical apparatus, adding far more manuscripts. This ultimately led to the 25th edition of 1963. The most significant papyri and recently discovered majuscules, (i.e., 0189), a few minuscules (33, 614, 2814), and rarely also lectionaries were also considered. However, while the critical apparatus was being added to and even altered, the text of the Nestle-Aland was not changed until the 26th edition (1979). Many of these changes to the text were a direct result of the papyri.

Returning to the First Century

The writers of the 27 books comprising the Christian Greek Scriptures were Jews.[174] (Romans 13:1-2) Either these men were apostles, intimate

---

[171] Ibid., 117

[172] James Ronald Royse, "Scribal Habits in Early Greek New Testament Papyri" (Ph.D. diss., Graduate Theological Union, 1981), 538–39.

[173] (Comfort and Barret, The Text of the Earliest New Testament Greek Manuscripts 2001, 506)

[174] Some believe that Luke was a Gentile, basing this primarily on Colossians 4:11, 14. Because Paul first mentioned "the circumcision" (Col 4:11) and thereafter talked about Luke (Col 4:14), the inference is drawn that Luke was not of the circumcision and therefore was not a Jew. However, this is by no means decisive. Romans 3:1-2 says, "Jews were entrusted with

traveling companions of the apostles, or were picked by Christ in a supernatural way, such as the apostle Paul. Being Jewish, they would have viewed the Old Testament as being the inspired, inerrant Word of God. Paul said, "all Scripture is inspired by God" (2 Timothy 3:16). These writers of the 27 New Testament books would have viewed the teachings of Jesus, or their books expounding on his teachings, as Scripture as well as the Old Testament. The teachings of Jesus came to most of these New Testament writers personally from Jesus, being taught orally; thereafter, they would be the ones who published what Jesus had said and taught orally. When it came time to be published in written form, it should be remembered that Jesus had promised them "The Helper, the Holy Spirit, whom the Father will send in my name, he will teach you all things and **bring to your remembrance** all that I have said to you." – John 14:26

The early first-century Christian copyists were very much aware of the traditions that the Jewish scribes followed in meticulously copying their texts. These copyists would have immediately understood that they were copying sacred texts. In fact, the early papyri show evidence of shared features with the Jewish Sopherim, men who copied the Hebrew Scriptures from the time of Ezra in the fifth-century B.C.E. to Jesus' day and beyond. They were extremely careful and were terrified of making mistakes.[175] We will find common features when we compare the Jewish Greek Old Testament with the Christian Greek Scriptures, such things as an enlarged letter at the beginning of each line, and the invention of the nomen sacrum[176] to deal with God's personal name. Marginal notes, accents, breathing marks, punctuation, corrections, double punctuation marks (which indicate the flow of text)–all of these show adoption of scribal practices of the Sopherim by Jewish Christian writers and scribes.

There are, unfortunately, fierce critics who reject any claims of veracity for these early manuscripts. Former evangelical Christian, now agnostic New Testament Bible scholar, Bart Ehrman writes,

> Not only do we not have the originals, we don't have the first copies of the originals. **We don't even have copies of the copies of the originals, or copies of the copies of the copies of the**

---

the whole revelation of God." Luke is one of those to whom such inspired revelations were entrusted.

[175] It is true that they took some liberties with the text, but these few places were the exception to the rule. They intentionally altered some passages that appeared to show irreverence for God or one of his spokespersons.

[176] Nomina sacra (singular: nomen sacrum) means "sacred names" in Latin, and can be used to refer to traditions of abbreviated writing of several frequently occurring divine names or titles in early Greek manuscripts, such as the following:

Lord ($\overline{KC}$), Jesus ($\overline{IH}$, $\overline{IHC}$), Christ ($\overline{XP}$, $\overline{XC}$, $\overline{XPC}$), God ($\overline{\Theta C}$), and Spirit ($\overline{\Pi NA}$).

originals. What we have are copies made later—much later. In most instances, they are copies made many *centuries* later. And these **copies all differ from one another, in many thousands of places.** As we will see later in this book, these copies **differ from one another in so many places that we don't even know how many differences** there are. Possibly it is easiest to put it in comparative terms: **there are more differences among our manuscripts than there are words in the New Testament.** (B. D. Ehrman, Misquoting Jesus: The Story Behind Who Changed the Bible and Why 2005, 10) (Bold mine)

As we read these remarks, it is easy to get a sense of hopelessness because "all feels lost, for there is certainly no way to get back to the originals." Correct? Ehrman has had a long history of creating hopelessness for his readers, as he carries on his alleged truth quest. He asserts that even in the very few numbers of places that we might be sure about the *wording*, we cannot be certain about the *meaning*.

Blinded by Misguided Perceptions

Ehrman clearly has been immensely impacted by the fact that we do not have the originals or immediate copies. Here we have a world-renowned textual and early Christianity scholar who is emphasizing that we do not have the originals, nor the direct copies, and since there are so many copyist errors, it is virtually impossible to get back to the Word of God at all. Even if by some stroke of fortune, we could, we cannot know the meaning with assurance. Ehrman is saying to the lay reader: we can no longer trust the text of the Greek New Testament as the Word of God. If so, we would have to conclude that all translations are untrustworthy as well.

Ehrman has exaggerated the negative to his readers to the detriment of the positive in New Testament textual criticism. Mark Minnick assesses the latter nicely: "Doesn't the existence of these variants undermine our confidence that we have the very words of God inspired? No! The fact is that because we know of them and are careful to preserve the readings of every one of them, *not one word of God's word has been lost to us.*"[177] The wealth of manuscripts that we have for establishing the original Greek New Testament is overwhelming, in comparison to other ancient literature. We can only wonder what Ehrman does with an ancient piece of literature

---

[177] Mark Minnick, "Let's Meet the Manuscripts," in *From the Mind of God to the Mind of Man: A Layman's Guide to How We Got Our Bible*, eds. James B. Williams and Randolph Shaylor (Greenvill, SC: Ambassador-Emerald International, 1999), p. 96.

that has only one copy, and that copy is hundreds or even over a thousand years removed from the time of the original.

Consider a few examples. Before beginning, it should be noted that some of the classical authors are centuries, some many centuries before the first century New Testament era, which is a somewhat unfair comparison. See the chart below.[178]

Author	Work	Writing Completed	Earliest MSS	Years Removed	Number of MSS
Homer	*Iliad*	800 B.C.E.	3rd century B.C.E.[179]	500	1,757
Herodotus	*History*	480–425 B.C.E.	10th cent. C.E.	1,350	109
Sophocles	*Plays*	496–406 B.C.E.	3rd cent. B.C.E.[180]	100-200	193
Thucydides	*History*	460–400 B.C.E.	3rd cent. B.C.E.[181]	200	96
Plato	*Tetralogies*	400 B.C.E.	895 C.E.	1,300	210
Demosthenes	*Speeches*	300 B.C.E.	Fragments from 1st cent. B.C.E.	1,000	340
Caesar	*Gallic Wars*	51-46 B.C.E.	9th cent. C.E.	950	251
Livy	*History of Rome*	59 B.C.E.–17 C.E.	5th cent. C.E.	400	150
Tacitus	*Annals*	100 C.E.	9th-11th cent. C.E.	750–950	33
Pliny, the Elder	*Natural History*	49–79 C.E.	5th cent. C.E. fragment	400	200
Eight Greek NT Authors	27 Books	50 – 98 C.E.	110-125 C.E.	12-27	5,800

The Greek New Testament evidence, as we've mentioned previously, is over 5,830+ Greek manuscripts that have been cataloged, over 9,284 versions, and over 10,000 Latin manuscripts, not to mention an

---

[178] The concept of this chart is taken from *The Bibliographical Test Updated - Christian Research* ... http://www.equip.org/article/the-bibliographical-test-updated/ May 04, 2017. However, some adjustments have been made as well as footnotes added.

[179] There are a number of fragments that date to the second century B.C.E. and one to the third century B.C.E., with the rest dating to the ninth century C.E. or later.

[180] Most of the 193 MSS date to the tenth century C.E., with a few fragments dating to the third century B.C.E.

[181] Some papyri fragments date to the third century B.C.E.

innumerable amount of church fathers' quotations. This places the Greek New Testament in a class by itself, because no other ancient document is close to this. However, there is even more. There are 62 Greek papyri, along with five majuscule manuscripts that date to the second and third centuries C.E.[182] Moreover, these early papyri manuscripts are from a region in Egypt that appreciated books as literature, and were copied by semi-professional and professional scribes, or at least highly skilled copyists. This region produced what are known as the most accurate and trusted manuscripts.

Were the Scribes in the Early Centuries Amateurs?

We could **go on nearly forever** talking about specific places in which the texts of the New Testament came to be changed, either accidentally or intentionally. As I have indicated, the examples are **not just in the hundreds but in the thousands.** The examples given are enough to convey the general point, however: there are lots of differences among our manuscripts, differences created by scribes who were reproducing their sacred texts. **In the early Christian centuries, scribes were amateurs** and as such were more inclined to alter the texts they copied—or more prone to alter them accidentally—than were scribes in the later periods who, starting in the fourth century, began to be

---

[182] Dr. **Daniel B. Wallace**, Executive Director of The Center for the Study of New Testament Manuscripts (CSNTM):

On 1 February 2012, I debated Bart Ehrman at UNC Chapel Hill on whether we have the wording of the original New Testament today. This was our third such debate, and it was before a crowd of more than 1000 people. I mentioned that **seven New Testament papyri had recently been discovered—six of them probably from the second century and one of them probably from the first.** These fragments will be published in about a year.

These manuscripts now increase our holdings as follows: we have as many as eighteen New Testament manuscripts (all fragmentary, more or less) from the second century and one from the first. **Altogether, about 33% of all New Testament verses are found in these manuscripts. But the most interesting thing is the first-century fragment.**

It was dated by one of the world's leading paleographers. He said he was 'certain' that it was from the first century. If this is true, it would be the oldest fragment of the New Testament known to exist. Up until now, no one has discovered any first-century manuscripts of the New Testament. The oldest manuscript of the New Testament has been P52, a small fragment from John's Gospel, dated to the first half of the second century. It was discovered in 1934.

Not only this, but the first-century fragment is from Mark's Gospel. **Before the discovery of this fragment, the oldest manuscript that had Mark in it was P45, from the early third century (c. 200–250 CE). This new fragment would predate that by 100 to 150 years.**— http://csntm.org/news

professionals. (B. D. Ehrman, Misquoting Jesus: The Story Behind Who Changed the Bible and Why 2005, 98) [Bold mine]

Let us take just a moment to discuss Ehrman's statement, "**in the early Christian centuries, scribes were amateurs....**" In this book, we established just the opposite. Literate or semi-professional copyist did the vast majority of our early papyri, with some being done by professionals. As it happened, the few poorly copied manuscripts became known first, establishing a precedent that was difficult for some to discard when the truckload of evidence came forth that showed just the opposite. (P. Comfort 2005, 18-19)

Ehrman is misrepresenting the situation to his readers when he states, "We don't even have copies of the copies of the originals or copies of the copies of the copies of the originals." The way this is worded, he is saying that we do not have copies that are three or four generations removed from the originals. Ehrman cannot know this because we have fifteen copies that are 75 to 100 years removed from the death of the apostle John in 100 C.E. There is the possibility that any of these could be only third or fourth generation removed copies. Furthermore, they could have been copied from a second or third generation. Therefore, Ehrman is misstating the evidence. Moreover, the uncertainty of this rhetoric is exposed by the above fact that we now have "seven New Testament papyri, [which] had recently been discovered, six of them probably from the second century and one of them probably from the first."[183]

Let us do another short review of two very important manuscripts: P75 and Vaticanus 1209 (B). P75 is also known as Bodmer 14, 15. As has already been stated, papyrus is writing material used by the ancient Egyptians, Greeks, and Romans that was made from the pith of the stem of a water plant. These are the earliest witnesses to the Greek New Testament. P75 contains most of Luke and John, dating from 175 C.E. to 225 C.E Vaticanus is designated internationally by the symbol "B" (and 03) and is known as an uncial manuscript written on parchment. It is dated to the mid-fourth-century C.E. [c. 350] and originally contained the entire Bible in Greek. At present, Vaticanus' New Testament is missing parts of Hebrews (Hebrews 9:14 to 13:25), all of First and Second Timothy, Titus, Philemon, and Revelation. Originally, this codex probably had approximately 820 leaves, of which 759 remain.

What kind of weight or evidence do these two manuscripts carry in the eyes of textual scholars? Vaticanus 1209 is a key source for our modern translations. When determining an original reading, this manuscript can

---

183

http://csntm.org/News/Archive/2012/2/10/EarliestManuscriptoftheNewTestamentDiscovered stand against other external evidence that would seem to the non-professional to be much more significant. P[75] also is one of the weightiest manuscripts that we have and is virtually identical to Vaticanus 1209, which dates 175 to 125 years later than P[75]. When textual scholars B. F. Westcott and F. J. A. Hort released their critical text in 1881, Hort said that Vaticanus preserved "not only a very ancient text but a very pure line of a very ancient text." (Westcott and Hort 1882, 251) Later scholars argued that Vaticanus was a scholarly recension: a critical revision or edited text. However, P[75] has vindicated Westcott and Hort because of its virtual identity with Vaticanus; it establishes that Vaticanus is essentially a copy of a second-century text, and likely, a copy of the original text, with the exception of a few minor points.

Kurt Aland[184] wrote, "P[75] shows such a close affinity with the Codex Vaticanus that the supposition of a recension of the text at Alexandria, in the fourth century, can no longer be held."[185] David C. Parker[186] says of P[75] that "it is extremely important for two reasons: "like Vaticanus, it is carefully copied; it is also very early and is generally dated to a period between 175 and 225. Thus, it pre-dates Vaticanus by at least a century. A careful comparison between P[75] and Vaticanus in Luke by C.M. Martini demonstrated that P[75] was an earlier copy of the same careful Alexandrian text. It is sometimes called proto-Alexandrian. It is our earliest example of a controlled text, one which was not intentionally or extensively changed in successive copying. Its discovery and study have provided proof that the Alexandrian text had already come into existence in the third century." (Parker 1997, 61) Let us look at the remarks of a few more textual scholars: J. Ed Komoszewski, M. James Sawyer, and Daniel Wallace.

> Even some of the early manuscripts show compelling evidence of being copies of a much earlier source. Consider again Codex Vaticanus, whose text is very much like that of P[75] (B and P75 are much closer to each other than B is to [Codex Sinaiticus]). Yet the papyrus is at least a century older than Vaticanus. When P[75] was discovered in the 1950s, some entertained the possibility that Vaticanus could have been a copy of P[75], but this view is no longer acceptable since the wording of Vaticanus is certainly more

---

[184] (1915 – 1994) was Professor of New Testament Research and Church History. He founded the Institute for New Testament Textual Research in Münster and served as its first director for many years (1959–83). He was one of the principal editors of The Greek New Testament for the United Bible Societies.

[185] K. Aland, "The Significance of the Papyri for New Testament Research," 336.

[186] Professor of Theology and the Director of the Institute for Textual Scholarship and Electronic Editing at the Department of Theology and Religion, University of Birmingham. Scholar of New Testament textual criticism and Greek and Latin paleography.

primitive than that of P75 in several places.' They both must go back to a still earlier common ancestor, probably one that is from the early second century. (Komoszewski, M. Sawyer and Wallace 2006, 78)

Comfort comments on how we can know that Vaticanus is not a copy of P[75]: "As was previously noted, Calvin Porter clearly established the fact that P[75] displays the kind of text that was used in making codex Vaticanus. However, it is unlikely that the scribe of B used P[75] as his exemplar because the scribe of B copied from a manuscript whose line length was 12–14 letters per line. We know this because when the scribe of Codex Vaticanus made large omissions, they were typically 12–14 letters long.[187] The average line length for P[75] is about 29–32 letters per line. Therefore, the scribe of B must have used a manuscript like P[75], but not P[75] itself."[188]

Ehrman suggests that the early Christians were not concerned about the integrity of the text, its preservation of accuracy. Let us consult the second-century evidence by way of Tertullian.[189]

> Come now, you who would indulge a better curiosity, if you would apply it to the business of your salvation, run over the apostolic churches, in which the very thrones[190] of the apostles are still pre-eminent in their places,[191] in which their own **authentic writings** are read, uttering the voice and representing the face of each of them severally.[192] (Bold mine)

What did Tertullian mean by "authentic writings"? If he was referring to the Greek originals—and it seems that he was, according to the Latin—it is an indication that some of the original New Testament books were still in existence at the time of his penning this work. However, let us say that it is

---

[187] Brooke F. Westcott and Fenton J. A. Hort, *Introduction to the New Testament in the Original Greek* (New York: Harper & Bros., 1882; reprint, Peabody, Mass.: Hendrickson, 1988), 233–34.

[188] (Comfort and Barret, The Text of the Earliest New Testament Greek Manuscripts 2001)

[189] Tertullian (160 – 220 C.E.), was a prolific early Christian author from Carthage in the Roman province of Africa.

[190] Cathedrae

[191] Suis locis praesident.

[192] Alexander Roberts, James Donaldson and A. Cleveland Coxe, The Ante-Nicene Fathers Vol. III: Translations of the Writings of the Fathers Down to A.D. 325 (Oak Harbor: Logos Research Systems, 1997), 260.

simply referring to copies that were well-preserved. In any case, this shows that the Christians valued the preservation of accuracy.

We need to visit an earlier book by Ehrman for a moment, *Lost Christianities*, in which he writes, "In this process of recopying the document by hand, what happened to the original of 1 Thessalonians? For some unknown reason, it was eventually thrown away, burned, or otherwise destroyed. Possibly, it was read so much that it simply wore out. The early Christians saw no need to preserve it as the `original' text. They had copies of the letter. Why keep the original?" (B. D. Ehrman 2003, 217)

Here Ehrman is arguing from silence. We cannot read the minds of people today, let alone read the minds of persons 2,000 years in the past. It is a known fact that congregations valued Paul's letters, and Paul exhorted them to share the letters with differing congregations. Paul wrote to the Colossians, and in what we know as 4:16, he said, "And when this letter has been read among you, have it **also read in the church of the Laodiceans; and see that you also read the letter from Laodicea.**" The best way to facilitate this would be to send someone to a congregation, have them copy the letter and bring it back to their home congregation. On the other hand, someone could make copies of the letter in the congregation that received it and deliver it to interested congregations. In 1 Thessalonians, the congregation that Ehrman is talking about here, at chapter five, verse 27, Paul says, "I put you under oath before the Lord to **have this letter read to all the brothers.**" What did Paul mean by "all the brothers"? It could be that he meant it to be used like a circuit letter, circulated to other congregations, giving everyone a chance to hear the counsel. It may merely be that, with literacy being so low, Paul wanted a guarantee that all were going to get to hear the letter's contents, and he simply meant for every brother and sister locally to have a chance to hear it in the congregation. Regardless, even if we accept the latter, the stress that was put on the reading of this letter shows the weight that these people were placed under concerning Paul's letters.[193] In addition, Comfort comments on how Paul and others would view apostolic letters:

> Paul knew the importance of authorized apostolic letters,
> for he saw the authority behind the letter that came from the first

---

[193] The exhortation ἐνορκίζω ὑμᾶς τὸν κύριον ἀναγνωσθῆναι τὴν ἐπιστολὴν πᾶσιν τοῖς ἀδελφοῖς ("I adjure you by the Lord that this letter be read aloud to all the brothers [and sisters]"), is stated quite strongly. ἐνορκίζω takes a double accusative and has a causal sense denoting that the speaker or writer wishes to extract an oath from the addressee(s). The second accusative, in this case τὸν κύριον ("the Lord"), indicates the thing or person by whom the addressees were to swear. The forcefulness of this statement is highly unusual, and in fact it is the only instance in Paul's letters where such a charge is laid on the recipients of one of his letters.—Charles A. Wanamaker, The Epistles to the Thessalonians: A Commentary on the Greek Text (Grand Rapids, Mich.: W.B. Eerdmans, 1990), 208-09.

Jerusalem church council. The first epistle from the church leaders who had assembled at Jerusalem was the prototype for subsequent epistles (see Acts 15). It was authoritative because it was apostolic, and it was received as God's word. If an epistle came from an apostle (or apostles), it was to be received as having the imprimatur [approval/authority] of the Lord. This is why Paul wanted the churches to receive his word as being the word of the Lord. This is made explicit in 1 Thessalonians (2:13), an epistle he insisted had to be read to all the believers in the church (5:27). In the Second Epistle to the Thessalonians, Paul indicated that his epistles carry the same authority as his preaching (see 2:15). Paul also told his audience that if they would read what he had written, they would be able to understand the mystery of Christ, which had been revealed to him (see Eph. 3:1–6). Because Paul explained the mystery in his writings (in this case, the encyclical epistle known as "Ephesians"), he urged other churches to read this encyclical (see Col. 4:16). In so doing, Paul himself encouraged the circulation of his writings. Peter and John also had publishing plans. Peter's first epistle, written to a wide audience (the Christian diaspora in Pontus, Galatia, Cappadocia, Asia, Bithynia—see 1 Pet. 1:1), was a published work, which must have been produced in several copies from the onset, to reach his larger, intended audience. John's first epistle was also published and circulated—probably to all the churches in the Roman province of Asia Minor. First John is not any kind of occasional epistle; it is more like a treatise akin to Romans and Ephesians in that it contains John's full explanation of the Christian life and doctrine as a model for all orthodox believers to emulate. The book of Revelation, which begins with seven epistles to seven churches in this same province, must have also been inititally published in seven copies, as the book circulated from one locality to the next, by the seven "messengers" (Greek *anggeloi*—not "angels" in this context). By contrast, the personal letters (Philemon, 1 and 2 Timothy, Titus, 2 John, 3 John) were not originally "published"; therefore, their circulation was small. Second Peter also had minimal circulation in the early days of the church. Because of its popularity, the book of Hebrews seemed to have enjoyed wide circulation—this was promoted by the fact that most Christians in the East thought it was the work of Paul and therefore was included in Pauline collections (see discussion below). The book of Acts was originally published by Luke as a sequel to his Gospel (see Acts 1:1–2). Unfortunately, in due course, this book got detached from Luke when the Gospel of

Luke was placed in one-volume codices along with the other Gospels.[194]

Peter, as we have seen, also had this to say about Paul's letters: "there are some things in them [Paul's letters] that are hard to understand, which the ignorant and unstable twist to their own destruction, **as they do the other Scriptures.**" (2 Pet 3:16) Peter viewed Paul's letters as being on the same level as the Old Testament, which was referred to as Scripture. In the second century (about 135 C.E.), Papias, an elder of the early congregation in Hierapolis, made the following comment.

> I will not hesitate to set down for you, along with my interpretations, everything I carefully learned then from the elders and carefully remembered, guaranteeing their truth. For unlike most people I did not enjoy those who have a great deal to say, but those who teach the truth. Nor did I enjoy those who recall someone else's commandments, but those who remember the commandments given by the Lord to the faith and proceeding from the truth itself. In addition, if by chance someone who had been a follower of the elders should come my way, I inquired about the words of the elders--what Andrew or Peter said, or Philip, or Thomas or James, or John or Matthew or any other of the Lord's disciples, and whatever Aristion and the elder John, the Lord's disciples, were saying. For I did not think that information from books would profit me as much as information from a living and abiding voice.[195]

As an elder in the congregation at Hierapolis, in Asia Minor, Papias was an unrelenting researcher, as well as a thorough compiler of information; he exhibited intense indebtedness for the Scriptures. Papias determined properly that any doctrinal statement of Jesus Christ or his apostles would be far more appreciated and respected to explain than the unreliable statements found in the written works of his day. We can compare Jude 1:17, where Jude exhorts his readers to preserve the words of the apostles.

Therefore, the notion that the "early Christians saw no need to preserve it as the 'original' text," is far too difficult to accept when we consider the above. Moreover, imagine a church in middle America being visited by Billy Graham. Now imagine that he wrote them a warm letter, but one also filled with some stern counsel. Would there be little interest in the preservation of those words? Would they not want to share it with

---

[194] (P. Comfort, Encountering the Manuscripts: An Introduction to New Testament Paleography and Textual Criticism 2005, 17)

[195] (Holmes, The Apostolic Fathers: Greek Texts and English Translations 2007, 565)

others? Would other churches not be interested in it? The same would have been even truer of early Christianity receiving a letter from an apostle like Peter, John, or Paul. There is no doubt that the "original" wore out eventually. However, they lived in a society that valued the preservation of the apostle's words, and it is far more likely that it was copied with care, to share with others, and to preserve. Moreover, let us acknowledge that their imperfections took over as well. Paul would have become a famous apostle who wrote a few churches, and there were thousands of churches toward the end of the first century. Would they have not exhibited some pride in the fact that they received a letter from the famous apostle Paul, who was martyred for the truth? Ehrman's suggestions are reaching and contrary to human nature. It is simply wishful thinking on his part.

However, Ehrman may not have entirely dismissed the idea of getting back to the original if he agreed with Metzger in their coauthored fourth edition of *The Text of the New Testament*. Metzger's original comments from previous editions are repeated there as follows.

> Besides textual evidence derived from New Testament Greek manuscripts and from early versions, the textual critic compares numerous scriptural quotations used in commentaries, sermons, and other treatises written by early church fathers. Indeed, so extensive are these citations that if all other sources for our knowledge of the text of the New Testament were destroyed, they would be sufficient alone for the reconstruction of practically the entire New Testament. (Metzger and Ehrman 2005, 126)

How are we to view the patristic citations? Let us look at another book for which Ehrman was coeditor and a contributor with other textual scholars: *The Text of the New Testament in Contemporary Research* (1995). The following is from Chapter 12, written by Gordon Fee (*The Use of the Greek Fathers for New Testament Textual Criticism*).

> In NT textual criticism, patristic citations are ordinarily viewed as the third line of evidence, indirect and supplementary to the Greek MSS, and are often therefore treated as of tertiary importance. When properly evaluated, however, patristic evidence is of primary importance, for both of the major tasks of NT textual criticism: in contrast to the early Greek MSS, the Fathers have the potential of offering datable and geographically certain evidence. (B. D. Ehrman 1995, 191)

To conclude, we have established that Ehrman has painted a picture that is not quite the truth of the matter for the average churchgoer while saying something entirely different for textual scholars. Moreover, he does not help the reader to appreciate just how close the New Testament manuscript evidence is to the time of the original writings, in comparison to manuscripts of other ancient works, many of which are few in number and hundreds, if not a thousand years removed.

In addition, Ehrman has exaggerated the variants in the Greek New Testament manuscripts by **not** qualifying the level of variants. In other words, he has not explained how he counts them to obtain such high numbers. Moreover, Ehrman's unqualified statement, "In the early Christian centuries, scribes were amateurs," has been discredited as well. Either literate or semi-professional copyist did **the vast majority** of the early papyri, with some being done by professionals.

CHAPTER 7 The Original or Earliest Text of the New Testament

This chapter may be somewhat controversial because many modern textual scholars are not certain that we can get back to the original text. Again, when we use the term "original" reading or "original" text in this publication, it is a reference to the exemplar manuscript by the New Testament author (e.g. Paul) and his secretary (e.g. Tertius)–if he used one–from which other copies were made for publication and distribution to the Christian communities. While this chapter will focus on the textual criticism process as a whole, its main focus will be the early text of the New Testament, namely, the first three centuries of Christianity. In other words, we will be considering the text of the New Testament from the middle of the first century up to the close of the fourth century C.E.

Whether it was in commentaries, the footnotes within our Bibles, or from the elder or pastor on Sunday, we have all read or heard something like "the *original* Greek word ..." For example, the *original* Greek word here is *hagiazo,* meaning, "to set apart to a sacred use" (Matt. 6:9). The *original* Greek word here is *kleros* and is related to the word *kleronomia,* "inheritance" (Col. 1:12; 1 Pet. 5:3). Perhaps the author or pastor is trying to provide a little Bible background, such as pointing out that the cubit is the *original* Greek word *pechus* in Matthew 6:27, which literally means "forearm." The publication or pastor may be emphasizing the nuances of different words for Christian services, such as the *original* Greek verb *diakoneo* (Matt. 20:26). One original Greek verb may emphasize the *subjection* that is involved in serving, such as a slave (*douleuo;* Col. 3:24), another could be the *sacredness* of service (*latreuo;* Matt. 4:10), while another might be focused on the *public nature* of the service provided (*leitourgeo;* Acts 13:2).

When incorporating a source, the author or pastor may mention something like *Mounce's Complete Expository Dictionary of Old & New Testament Words.* It will be used to explain the original Greek word, such as *epikaleo,* which means, "*to receive an appellation or surname ... to call upon, invoke ... to appeal to.*"[196] Paul used this same word when he declared, "I appeal to Caesar!" (Acts 25:11, NASB) A common way of expressing it is, "in the original Greek, this term basically "denotes" (the meaning, especially a specific or literal one) or "connotes (to imply or

---

[196] William D. Mounce, *Mounce's Complete Expository Dictionary of Old & New Testament Words* (Grand Rapids, MI: Zondervan, 2006), 1152.

suggest something in addition to the literal or main meaning)." When Paul wrote about "the mind of the spirit," he used an *original* Greek word that **denotes** 'a way of thinking' or 'mindset.' The *original* Greek word for our English transliteration "amen," **connotes** 'certainty,' 'truthfulness,' 'faithfulness,' and 'absence of doubt.' We can see that getting back to the word in the *original* language can add considerable insight into the Scriptures. Therefore, our getting back to the actual words of the *original* language that the New Testament Bible author penned is, indeed, the goal of these two authors.

The importance of the actual words is constantly evident when we examine the text of the original. Let's look at one example: a story that we all know. On the return trip home after the festivals in Jerusalem, Joseph and Mary thought that Jesus was somewhere with the family, so at first, his not being present was no cause for alarm. Three days later, when Mary and Joseph came back to Jerusalem to find Jesus, he was in the temple, "sitting in the midst of the teachers and listening to them and **questioning them**" (Luke 2:44-46, UASV). Other translations read, "Listening to them and **asking them questions**" (RSV, NASB, ESV, LEB, and HCSB). However, that rendering does not really capture the original language word.

Luke 2:46 English Standard Version (ESV)	Luke 2:46 New American Standard Bible (NASB)	Luke 2:46 Updated American Standard Version (UASV)
46 After three days they found him in the temple, sitting among the teachers, listening to them and **asking them questions**.	46 Then, after three days they found Him in the temple, sitting in the midst of the teachers, both listening to them and **asking them questions**.	46 Then, it occurred, after three days they found him in the temple, sitting in the midst of the teachers and listening to them and **questioning them**.

This was no 12-year-old boy asking questions out of curiosity. The Greek word *erotao* is the Greek word for "ask," "question," and is a synonym of *eperotao*. The latter of the two was used by Luke and is much more demanding, as it means, "to ask a question, to question, interrogate someone, questioning as used in judicial examination" and, therefore, could include counter questioning. Therefore, Jesus, at the age of twelve, did not ask childlike questions looking for corresponding answers but was likely challenging the thinking of these Jewish religious leaders. What was the response of those Jewish religious leaders? The account goes on to say, "And all who heard Him **were amazed** at His understanding and His answers" – Luke 2:47, NASB.

What Is Meant by 'Establishing the Original Text'?

Because the terms *original* and *autograph* are used interchangeably, it can cause confusion at times if not differentiated. As was explained in the introduction, the **Autograph** (self-written) was the text actually written by a New Testament author, or the author and scribe as the author dictated to him. If the scribe was taking down dictation (Rom. 16:22; 1 Pet. 5:12), he might have done so in shorthand.[197] Whether by shorthand or longhand, we can assume that both the scribe and the author would check the scribe's work. The author would have authority over all corrections since Holy Spirit did not move the scribe. If the inspired author wrote everything down himself as the Spirit moved him, the finished product would be the autograph. This text is also often referred to as the **Original**. Hence, the terms *autograph* and *original* are often used interchangeably. Sometimes textual critics prefer to make a distinction, using "original" as a reference to the text that is correctly attributed to a biblical author. This is a looser distinction, one that does not focus on the process of how a book or letter was written. Once more, the term "original" reading or "original" text in this publication is a reference to the exemplar manuscript by the New Testament author (e.g. Paul) and his secretary (e.g. Tertius) from which other copies was made for publication and distribution of the Christian communities.

Some readers may find it disconcerting that ancient copies of the New Testament are not inspired, and thousands of variations crept into them over the first fourteen centuries. This is not the complete picture, however, because we have the next five centuries of restoration work done by hundreds of textual scholars around the world. If asked, "Are our copies inspired, without error?" the short answer would have to be **no**. But what if we have the exact representation of the original?

If we can get back to what was written in the original 27 books that were first published, would we not have a copy of the inspired original? We know that 2 Timothy 3:16 informs us, "all Scripture is inspired by God," meaning that the actual words in the autographs were a product of inspiration. Moreover, the inspired authors were as 2 Peter 1:21 informs us, "men [who] spoke from God as they were carried along by the Holy Spirit." Nevertheless, if dictation were the process of composition for some of the New Testament books, they would have still needed to be checked for

---

[197] "The usual procedure for a dictated epistle was for the amanuensis to take down the speaker's words (often in shorthand) and then produce a transcript, which the author could then review, edit, and sign in his own handwriting. Two New Testament epistles provide the name of the amanuensis: Tertius for (Romans 16:22) and Silvanus (another name for Silas) for 1 Peter 5:12" Philip Comfort, *Encountering the Manuscripts: An Introduction to New Testament Paleography & Textual Criticism* (Nashville, TN: Broadman & Holman, 2005), 06.

scribal errors, because the amanuensis, i.e., the author's scribe (secretary), was not moved along by Holy Spirit in the same sense. Therefore, the author would review the dictated draft if he used a scribe, making any corrections necessary. After that, the scribe would make a corrected copy, which if approved by the author, would become the officially published edition, and would have been signed by the author. In the final analysis, a textual committee, e.g. NA28/UBS5 has the potential to give us the exact wording of the original, and would, in essence, be giving us the restored edition of the original.

Today we have a storehouse of external evidence: original language manuscripts, versions, apostolic quotations, and lectionaries that take us ever closer to the recovery of the original. Textual scholar Paul D. Wegner, author of *A Student's Guide to Textual Criticism of the Bible*, has addressed this for both the Old and the New Testaments:

> Careful examination of these manuscripts has served to strengthen our assurance that our Modern Greek and Hebrew texts are very close to the original autographs, even though we do not have those autographs. (2006, 301)[198]

The traditional goal of scholars within textual criticism has been to get back to the *original* through the practice of applying the rules and principles of textual criticism. These rules and principles go back to the early textual scholars such as Johann Jakob Griesbach (1745-1812),[199] Friedrich Constantin von Tischendorf (1815-1874), Brook Foss Westcott (1825-1901, Fenton John Anthony Hort (1828-1892), Frederick G. Kenyon (1863-1952), Kirsopp Lake (1872-1946), Eberhard Nestle (1851-1913),[200] and his son Erwin Nestle (1883-1972). Kurt Aland (1915-1994) is the lynchpin between the older generation of textual scholars and modern textual scholarship. Bruce M. Metzger (1914-2007), Ernest Cadman Colwell (1901-1974), Jacob Harold Greenlee (1918-2015), Gordon D. Fee (1934-) and Philip W. Comfort (1950-) join Aland, among many, many others.

---

[198] Paul D. Wegner, *A Student's Guide to Textual Criticism of the Bible* (InterVarsity Press, Downers Grove 2006), 301.

[199] J. J. Griesbach is the one who really laid the foundation for the rules and principles for New Testament textual criticism.

[200] In 1898, Eberhard Nestle published a significant handbook of textual criticism, and in 1898 published the first edition of a Greek New Testament under the title Novum Testamentum Graece cum apparatu critico ex editionibus et libris manu scriptis collecto. The text of this Greek New Testament was a combination of the editions of Constantin von Tischendorf, The New Testament in the Original Greek of Westcott and Hort, and the edition of Richard Francis Weymouth. Wherever two of these three editions agree, this was the preferred reading by Nestle.

J. Harold Greenlee wrote, "Textual criticism is the study of copies of an ancient writing to try to determine the exact words of the text as the author originally wrote them."[201] This is the fundamental thought found in almost all introductory-intermediate textbooks on textual criticism throughout the twentieth century. The traditional approach was to look at all of the evidence, internal (largely contextual) and external (e.g. dating); however, the priority or weight in determining the original reading was given to the oldest manuscripts, which also display the harder readings, contributing to their trustworthiness. Most modern critical texts were the product of this approach. However, the Alands and others have shifted the emphasis to internal evidence,[202] as opposed to external evidence.[203]

Currently, there are literally hundreds of textual scholars who realize without knowing what the original words of the original text were; then, there is no way to accurately translating the Scriptures, interpreting the Scriptures, or defending the Scriptures. As Hill and Kruger put it,

> While the complexities in recovering the original text need to be acknowledged, that is a separate question from whether the concept of an original text is incoherent and should therefore be abandoned as a goal of the discipline. Unfortunately, these two questions are often mingled together without distinction. Although recovering the original text faces substantial obstacles (and therefore the results should be qualified), there is little to suggest that it is an illegitimate enterprise. If it were illegitimate, then we would expect the same would be true for Greek and Roman literature outside the New Testament. ... Recognizing the historical value of such scribal variations need not be set in opposition to the goal of recovering the original text. These two aspects of textual criticism are complementary, not mutually exclusive. Indeed, it is only when we can have some degree of assurance regarding the original text that we are even able to recognize that later scribes occasionally changed it for their own

---

[201] Greenlee, J. Harold (2008). *The Text of the New Testament, From Manuscript to Modern Edition* (p. 2). Baker Publishing Group. Kindle Edition.

[202] Internal evidence is evidence that comes from the text itself, such as *the reading from which the others most likely arose is probably the original*, and *the harder reading is to be preferred*.

[203] External evidence is manuscript evidence: its date, geographical location, and relationship to other known manuscripts. Textual scholars generally prefer the readings supported by the Alexandrian family of witnesses. The Byzantine family of manuscripts tends to be rejected because of its being less trustworthy, but most critics now grant that it should still be considered.

theological purposes. Without the former we would not have the latter. – (Hill and Kruger 2012, Loc. 233-250 KDP)

Those Who Doubt the Recovery

The majority of scholars today believe that recovering the complete original Greek New Testament is outside the realm of possibility. Lee Martin MacDonald writes, "The traditional goal of textual criticism has been to establish the 'original' or earliest possible biblical text, but the overwhelming number of textual variants and the overlapping of several textual traditions make that goal a significant if not impossible challenge. Some scholars continue in the hope of recovering the originals and eliminating all ambiguities in the present texts, but they appear to be in the minority."[204]

MacDonald's comments are on point, and it is likely even graver than he has remarked. However, his comment about "the traditional goal of textual criticism" being "to establish the 'original' or [italics mine] earliest possible biblical text," is not exactly the longstanding traditional objective, as it was, in fact, "to establish the original"–not "the earliest possible biblical text." We (Wilkins and Andrews) remain in that group of scholars who aim at establishing the original.[205]

The traditional goal of the 19th century and early 20th-century textual scholars was to make the critical text a mirror image of the "original text." This was their goal even if they were aware that it would never be a one-hundred-percent success. In fact, we can go back to Richard Bentley (1662-1742), who believed, in reality, that he could establish the original text in the majority of places where variants existed. The goal of the contemporary textual scholar is to get back to the "initial text." In the Editio Critica Maior (ECM), a critical edition of the Greek New Testament, we find that the "initial text is the form of a text that stands at the beginning of a textual tradition."[206] According to Gerd Mink, "the initial text preceded the textual tradition and has not survived in any manuscript." He goes on to say, "We cannot know this text with certainty, but can only reconstruct it

---

[204] L. M. McDonald, *Forgotten Scriptures: The Selection and Rejection of Early Religious Writings* (Louisville: Westminster John Knox Press, July 13, 2009), 184.

[205] Again, when we employ the term "original" reading or "original" text in this publication, it is a reference to the exemplar manuscript composed by the New Testament author (e.g., Paul) and recorded by his secretary (e.g., Tertius), if he used one, from which all other copies ultimately were derived for publication and distribution to the Christian communities.

[206] ECM/1–2Peter, 23*n. 4

hypothetically."[207] He also says, "The initial text is not identical with the original, the text of the author. Between the autograph and the initial text considerable changes may have taken place which may not have left a single trace in the surviving textual tradition."[208] In short, the general, basic consensus is that the "initial text" is the earliest possible text for each of the twenty-seven books of the New Testament.

Early Christianity gave rise to what is known as "local texts." Christian congregations in and near cities, such as Alexandria, Antioch, Constantinople, Carthage, or Rome, were making copies of the Scriptures in the form that would become known as a text-type. In other words, manuscripts grew up in certain areas, just like a human family, becoming known as their text-type, having their own characteristics. The reality is not as simple as this because there are mixtures of text-types within each text-type. However, each text-type resembles itself more than it does the others. It should also be remembered that most of our extant manuscripts are identical in more than seventy-five percent of their texts. Thus, it is the percentage of variant readings that identifies a manuscript as a particular text-type, i.e., "agreement in error" or variation from the original.

Therefore, the process of classifying manuscripts has for many years been to classify them as a particular text-type, such as Alexandrian, Western, Caesarean, or Byzantine. However, these days are fading, because technology has allowed the textual scholar to carry out a more comprehensive comparison of all readings in all manuscripts, possibly making all previous classifications meaningless, or nearly so. This new method is known as The Coherence-Based Genealogical Method (CBGM), which will be explained at great length in THE TEXT OF THE NEW TRSTAMENT by Don Wilkins. In this method, an "initial text" is "relatively close to the form of the text from which the textual tradition of a New Testament book has originated." (Stephen C. Carlson)[209] In addition, "D. C. Parker's essay asserts the impossibility of the attempt to recover a single original text, and hence the editor or critic must be content with the text

---

[207] This presentation is based on lectures given by the author at the Münster Colloquium on the Textual History of the Greek New Testament. http://www.uni-muenster.de/INTF/Colloquium2008_programme.pdf

[208] Gerd Mink, "Problems of a Highly Contaminated Tradition, the New Testament: Stemmata of Variants as a Source of a Genealogy for Witnesses," in Studies in Stemmatology, vol. 2 [ed. Pieter van Reenen, August den Hollander, and Margot van Mulken; Amsterdam: John Benjamins, 2004], 25).

[209] http://textualcriticism.scienceontheweb.net/RECON/Carlson-CBGM1.html

from which the readings in the extant manuscripts are genealogically descended (p. 21)."[210]

Believing that We Can Establish the Original

B. F. Westcott and F. J. A. Hort believed that they had established the original text with their *New Testament in the Original Greek* (1881). They write, "This edition is an attempt to present exactly the original words of the New Testament, so far as they can be determined from surviving documents."[211] We notice that Westcott and Hort qualified their goal with "as far as can be determined from surviving documents." The producers of the 5th edition of the *Greek New Testament,* United Bible Societies' Corrected Edition (2014)[212] and Kurt and Barbara Aland in their 28th edition of the *Nestle-Aland Greek New Testament* (2012)[213] believe that these critical texts are the most anyone has achieved in establishing the original.[214] However, it must be said that the NA28 has been shifted to the goal of establishing the "initial text." Westcott and Hort looked to the **earliest manuscripts** of their day as their foundation for the original text; the Alands, while appreciating the early texts, did move away to the reasoned eclectic approach, an approach that focuses more heavily on internal evidence rather than external evidence.[215] Nevertheless, their clearly stated goal was "an assurance of certainty in establishing the original text."[216] Sadly, as MacDonald stated above, many modern textual scholars have abandoned

---

[210] The Textual History of the Greek New Testament: Changing Views in Contemporary Research (Peter Rodgers Review) .., http://peter-rodgers.com/#articles (accessed July 7, 2014).

[211] B. F. Westcott; F. J. A. Hort, *The New Testament In the Original Greek,* Cambridge/London, 1881.

[212] Referred to as UBS5

[213] Referred to as NA27. It should be noted that the Greek text of the NA27 and the UBS4 are exactly the same, but their apparatuses are different. The NA27 is more for the scholar, the pastor, and the Bible student and deals with far more variants and offers more evidence for each variant, while the UBS4 is more for the Bible translator and includes only variants deemed important to Bible translation.

[214] Aland and Aland in their book, *The Text of the New Testament,* make the clear statement that the text of the Greek New Testament, United Bible Societies (UBS3) and the Nestle-Aland Greek New Testament (NA26) "comes closer to the original text of the New Testament than did Tischendorf or Westcott and Hort not to mention von Soden." (Aland and Aland, The Text of the New Testament 1995, 24)

[215] This approach addresses textual criticism by looking to internal and external evidence. However, many who use this approach do lean too heavily on internal evidence. In addition, while they value early manuscripts, they choose the best reading from a consideration of all manuscripts, believing that any of them can carry the original, avoiding preferences.

[216] (Aland and Aland, The Text of the New Testament 1995, 291-2)

the hope of ever establishing the original text, or accepting that the above-mentioned critical texts might live up to that claim. I (Andrews) personally find it ironic that the idea of establishing the original text became less and less of concern to the textual scholar over the 20th century as liberal-progressive scholarship consumed conservative scholarship throughout that same century. The reader must determine his own view as to whether there is any correlation.

On the objective of getting back to the original, the authors of *The Early Text of the New Testament* write, "However, while the complexities in recovering the original text need to be acknowledged, that is a separate question from whether the concept of an original text is incoherent and should, therefore, be abandoned as a goal of the discipline. Unfortunately, these two questions are often mingled together without distinction. Although recovering the original text faces substantial obstacles (and therefore the results should be qualified), there is little to suggest that it is an illegitimate enterprise. If it were illegitimate, then we would expect the same would be true for Greek and Roman literature outside the New Testament. Are we to think that an attempt to reconstruct the original word of Tacitus, or Plato, or Thucydides is misguided? Or that it does not matter? Those who argue that we should abandon the concept of an original text for the New Testament often give very little (if any) attention to the implications of such an approach for classical literature." (Hill and Kruger 2012, 4)

Westcott and Hort sought to establish the original text by choosing what they felt was the most faithful text or family of texts, the Alexandrian family (especially the Codex Vaticanus, designated B), and worked from there to establish their critical text. Again, modern scholarship has abandoned both the idea of establishing the original and of choosing a trusted text or family of texts as a foundation. Since the mid-19th century, they have been using "eclecticism," now known as "reasoned eclecticism."[217] In this, all manuscripts are placed on equal footing. They simply look to all text-types and decide which variant gave rise to all others, assigning more weight to internal evidence than to the external evidence of manuscripts. The last few decades have seen the rise of the newest form of NTTC, The Coherence-Based Genealogical Method (CBGM).

Philip Comfort, the author of, *Encountering the Manuscripts: An Introduction to New Testament Paleography and Textual Criticism* (2005), has abandoned the possibility of establishing the original text. Comfort finds this hope in the very earliest papyri and the Alexandrian text. He

---

[217] Nonetheless, the oldest manuscripts, which are of the Alexandrian text-type, seem to be the favored, and text of the United Bible Society, 5th ed. and Nestle-Aland, 28th ed. has an Alexandrian disposition.

believes that the very early Alexandrian (Egyptian) text represents what the whole of the Christian writings must have looked like at that time. Writings of the early church fathers such as Irenaeus, Marcion, and Hippolytus reflect the Alexandrian form of the text. New Testament textual scholar Larry W. Hurtado holds this position as well. We will quote his position extensively.

> All indications are that early Christians were very much given to what we today would call "networking" with one another, and that includes translocal efforts. Indeed, the Roman period generally was a time of impressive travel and translocal contacts, for trading, pilgrimages, and other purposes.[218] Eldon Epp has marshaled evidence that the early Christian papyri, mainly from Egypt, reflect "extensive and lively interactions between Alexandria and the outlying areas, and also between the outlying areas [of Egypt] and other parts of the Roman world ... and ... the wide circulation of documents in this early period."[219] In another essay, Epp also demonstrated how readily people expected to send and receive letters all across the Roman Empire, reflecting more broadly a "brisk 'intellectual commerce' and dynamic interchanges of people, literature, books, and letters between Egypt and the vast Mediterranean region."[220]
>
> In illustration of this, note that we have at least three copies of the Shepherd of Hermas that are dated to the late second/early third century, at most only a few decades later than the composition of this text. Thus, this Roman-provenance writing made its way to Egypt very quickly and was apparently received positively. Even more striking is the appearance of a copy of Irenaeus's Against Heresies that has been dated to the late second or early third century. Again, within a very short time, we have

---

[218] See Lionel Casson, Travel in the Ancient World (London: Allen & Unwin, 1974); and Richard Bauckham's discussion in his essay, "For Whom Were the Gospels Written?" in The Gospels for All Christians: Rethinking the Gospel Audiences, ed. Richard Bauckham (Grand Rapids: Eerdmans, 1998), 32 (9-48).

[219] Eldon Jay Epp, "The Significance of the Papyri for Determining the Nature of the New Testament Text in the Second Century: A Dynamic View of Textual Transmission," in Gospel Traditions in the Second Century: Origins, Recensions, Text, and Transmission, ed. William L. Petersen (Notre Dame: University of Notre Dame Press, 1989), 81 (71-103).

[220] Eldon Jay Epp, "New Testament Papyrus Manuscripts and Letter Carrying in Greco-Roman Times," in The Future of Early Christianity: Essays in Honor of Helmut Koester, ed. Birger A. Pearson (Minneapolis: Fortress Press, 1991), 55 (35-56). As another particular piece of evidence of Christian networking across imperial distances, Malcolm Choat pointed me to a third-century letter sent from an unknown individual Christian in Rome to fellow Christians in Egypt (P. Amherst 1.3), requesting certain financial transactions. For discussion see Charles Wessely, "Les plus ancients monuments du Christianisme ecrits sur papyrus," Patrologia Orientalis, Tomas Quartus (Paris: Librairie de Paris, 1908), 135-38.

a writing composed elsewhere (Gaul) finding its way to Christians in Oxyrhynchus (about 120 miles south of Cairo). We could also note the several early copies of writings of Melito of Sardis (Roman Asia Minor). In short, the extant manuscript evidence fully supports the conclusion that the Oxyrhynchus material reflects a broad, translocal outlook.

... We shall explore the implications of the papyrus evidence, on the working assumption that though largely of Egyptian provenance, these early Christian papyri reflect attitudes, preferences, and usages of many Christians more broadly in the second and third centuries. We turn now to consider what we might infer from the list of textual witnesses provided to us in these papyri.[221]

Distribution of Papyri Witnesses for Each New Testament Book					
NT Book	Total	Early	NT Book	Total	Early
Matthew	23	11	1 Timothy	0	0
Mark	3	2	2 Timothy	0	0
Luke	10	6	Titus	2	1
John	30	19	Philemon	2	1
Acts	14	7	Hebrews	8	4
Romans	10	5	James	6	4
1 Corinthians	8	3	1 Peter	3	1
2 Corinthians	4	2	2 Peter	2	1
Galatians	2	1	1 John	2	1

[221] Larry W. Hurtado, *The Earliest Christian Artifacts: Manuscripts and Christian Origins* (Grand Rapids: William B. Eerdmans, 2006), 26-27.

Ephesians	3	3	2 John	1	0
Philippians	3	2	3 John	1	0
Colossians	2	1	Jude	3	2
1 Thessalonians	4	3	Revelation	7	4
2 Thessalonians	2	2			

It appears that some of the answers to establishing the original text of the Christian Greek Scriptures lie within the Westcott and Hort approach. There are 13 papyrus manuscripts that date from about 125–200 C.E. (including seven new papyri about to be released, one of which is claimed to be from the first century), and there are another 65 papyrus manuscripts that date from the 4th century C.E.[222] It is from these manuscripts, especially the earliest ones, that we are going to be aided in establishing the original text.[223] Tregelles (1813-75), Tischendorf (1815-74), and Westcott (1825-1901) and Hort (1828-92) hung their textual hats on the two best manuscripts of their day, i.e., Sinaiticus (c. 360) and Vaticanus (c. 350), both of the Alexandrian text-type.

P75 (c.175–225) contains most of Luke and John and has vindicated Westcott and Hort for their choice of Vaticanus as the premium manuscript for establishing the original text. After careful study of P75 against the Vaticanus Codex, scholars have found that they are just short of being identical. In his introduction to the Greek text, Hort argues that the Vaticanus Codex is a "very pure line of very ancient text."[224]

Those who have abandoned all hope of such a venture would argue differently, saying "oldest is not necessarily best." For these scholars, the original reading could be found in any manuscript, which is true to a degree. They continue with the approach that the reading that produced the other readings is likely the original. While on the surface this sounds

---

[222] As of 2014, there are 127 papyri.

[223] It should be noted that Andrews is not arguing for setting aside all manuscripts except the early papyri. Rather, he is merely suggesting that our best evidence lies within these early papyri.

[224] B. F. Westcott and F. J. A. Hort, Introduction [and] Appendix, Vol. 2 of *New Testament in the Original Greek* (London: Macmillan and Company, 1881), 251.

great, it is not as solid a principle as one might think. On this issue, Comfort writes:

> For example, two scholars, using this principle to examine the same variant, may not agree. One might argue that a copyist attempting to emulate the author's style produced the variant; the other could claim the same variant has to be original because it accords with the author's style. Or, one might argue that a variant was produced by an orthodox scribe attempting to rid the text of a reading that could be used to promote heterodoxy or heresy; another might claim that the same variant has to be original because it is orthodox and accords with Christian doctrine (thus a heterodoxical or heretical scribe must have changed it). Furthermore, this principle allows for the possibility that the reading selected for the text can be taken from any manuscript of any date. This can lead to subjective eclecticism.[225]

When we look deeper into reasoned eclecticism and the local-genealogical method,[226] we find that they lean more heavily on the side of the internal evidence as opposed to external evidence. It is the position of this author that the greater weight should be placed on the external evidence if we are to recover the original text. Westcott and Hort held this position as well. They wrote, "Documentary attestation has been in most cases allowed to confer the place of honour as against internal evidence." (Westcott and Hort 1882, 17) Ernest Colwell, who was of the same mindset, suggested in 1968 that we needed to get back to the principles of Westcott and Hort. Sadly, textual scholarship has largely strayed from those principles.

With what we have already discussed as to the level of skilled copying of the early papyri, apparently, the scribal practices of Alexandria, Egypt, have played a significant role in this. As historical records have shown, Alexandria had an enormous Jewish population. We can imagine a large, predominately Jewish, Christian congregation early on as the gospel made its way throughout that land. This congregation would have maintained deep ties with their fellow Christians in Jerusalem and Antioch. Then, there was the Didaskelion catechetical school of Alexandria that had some of the most influential Church Fathers as head instructors. As has already been noted, Pantaenus took over and was in charge from about 160–180 C.E., Clement being his greatest student, and Origen, who brought this school to Caesarea in 231, establishing a second school and scriptorium.

---

[225] P. W. Comfort (1992), 38–39.

[226] This method holds that a variant can be established as original and can come from any given manuscript(s).

As the Greek Septuagint originated from Alexandria, and the vast majority of the earliest New Testament papyri also had their origins in Egypt (Fayum and Oxyrhynchus), it is quite clear that the above-mentioned Church Fathers would have accessed the Septuagint and the Christian Greek Scriptures in their writings and evangelistic work. Origen, who learned from both Clement and Pantaenus, wrote more than the earliest leaders of Christianity, and his writings are a reflection of the early New Testament papyri, as is true with Clement and his writings. Considering that Clement studied under Pantaenus, it is not difficult to surmise that his writings would also be a reflection of the early New Testament papyri. Therefore, it truly is not unreasonable to suggest that going in reverse chronologically: Origen, Clement, Pantaenus, and those who studied with Pantaenus and brought him into Christianity from Stoic philosophy, were using Alexandrian family texts-types that were mirror-like reflections of the original texts of the Christian Greek Scriptures. Church historian Eusebius helps us to appreciate just how early this school was; note how he expresses it:

> About the same time, a man most distinguished for his learning, whose name was Pantaenus, governed the school of the faithful. There had been a school of sacred learning *established there from ancient times* [italics mine], which has continued down to our own times, and which we have understood was held by men able in eloquence and the study of divine things. The tradition is that this philosopher was then in great eminence, as he had been first disciplined in the philosophical principles of those called stoics.[227]

What we have learned thus far is that in the second and third centuries C.E., the scholarship and scribal practices of Alexandria had a tremendous impact on all of Egypt and as far south as the Fayum and Oxyrhynchus. This means that the standard text of the Christian Greek Scriptures reflecting the originals came up out of Egypt during the second century. The Alexandrian Library had been a force for influencing rigorous scholarship and setting high standards from the third century B.C.E. onward. Is it mere coincidence that the four greatest libraries and learning centers were located in the very places that Christianity had its original growth: Alexandria, Pergamum near Ephesus, Rome, and Antioch? The congregations within these cities and nearby ones would be greatly influenced by their book production.

However, some improvements can be made to these critical texts, because the editors of the 26th to 28th editions of the Nestle-Aland text made revisions setting the text further apart from the Westcott and Hort

---

[227] Eusebius, *Ecclesiastical History* 5:10:1.

text of 1881. In this, they have ignored the testimony of the earliest manuscripts and Codex Vaticanus and have rejected many readings by relegating them to the margin, or to the critical apparatus, leaving an inferior reading in the main text. It is as Comfort says in his *New Testament Text and Translation Commentary*:

> ...the resultant eclectic text exhibits too much dependence on internal evidence, emphasizing the 'local' aspect of the 'local-genealogical' method, to use Aland's language. This means that the decision-making, on a variant-unit-by-variant-unit basis, produced a text with an uneven documentary presentation. Furthermore, the committee setting, with members voting on each significant textual variant cannot help but produce a text with uneven documentation. All eclectic texts reconstruct a text that no ancient Christian actually read, even though they approach a close replication of the original writings. However, the NU edition's eclecticism extends even to following different manuscripts within the same sentence. (P. W. Comfort 2008, p. XV)

The Reliability of the Early Text

Even though many textual scholars credited the Aland's *The Text of the New Testament* with their description of the text as "free," that was not the entire position of the Alands. They did describe different texts' styles, such as "at least normal," "normal," "free," and "strict," seemingly to gauge or weigh the textual faithfulness of each manuscript. However, like Kenyon, they saw a need based on the evidence, which suggested a rethinking of how the evidence should be described,

> We have inherited from the past generation the view that the early text was a 'free' text, and the discovery of the Chester Beatty papyri seemed to confirm this view. When P[45] and P[46] were joined by P[66] sharing the same characteristics, this position seemed to be definitely established. P[75] appeared in contrast to be a loner with its "strict" text anticipating Codex Vaticanus. Meanwhile the other witnesses of the early period had been ignored. It is their collations which have changed the picture so completely.[228]

While we have said this once, it bears repeating, as *some* of the earliest manuscripts that we now have evidence that a professional scribe copied them. *Many* of the other papyri confirm that a semiprofessional hand copied them, while *most* of these early papyri give evidence of being

---

[228] (Aland and Aland, The Text of the New Testament 1995, 93-5)

produced by a copyist who was literate and experienced. Therefore, either literate or semiprofessional copyist did the vast majority of the early extant papyri, with some being done by professionals. As it happened, the few poorly copied manuscripts became known first, establishing a precedent that was difficult for some to shake when the enormous amount of evidence emerged that showed just the opposite.

After a detailed comparison of the papyri, Kurt and Barbara Aland concluded that these manuscripts from the second to the fourth centuries are of three kinds (at least normal, normal, free, and strict). "It is their collations which have changed the picture so completely." (p. 93)

1. **Normal Texts**: The normal text is a relatively faithful tradition (e.g., P^{52}, which departs from its exemplar only occasionally, as do New Testament manuscripts of every century. It is further represented in P^4, P^5, P^{12}(?), P^{16}, P^{18}, P^{20}, P^{28}, P^{47}, P^{72} (1, 2 Peter) and P^{87}.[229]

2. **Free Texts**: This is a text dealing with the original text in a relatively free manner with no suggestion of a program of standardization (e.g., p^{45}, p^{46} and p^{66}), exhibiting the most diverse variants. It is further represented in P^9 (?), P^{13}(?), P^{29}, P^{37}, P^{40}, P^{69}, P^{72} (Jude) and P^{78}.[230]

3. **Strict Texts**: These manuscripts transmit the text of the exemplar with meticulous care (e.g., P^{75}) and depart from it only rarely. It is further represented in P^1, P^{23}, P^{27}, P^{35}, P^{36}, P^{64+67}, P^{65}(?), and P^{70}.[231]

Bruce M. Metzger (1914 – 2007) was an editor with Kurt and Barbara Aland of the United Bible Societies' standard Greek New Testament and the Nestle-Aland Greek New Testament. In his *A Textual Commentary on the Greek New Testament*, Second Edition (1971, 1994), and other works, we have his view of the Alexandrian text-type as follows.

> The *Alexandrian text*, which Westcott and Hort called the *Neutral text* (a question-begging title), is usually considered to be the best text and the most faithful in preserving the original. Characteristics of the Alexandrian text are brevity and austerity. That is, it is generally shorter than the text of other forms, and it does not exhibit the degree of grammatical and stylistic polishing that is characteristic of the Byzantine type of text. Until recently, the two chief witnesses to the Alexandrian text were codex Vaticanus (B) and codex Sinaiticus (ℵ), parchment manuscripts dating from about the middle of the fourth century. With the

---

[229] Ibid., 95

[230] Ibid., 59, 64, 93

[231] Ibid., 64, 95

acquisition, however, of the Bodmer Papyri, particularly P[66] and P[75], both copied about the end of the second or the beginning of the third century, evidence is now available that the Alexandrian type of text goes back to an archetype that must be dated early in the second century. The Sahidic and Bohairic versions frequently contain typically Alexandrian readings.

It is best if textual scholars focus their attention on the categories the Alands set out, as opposed to their over-generalization that the early period of copying was "uncontrolled" and "free." The Alands' rating system consisted of "at least normal," "normal," "strict," and "free," designed to evaluate the textual faithfulness of each manuscript. It seems that these terms were meant to gauge the level of control that the scribe showed in copying his exemplar. Manuscripts labeled "at least normal" referred to a copyist who at least gave some consideration to his task, namely, producing an accurate copy of the exemplar. "Normal," on the other hand, referred to a copyist who permitted what was deemed a normal amount of variants within a copying of the exemplar. Therefore, "strict" referred to a scribe who allowed very few variants in his copy of the exemplar. Lastly, "free" would refer to a copyist who showed almost no regard for being faithful to the exemplar that he was copying.

It behooves the textual scholar to give much attention to the study of scribal habits, which really began with Ernest Colwell in 1969, who analyzed the scribal habits in P[45], P[66], and P[75] by examining their singular readings.[232] Singular readings are variant readings that are found only in the manuscript being examined, not in any other extant documents. By studying these singular readings of a particular manuscript, we see into the habits of that scribe, namely, his pattern of textual variations, his interactions with the text. Colwell's investigation was followed by a much more extensive study of singular readings by James Royse of the same manuscripts some twelve years later.[233] Then, we had Philip Comfort in his doctoral dissertation in 1997.[234] Comfort explains that his objective was "to determine what it was in the text that prompted the scribes of P[45], P[66], and

---

[232] Ernest C. Colwell, "*Method in Evaluating Scribal Habits: A Study of P45, P66, P75*," in *Studies in Methodology in Textual Criticism of the New Testament,* New Testament Tools and Studies 9 (Leiden: Brill, 1969).

[233] James Ronald Royse, "*Scribal Habits in Early Greek New Testament Papyri*" (Ph.D. diss., Graduate Theological Union, 1981). According to Royse, this investigation of singular readings does not apply to lectionaries, patristic sources, and versions, just New Testament papyri, uncials, and minuscules.

[234] Philip Comfort, "*The Scribe as Interpreter: A New Look at New Testament Textual Criticism according to Reader Reception Theory*," D. Litt. et Phil, dissertation, University of South Africa (1997).

P[75] to make individual readings." Comfort suggests that we forgo the categories of the Alands and "that textual critics could use the categories "reliable," "fairly reliable," and "unreliable" to describe the textual fidelity of any given manuscript." This author would agree. Moreover, he shows "that many of the early papyri are 'reliable,' several 'fairly reliable,' and a few 'unreliable.'" Comfort then logically explains, "One of the ways of establishing reliability (or lack thereof) is to test a manuscript against one that is generally proven for its textual fidelity. For example, since many scholars have acclaimed the textual fidelity of P[75] (both for intrinsic and extrinsic reasons), it is fair to compare other manuscripts against it in order to determine their textual reliability." (P. Comfort 2005, 268)

How do we know that the critical text NA28 and the UBS5 are reliable? In 1989, Eldon J. Epp noted that the papyri have added virtually no new substantial variants to the variants already known from our later manuscripts.[235] Even with the discovery of many other papyri over the last 25 years, the situation has remained the same. It can be said that after 135 years of early manuscript discoveries since Westcott and Hort of 1881, the above critical editions of the Greek New Testament have gone virtually unchanged. (Hill and Kruger 2012, 5) Hill and Kruger go on to say, "It also means that the fourth-century 'best texts,' the 'Alexandrian' codices Vaticanus and Sinaiticus, have roots extending throughout the entire third century and even into the second." (p. 6)

The most reliable of the earliest texts are P[1], P[4, 64, 67], P[23], P[27], P[30], P[32], P[35], P[39, P49, 65], P[70], P[75], P[86], P[87], P[90], P[91], P[100], P[101], P[106], P[108], P[111], P[114], and P[115]. The copyists of these manuscripts allowed very few variants in their copies of the exemplars.[236] They had the ability to make accurate judgments as they went about their copying, resulting in superior texts. Whether their skills in copying were a result of their belief that they were copying a sacred text, or from their training, cannot be known. It could have been a combination of both. These papyri are of great importance when considering textual problems and are considered by many textual scholars to be a good representation of the original wording of the text that was first published by the biblical author. Still, "many of these manuscripts

---

[235] E. J. Epp, 'The Significance of the Papyri for Determining the Nature of the New Testament Text in the Second Century: A Dynamic View of Textual Transmission', in W. L. Petersen, ed., *The Gospel Traditions in the Second Century* (Notre Dame: University of Notre Dame Press, 1989), 101.

[236] In 1988, the Alands, in the second edition of *The Text of the New Testament* (93-95), categorized thirty of the forty-four earliest manuscripts (40 papyri and 4 parchment) as "at least normal," "normal," and "strict," with the other fourteen being categorized as "free" or "like Codex Bezae (D)." At that time, the Alands did not rate P[90] [2nd], P[92], [3rd/4th] and P[95] [3rd], likely because they had only recently been discovered. However, we now have the Aland classification of "strict."

contain singular readings and some 'Alexandrian' polishing, which needs to be sifted out." (P. Comfort 2005, 269) Nevertheless, again, they are the best texts and the most faithful in preserving the original. While it is true that some of the papyri are mere fragments, some contain substantial portions of text. We should note too that text types really did not exist per se in the second century, and it is a mere convention to refer to the papyri as Alexandrian, since the best Alexandrian manuscript, Vaticanus, did exist in the second century by way of $\mathfrak{P}^{75}$.[237] It is not that the Alexandrian text existed, but rather $\mathfrak{P}^{75}$/Vaticanus evidence that some very strict copying with great care was taking place.[238] Manuscripts that were not of this caliber of strict and careful copying were the result of scribal errors and scribes taking liberties with the text. Therefore, even though $\mathfrak{P}^5$ may be categorized as a Western text-type, it is more a matter of negligence in the copying process.

The Aland Classification of Papyri as of 2002[239]

Strict	At Least Normal	Normal	Free	Like D
$\mathfrak{P}^1$, $\mathfrak{P}^{23}$, $\mathfrak{P}^{27}$, $\mathfrak{P}^{35}$, $\mathfrak{P}^{39}$, $\mathfrak{P}^{64/67}$, $\mathfrak{P}^{65(?)}$, $\mathfrak{P}^{70}$, $\mathfrak{P}^{75}$, $\mathfrak{P}^{77}$, $\mathfrak{P}^{102}$, $\mathfrak{P}^{103}$, $\mathfrak{P}^{104}$, $\mathfrak{P}^{106}$, $\mathfrak{P}^{108}$, $\mathfrak{P}^{109}$, $\mathfrak{P}^{111}$	$\mathfrak{P}^{15}$, $\mathfrak{P}^{22}$, $\mathfrak{P}^{30}$, $\mathfrak{P}^{32}$, $\mathfrak{P}^{49}$, $\mathfrak{P}^{53}$	$\mathfrak{P}^4$, $\mathfrak{P}^5$, $\mathfrak{P}^{12(?)}$, $\mathfrak{P}^{16}$, $\mathfrak{P}^{18}$, $\mathfrak{P}^{20}$, $\mathfrak{P}^{28}$, $\mathfrak{P}^{47}$, $\mathfrak{P}^{52}$, $\mathfrak{P}^{72}$ (1, 2 Pet.), $\mathfrak{P}^{87}$, $\mathfrak{P}^{90}$, $\mathfrak{P}^{101}$, $\mathfrak{P}^{107}$	$\mathfrak{P}^{45}$, $\mathfrak{P}^{46}$, $\mathfrak{P}^{66}$, $\mathfrak{P}^{9(?)}$, $\mathfrak{P}^{13(?)}$, $\mathfrak{P}^{29}$, $\mathfrak{P}^{37}$, $\mathfrak{P}^{40}$, $\mathfrak{P}^{69}$, $\mathfrak{P}^{72}$(Jude), $\mathfrak{P}^{78}$, $\mathfrak{P}^{95}$	$\mathfrak{P}^{38}$, $\mathfrak{P}^{48}$
Early Uncials 0220	0162, 0189		0171	

[237] The Coherence Based Genealogical Method, which was developed by Gerd Mink and assists scholars in developing genealogical trees of manuscripts, will be discussed in far greater detail in Chapter XIII by Wilkins; but we should note here that it has no relation to the traditional text-type model. It is for this reason that scholars such as Holger Strutwolf have suggested that we abandon any references to the manuscripts by the tradition text-types.

[238] "What we do know, from the manuscript evidence, is that several of the earliest Christian scribes were well-trained scribes who applied their training to making reliable texts, both of the Old Testament and the New Testament. We know that they were conscientious to make a reliable text in the process of transcription (as can been seen in manuscripts like P4+64+67 and P75), and we know that others worked to rid the manuscript of textual corruption. This is nowhere better manifested than in P66, where the scribe himself and the *diorthotes* (official corrector) made over 450 corrections to the text of John. As is explained in the next chapter, the *diorthotes* of P66 probably consulted other exemplars (one whose text was much like that of P75) in making his corrections. This shows a standard Alexandrian scriptoral practice at work in the reproduction of a New Testament manuscript." (P. Comfort, Encountering the Manuscripts: An Introduction to New Testament Paleography and Textual Criticism 2005, 264)

[239] The table is copied from (Hill and Kruger 2012, 11)

As Hill and Kruger put it, "if one accepts the Alands' analyses, in 2002, forty out of fifty-five (or just under 73 percent) of the earliest NT manuscripts had Normal to Strict texts, and fifteen (or just over 27 percent) had Free to Like D texts. The single largest category, consisting of eighteen out of fifty-five (or nearly a third) of the earliest manuscripts, is the category of Strict text." (Hill and Kruger 2012, 11) Therefore, it would be difficult to follow in the footsteps of previous authors who cite the Alands as their source in describing the early period of copying the Greek New Testament as "free," or "wild," "in a state of flux," "chaotic," "a turbid textual morass," and so on.

The Primary Task of a Textual Scholar

The long-held task of the textual scholar has been to recover the original reading. Samuel Prideaux Tregelles (1813-1875) stated that the objective "of all textual criticism is to present an ancient work, as far as possible, in the very words and form in which it proceeded from the writer's own hand. Thus, when applied to the Greek New Testament, the result proposed is to give a text of those writings, as near as can be done on existing evidence, such as they were when originally written in the first century."[240] B. F. Westcott (1825-1901) and F. J. A. Hort (1828-1892) said it was their goal "to present exactly the original words of the New Testament, so far as they can now be determined from surviving documents."[241] Throughout the twentieth century, leading textual scholars such as Bruce M. Metzger (1914-2007) and Kurt Aland (1915-1994) had the same goals for textual criticism. By it Griesbach (1745-1812), Tregelles, Tischendorf (1815-1874), Westcott and Hort, Metzger, Aland, and other prominent textual scholars since the days of Erasmus (1466-1536) all gave their lives to the restoration of the Greek New Testament.

However, sadly, "more dominant in text critics' thinking now is the need to plot the changes in the history of the text."[242] While Bart Ehrman, David Parker, and J. K. Elliot are correct that we could never restore or establish the original words of the authors of the twenty-seven Greek New Testament books beyond question, it should still remain the goal, as opposed to the pessimistic attitude of late. If we sidestep the traditional goal of textual criticism, we are really abandoning textual criticism itself. While the textual scholar wants to track down the variants to the text through the centuries, this can only be done by realizing there was a

---

[240] Tregelles, *An Account of the Printed Text of the Greek New Testament*, 174.

[241] Westcott and Hort, *Introduction to the New Testament in the Original Greek*, 1.

[242] J. K. Elliott, "The International Greek New Testament Project's Volumes on the Gospel of Luke: Prehistory and Aftermath," NTTRU 7, 17.

beginning, i.e., the twenty-seven original texts. How does one identify an alteration in the text without knowing from what it was altered? While the NA28/UBS5 critical edition cannot be considered a 100% reproduction of the original twenty-seven books, textual scholarship should always work in that direction, or otherwise, what is the purpose? The author of this publication is in harmony with the words of Paul D. Wegner, who writes, "Textual criticism is foundational to exegesis and interpretation of the text: we need to know what the wording of the text is before we can know what it means." (Wegner 2006, 230)

The sad state of affairs is that textual scholarship as a whole is unwittingly or knowingly moving the goal posts for some unknown reason. In textual criticism, it is now the earliest knowable text, in biblical hermeneutics, it dissecting a text until you no longer have the text, in Bible translation, it is going beyond what the Word of God is in the receptor language (e.g., English, Spanish, German) into what the translator thinks the original author meant. How is it possible for no one to see the danger of what is happening? What has happened right before our eyes are the goal of an early text not the original, Bible books by unknown authors, not the ones bearing their name, with Jesus not saying half of what the Gospels claim he said, in mini-commentary, interpretive translations by translators that are of the biblical criticism mindset.

CHAPTER 8 How Did the Spread of Early Christianity and the Persecution of the Early Church Impact the Text of the New Testament?

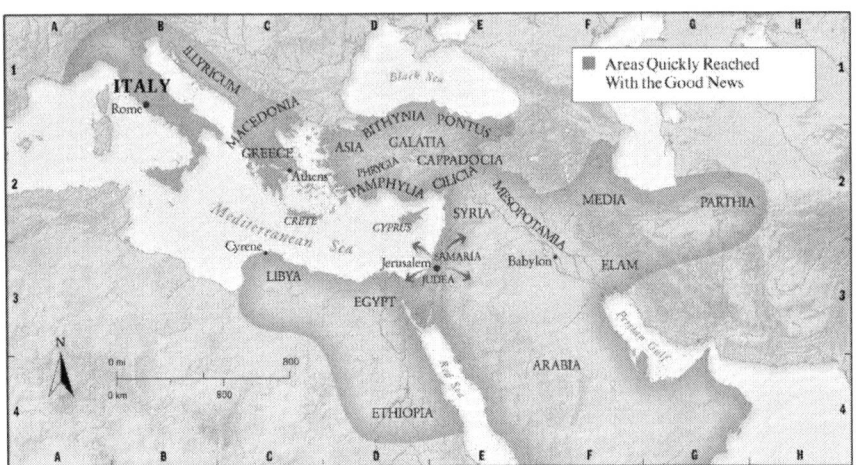

The Foretold Apostasy

Within just a few short decades after the death of the apostle John, divisions were already evident among the early Christians. Historian Will and Ariel Durant write: "Celsus [Greek Philosopher and second-century opponent of Christianity] himself had sarcastically observed that Christians were 'split up into ever so many factions, each individual desiring to have his own party.' About 187 AD Irenaeus listed twenty varieties of Christianity; about 384 AD Epiphanius counted eighty." (*The Story of Civilization: Part III, Caesar and Christ*) While this and what lies below is all true, the first century Christianity that Jesus Christ started, and the apostles grew went from 120 Christians in the upper room of Pentecost 33 C.E. to shortly over one million by 130 C.E. This in a world of only a one hundred million in population.

2 Thessalonians 2:1a, 3 Updated American Standard Version (UASV)

2 Now we request you, brothers, with regard to the coming of our Lord Jesus Christ … ³ Let no one deceive you in any way, for it will not come unless **the apostasy comes first**, and the man of lawlessness is revealed, the son of destruction,

Apostasy: (Gr. *apostasia*) The term literally means "to stand away from" and is used to refer to ones who 'stand away from the truth.' It is abandonment, a rebellion, an apostasy, a refusal to accept or acknowledge true worship. In Scripture, this is used primarily concerning the one who rises up in defiance of the only true God and his people, working in opposition to the truth. – Ac 21:21; 2 Thess. 2:3.

On this text, New Testament scholar Knute Larson writes, "Before that great day comes, Paul declared, the rebellion must occur. The word used here is *apostasia* or apostasy. Before the day of the Lord, there will be a great denial, a deliberate turning away by those who profess to belong to Christ. It will be a rebellion. Having once allied themselves with Christ, they will abandon him. Within the recognized church there will come a time when people will forsake their faith. Throughout history, there have been defections from the faith. But the apostasy about which he wrote to the Thessalonians would be of greater magnitude and would signal the coming of the end." (Larson 2000, 105)

The apostle Paul says to the Ephesian elders; there is but "one Lord, one faith, one baptism." (Eph. 4:5) Paul penned those words about 60 C.E., and he was informing them that there was but one Christian faith. Yet, today we see more varieties of Christian faith than we care to count, all claiming that they are the truth and the way. Whenever a brave soul dares to be truthful and bring up that there are doctrinal differences, different doctrinal position, and different standards of conduct, he is shouted down as an alarmist. They claim that most of these denominations are the same on the essential doctrines, i.e., the salvation doctrines. Well, this actually is not true and is an attempt at hiding the truth, because even the salvation doctrines have anywhere from three to five different interpretations. Regardless, we must concern ourselves with a crucial question from Jesus Christ, "when the Son of Man comes, will he find faith on earth?" (Lu 18:8) This is a whole other discussion. We concern ourselves with how these divisions came about in the first place.

As has already been stated in another blog article, but bears repeating, the blame lies with Satan. He attempted to have Jesus killed as a baby, he tempted Jesus in the wilderness after his baptism, and he attempted persecution right from the start. Peter wrote, "Be sober-minded; be watchful. Your adversary, the devil, prowls around like a roaring lion, seeking someone to devour." (1 Pet. 5:8) Initially, the persecution of this young Christian body came from Jewish religious leaders, and then from the Roman Empire itself. With "all authority in heaven" (Matt. 28:20) Jesus watched on, as the Holy Spirit guided and directed them, this infancy Christian congregation endured the best that Satan and his henchman had to offer. (See Rev. 1:9; 2:3, 19) As we know from Scripture, Satan is not one to give up, so he devised a new plan, divide and conquer. Yes, he would cause divisions within the Christian congregation. Satan broke out the ultimate weapon— **the apostasy.** We need not to believe that all of a sudden, the apostasy came into the Christian congregation. No, Jesus was watching from heaven, and he made sure that he warned them while he was here on earth of what was to come, and he made the young Christian congregation aware of what was coming and when it was getting started. – Colossians 1:18

In the Greek New Testament, the noun "apostasy" (Gr., *apostasia*) has the sense of "desertion, abandonment or rebellion." (Acts 21:21, ftn.) There it predominantly is alluding to abandonment; a drawing away from or abandoning of pure worship.

"[Jesus] Be Aware of False Prophets . . .

[Peter] There Will Be False Teachers Among You."

Matthew 7:15 Updated American Standard Version (UASV)

[15] "Beware of the false prophets, who come to you in sheep's clothing, but inwardly are ravenous wolves.

Jesus was well aware of what Satan would try to accomplish step-by-step, and that divisions through those from within were on the list. New Testament scholar Stuart K. Weber says, "Jesus had an important reason for inserting the wolf metaphor (Acts 20:27–31)—to alert his listeners to the danger of a false prophet. If the false prophets were thought of as a source of bad fruit, then the disciples might think it was enough simply to recognize and ignore the false prophet, refusing to consume his bad fruit, and awaiting God's judgment on him. But the wolf metaphor attributes a more active and malicious motive to the false prophet. He is actually an enemy of the sheep, and, if not confronted, will get his way by destroying the sheep." (Weber 2000, 101)

Weber mentions Acts 20:28-30, where Paul, about **56 C.E.**, warned the Ephesian elders,

Acts 20:28-30 Updated American Standard Version (UASV)

[28] Pay careful attention to yourselves and to all the flock, in which the Holy Spirit has made you overseers, to care for the congregation[6] of God, which he obtained with the blood of his own Son.* [29] I know that after my departure fierce wolves will come in among you, not sparing the flock; [30] and **from among your own selves** men will arise, **speaking twisted things, to draw away the disciples after them.**

* Lit *with the blood of his Own.*

Yes, these, who standoff from the Truth and the Way, would not be seeking their own disciples, but rather they would be seeking, "to draw away the disciples after them." i.e., the disciples of Christ. Jesus was well aware that the easiest way to defeat any group is to divide them, and so was Satan, who had been watching humanity for over 4,000 years, and especially the Israelites (Isaac and Ishmael / Jacob and Esau / Israel and Judah), as "Satan disguises himself as an angel of light. So, it is no surprise if his servants, also, disguise themselves as servants of righteousness." – 2 Corinthians 11:14-15.

The apostle Peter also spoke of these things about **64 C.E.**, "there will be false teachers among you, who will secretly bring in destructive heresies … in their greed they will exploit you with false words." (2 Pet. 2:1, 3) These abandoned the faithful words, became false teachers, rising within the Christian congregation, sharing their corrupting influence, intending to hide, disguise, or mislead.

These dire warnings by Jesus and the New Testament Authors had their beginnings in the first century C.E. Yes, they began small, but burst forth on the scene in the second century.

"[Paul says it] Is Already at Work"

About **51 C.E.**, some 18-years after Jesus' death, resurrection and ascension, division was already starting to creep into the faith, "the mystery of lawlessness is already at work." (2 Thess. 2:7) Yes, the power of **the man of lawlessness** was already present, which is the power of Satan, the god of this world (2 Cor. 4:3-4), and his tens of millions of demons, are hard at work behind the scenes.

There were even some divisions beginning as early as **49 C.E.**, when the elders wrote a letter to the Gentile believers, saying,

Acts 15:24 Updated American Standard Version (UASV)

24 Since we have heard that some went out from among us and troubled you with words, unsettling your souls,[*] although we gave them no instructions,

[*] This means that some, who left the Christian faith and were not trying to subvert (undermine) the faith of others.

Here we see that some *within* were being very vocal about their opposition to the direction the faith was heading. Here, it was over whether the Gentiles needed to be circumcised, suggesting that they needed to be obedient to the Mosaic Law. (Ac 15:1, 5)

As the years progressed throughout the first-century, this divisive "talk [would] spread like gangrene." (2 Tim. 2:17, c. 65 C.E.) About **51 C.E.**,

They had some in Thessalonica, at worst, going ahead of, or at best, misunderstanding Paul, and wrongly stating by word and a bogus letter "that the day of the Lord has come." (2 Thess. 2:1-2) In Corinth, about **55 C.E.**, "some of [were saying] that there is no resurrection of the dead. (1 Cor. 15:12) About **65 C.E.**, some were "saying that the resurrection has already happened. They [were] upsetting the faith of some." (2 Tim 2:16-18)

Throughout the next three decades, no inspired books were written. However, by the time of the Apostle John's letter writing days of 96-98 C.E., he tells us "Now many antichrists have come. Therefore we know that it is the last hour." (1 John 2:18) These are ones, "who denies that Jesus is the Christ" and ones who not confess "Jesus Christ has come in the flesh is from God." (1 John 2:22; 4:2-3)

From 33 C.E. to 100 C.E., the apostles served Christ as a restraint against "the apostasy" that was coming. Paul stated in 2 Thessalonians 2:7, "For the mystery of lawlessness is already at work. Only he [Apostle by Christ] who now restrains it [the apostasy] will do so until he **[apostles]** is out of the way." 2 Thessalonians 2:3 said, "Let no one deceive you in any way **[misinterpretation or false teachers of Paul's first letter]**. For that day **[presence, parousia (second coming) of Christ]** will not come, unless the apostasy comes first, and the man of lawlessness **[likely one person, or maybe an organization / movement, empowered by Satan]** is revealed, the son of destruction."

We must keep in mind that the meaning of any given text is what the author meant by the words that he used, as should have been understood by his audience, and had some relevance/meaning for his audience. The rebellion [apostasy] began slowly in the first century and would break forth after the death of the last apostle, i.e., John. As a historian, Ariel Durant informed us earlier, by 187 C.E., there were 20 varieties of Christianity, and by 384 C.E., there were 80 varieties of Christianity. Christianity would become one again, a universal religion, i.e., Catholicism.

Gnostic Belief

Marcion (85-c.160) was a semi-Gnostic, who believed that the teachings of Jesus were irreconcilable with the actions of the God of the Old Testament. He viewed the God of the Old Testament, Jehovah, to be vicious, violent and cruel, an oppressor who gave out material rewards to those worshiping him. In contrast, Marcion described the New Testament God, Jesus Christ, as a perfect God, the God of unadulterated love and compassion, of kindness and quick to forgive.

Montanus (late second century) was a "prophet" from Asia Minor, who believed that their revelation came directly from the Holy Spirit, which superseded the authority of Jesus, Paul, Peter, John, James, anyone really. They believed in the imminent return of Christ and the setting up of the New Jerusalem in Pepuza. He was more concerned about Christian conduct than he was Christian doctrine, wanting to get back to the Christian values of the first century. However, he took this to the extreme, just as John Calvin would some 1,300 years later in the 16th century. Montanism was a movement focused on prophecy, especially the founder's views, being seen as the light for their time. They believed that the apostle and prophets had the power to forgive sin.

Valentinus (c.100-c.160) was a Greek poet, who founded his school in Rome, and most prominent early Christian gnostic theologian. He claimed that though Jesus' heavenly (spiritual) body was of Mary, he was not actually born from her. This belief came about because Gnostics viewed all matter as evil. Therefore, if Jesus had really been a real human person with a physical body, he would have been evil. Another form of Gnosticism was Docetism, which claimed that Jesus Christ was not a real person, i.e., it was a mere appearance and illusion, which would have included his death and resurrection.

Manes (c. 216-274) was the prophet and the founder of Manichaeism, a gnostic religion. He sought to combine elements of Christianity, Buddhism, and Zoroastrianism, based on a rigid dualism of good and evil, locked in an eternal struggle. He believed that salvation is possible through education, self-denial, fasting, and chastity. He also believed that he was an "apostle of Jesus Christ," (Ramsey 2006, 272) although, strictly speaking, his religion was not a movement of Christian Gnosticism in the earlier approach.

Beginning with the Council of Nicaea in 325 C.E., Emperor Constantine legalized Christianity in an attempt at reunited the empire. He fully understood that religious division was a threat to the continuation of the Roman Empire. However, it was Emperor Theodosius I (347 – 395 C.E.), who banned paganism and imposed Christianity as the State religion of the Roman Empire. The Roman Catholic Church can trace its existence back to the council of Nicaea in 325 C.E. at best. Protestantism had its beginnings in the Reformation of the 16th century. However, there were dissensions in within Catholicism for a thousand years.

Returning to the First Century Again

The early Christian congregations were not isolated from one another. The Roman roads and maritime travel connected all the regions from Rome to Greece, to Asia, to Syria and Palestine, and Egypt.[243] Following the days

---

[243] People of the first three centuries sent and received letters and books from all over the Roman Empire. Hurtado has given us two examples: the Shepherd of Hermas was written

of Pentecost 33 C.E., Jewish or Jewish proselyte Christians returned to Egypt with the good news of Christ (Acts 2:10). Three years after that, the Ethiopian eunuch traveled home with the good news as well (Acts 8:26–39). Apollos of Alexandria, Egypt, a renowned speaker, left Egypt with the knowledge of John the Baptizer and arrived in Ephesus in about 52 C. E. (Acts 18:24-25) The apostle Paul traveled approximately 10,282 miles throughout the Roman Empire establishing congregations.[244] The apostles were a restraint to the apostasy and division within the whole of the first-century Christian congregation (2 Thess. 2:6-7; 1 John 2:18). It was not until the second century that the next generation of Christian leaders gradually caused divisions.[245] However, the one true Christianity that Jesus started, and the apostles established was strong, active, and able to defend against Gnosticism, Roman persecution, and Jewish opposition.

It is conceivable that by 55 C.E. there would have been a thriving congregation in Alexandrian Egypt, with its huge Jewish population.[246] "Now those who had been scattered because of the persecution that arose over Stephen went through as far as Phoenicia and Cyprus and Antioch, speaking the word to no one except Jews" (Acts 11:19). While this indicates a traveling north to Antioch, it does not negate traveling south to Egypt. Antioch obviously is mentioned because it played a significant role as a commencement for first century Christianity, in particular for the apostle Paul.

The Coptic Church claims the Gospel writer Mark as its founder and first patriarch. Tradition has it that he preached in Egypt just before the middle of the first century. At any rate, Christianity spread to Egypt and North Africa at an early date. In fact, it became a prominent religious center, with a noted scholar named Pantaenus, who founded a catechetical school in Alexandria, Egypt, about 160 C.E. In about 180 C.E. another prominent scholar, Clement of Alexandria, took over his position. Clement put this religious, educational institution on the map as a possible center for the whole of the Christian church throughout the Roman Empire. The persecution that came circa the year 202 C.E. forced Clement to flee Alexandria, but one of the most noted scholars of early Christian history,

---

in Rome and found its way to Egypt within a few decades; Irenaeus' Against Heresies was written in Gaul and made it to Egypt (Oxyrhynchus) within short order.

[244] http://orbis.stanford.edu/

[245] This apostasy and divisiveness did not just come into the Christian congregation from nowhere. It started developing in the first century but was restrained by apostolic authority.

[246] Macquarie University, *Ancient History Documentary Research Center* (AHDRC), Papyri from the Rise of Christianity in Egypt (PCE),

http://www.anchist.mq.edu.au/doccentre/PCEhomepage.html.

Origen, replaced him. In addition, Origen took this scholarly environment to Caesarea in 231 C.E. and started yet another prominent school and scriptorium (i.e. a room for copying manuscripts).

What does all this mean? While we cannot know absolutely, textual scholar Philip W. Comfort[247] and others believe that the very early Alexandrian manuscripts that we now possess are a reflection of what would have been found throughout the whole of the Greco-Roman Empire about 125–300 C.E. If we were to discover other early manuscripts from Antioch, Constantinople, Carthage, or Rome, they would be very similar to the early Alexandrian manuscripts. This means that these early manuscripts are a primary means of establishing the original text, and we are in a far better position today than were Westcott and Hort in 1881.

In addition, we can assume an effort on the part of copyists to preserve the originals unchanged, because the authors themselves spoke of their writings as being authoritative and said that no one should alter what they had published or taught. The apostle Paul wrote to the Galatians that they should consider as "accursed" anyone (even angels) who proclaimed a gospel contrary to the one they had preached. (Gal. 1:6-9) Paul went on to write, "the gospel that was preached by me is not according to man [I.e., human origin]. For I neither received it from man, nor was I taught it, but I received it through a revelation [Lit., uncovering; disclosure] of Jesus Christ." (Gal. 1:11-12) The apostle Paul charged that 'the Corinthian Christians had put up with false teachers, readily enough, who proclaim another Jesus and another gospel.' (2 Cor. 11:3-4) Paul and Silas wrote to the Thessalonians that they constantly thanked God that when the Thessalonians received the word of God, which they had heard from them, they accepted it not as the word of men, but for what it really was, the **word of God**. (1Thess. 2:3) Paul then closed that letter by commanding them "by the Lord, have this letter read aloud to all the brothers." (1 Thess. 5:27) In 2 Thessalonians Paul 'requested that they not be quickly shaken from their composure or be disturbed either by a spirit or a word or a letter as if from us.' (2:2) Paul closed the letter with a greeting in his own hand, to authenticate it. (3:17) Lastly, John closed the book of Revelation with a warning to everyone about adding to or taking away from what he had written therein. (Rev. 22:18-19) The New Testament authors were well aware that future scribes could intentionally alter the Word of God, so they warned them of the consequences.

Let's look at yet another author of the New Testament. The apostle Peter wrote about 64 C.E.,

---

[247] Philip W. Comfort, *The Quest for the Original Text of the New Testament* (Eugene, Oregon: Wipf and Stock Publishers, 1992).

2 Peter 1:12-18 Updated American Standard Version (UASV)

[12] Therefore, I will always be ready to remind you of these things, though you know them and are established in the truth that is present with you. [13] I consider it right, as long as I am in this tabernacle,[248] to stir you up by way of reminder, [14] knowing that the putting off of my tabernacle[249] is soon,[250] just as also our Lord Jesus Christ made clear to me. [15] So I will make every effort so that after my departure, you may be able to recall these things for yourselves.[251]

Prophetic Word Made More Sure

[16] For we did not follow cleverly devised myths when we made known to you the power and coming[252] of our Lord Jesus Christ, but we were eyewitnesses of his majesty. [17] For when he received honor and glory from God the Father, and the voice was brought[253] to him by the Majestic Glory, "This is my beloved Son, with whom I am well pleased," [18] and we ourselves heard this very voice brought from heaven, when we were with him on the holy mountain.

Peter was making it clear that he was sharing firsthand accounts and not devised tales. Here again, like the other New Testament authors, Peter warned his readers of false teachers, who corrupted the truth and distorted the Scriptures, such as Paul's letters. Like Paul and John, Peter warned that this would be done to the offenders' own destruction.

2 Peter 3:15-16 Updated American Standard Version (UASV)

[15] and regard the patience of our Lord as salvation; just as also our beloved brother Paul, according to the wisdom given him, wrote to you, [16] as also in all his letters, speaking in them of these things, in which

---

[248] Or *earthly dwelling* or *tent*; that is, *his earthly body*

[249] Or *earthly dwelling* or *tent*; that is, *his earthly body*

[250] Or *is coming swiftly*

[251] Lit *to call these things to remembrance*

[252] **Presence; Coming:** (Gr. *parousia*) The Greek word which is rendered as "presence" is derived from *para*, meaning "with," and *ousia*, meaning "being." It denotes both an "arrival" and a consequent "presence with." Depending on the context, it can mean "presence," "arrival," "appearance," or "coming." In some contexts, this word is describing the presence of Jesus Christ in the last days, i.e., from his ascension in 33 C.E. up unto his second coming, with the emphasis being on his second coming, the end of the age of Satan's reign of terror over the earth. We do not know the day nor the hours of this second coming. (Matt 24:36) It covers a marked period of time with the focus on the end of that period. – Matt. 24:3, 27, 37, 39; 1 Cor. 15:23; 16:17; 2 Cor. 7:6-7; 10:10; Php 1:26; 2:12; 1 Thess. 2:19; 3:13; 4:15; 5:2.

[253] Or *borne* or *made*

186

are some things hard to understand, which the untaught and unstable distort, as they do also the rest of the Scriptures, to their own destruction.

Yes, "It is especially interesting that Peter writes of the distortion of Paul's letters along with 'the other Scriptures.' The implication is that the letters of Paul were already regarded as Scripture at the time Peter wrote."[254] Verse 16 shows that Peter

...is aware of several Pauline letters. This knowledge again raises the dating issue. We know that Paul himself on one occasion had requested that churches share his letters: 'After this letter has been read to you, see that it is also read in the church of the Laodiceans and that you, in turn, read the letter from Laodicea' (Col 4:16). However, it is a big jump in time from Colossians to the first concrete evidence we have of people who know more than one letter. This evidence shows up in *1 Clement*, who not only knows Romans but can also write to the Corinthians, 'Take up the epistle of the blessed Apostle Paul' (*1 Clem.*[255] 47:1). It appears later in *2 Clement* and in Ignatius's *Ephesians*.[256] Thus, we are on solid ground when we accept that a collection of the Pauline letters existed by the end of the first century.[257] It is also likely that some Pauline letters circulated independently of a collection (which is what one would expect as one church hears that another has a letter that might prove helpful in their situation),[258] and that there were collections of a few Pauline letters before there was a collection of all of his letters.[259] All of this is quite logical since Paul was a valued teacher in his circle of communities and, as he left an area and especially as he died, his letters were his continuing voice. Thus churches would share letters and, as they obtained funds (a few hundred dollars to a couple thousand dollars in

---

[254] Allen Black and Mark C. Black, *1 & 2 Peter*, The College Press NIV Commentary (Joplin, MO: College Press Pub., 1998), 2 Pe 3:16.

[255] *1 Clem.* First Epistle of Clement to the Corinthians

[256] Ignatius, *Eph.* 12:2, refers to Paul, "who in all his Epistles makes mention of you in Christ Jesus." (Although one wonders how Ignatius thought the Ephesians were mentioned in every Pauline letter he knew.) On the evidence for 2 Clement's knowledge of a collection, see Karl P. Donfried, *The Setting of Second Clement in Early Christianity* (NovTSup 38; Leiden: E. J. Brill, 1974), 93–95.

[257] Jack Finegan, "The Original Form of the Pauline Collection," *HTR* 49 (1956) 85–104. See also Walter Schmithals, "Zur Abfassung und ältesten Sammlung der pauli nischen Hauptbriefe" ["On the Composition and Earliest Collection of the Major Epistles of Paul"], *ZNW* 51 (1960) 225–45.

[258] Harry Gamble, "The Redaction of the Pauline Letters and the Formation of the Pauline Corpus," *JBL* 94 (1971) 403–18.

[259] Mary Lucetta Mowry, "The Early Circulation of Paul's Letters," *JBL* 63 (1944) 73–86.

today's money), they would make copies. Copies would turn into collections, especially since it was possible to use one scroll for several of the shorter letters. Probably by the end of the first century, the complete collection (i.e., all extant letters) was circulating to at least a limited degree (remember, these copies did not come cheap). The issue is which stage in this process 2 Peter is indicating.[260]

This author would argue that the stage to which Peter was referring was the time when "there were collections of a few Pauline letters before there was a collection of all of his letters." It is most likely that Peter's first letter was written about 62-64 C.E., while **Peter's second letter was written about 64 C.E.**[261] At the time Peter penned his second letter, several of Paul's letters from the 50's was available to Peter (Romans [56], 1 & 2 Corinthians [55], Galatians [50-52], and 1 & 2 Thessalonians [50, 51]). He could have had access to those from the early 60's as well (Ephesians [60-61], Philippians [60-61], Colossians [60-61], Titus [61-64], Philemon [60-61], and Hebrews [61]). The only ones that were clearly unavailable would have been 1 & 2 Timothy [61, 64] and possibly Titus [61-64]. Thus, from Peter's reference to "in all his [Paul's] letters, speaking in them of these things," we garner several insights. It highly suggests (1) there were collections of Paul's letters, (2) Peter and the early church viewed them as "Scripture" in the same sense as the Old Testament Scriptures, (3) they were not to be changed, and (4) that apostolic authors' written works were being collected and preserved for posterity.

Second-Century Manuscripts: Once we enter the second century almost all firsthand witnesses of Jesus Christ would have died, and most of the younger traveling companions, fellow workers and students of the apostles, would be advancing into old age. However, there were some, like Polycarp who was born to Christian parents about 69 C.E. in Asia Minor, in Smyrna. As he grew into a man, he became known for his kindness, self-discipline, compassionate treatment of others, and thorough study of God's Word. Soon enough he became an elder in the Christian congregation at Smyrna. Polycarp was very fortunate to live in a time when he was able to learn from the apostles themselves. In fact, the apostle John was one of his teachers.

By any standard, Polycarp must be reckoned as one of the more notable figures in the early postapostolic church. Already bishop of Smyrna in Asia Minor when his friend and mentor, Ignatius of Antioch

---

[260] Peter H. Davids, *The Letters of 2 Peter and Jude*, The Pillar New Testament Commentary (Grand Rapids, MI: William B. Eerdmans Pub. Co., 2006), 302–303.

[261] Clinton E. Arnold, *Zondervan Illustrated Bible Backgrounds Commentary: Hebrews to Revelation.*, vol. 4 (Grand Rapids, MI: Zondervan, 2002), 153.

[c. 35 C.E. – c. 108 C.E.], addressed one of his letters to him (ca. A.D. 110; cf. above, p. 131), he died a martyr's death (see the *Martyrdom of Polycarp*) several decades later at age eighty-six (ca. 155–160), having served as bishop for at least forty and possibly sixty or more years. Irenaeus (who met Polycarp as a child) and Eusebius both considered him a significant link in the chain of orthodox apostolic tradition. His life and ministry spanned the time between the end of the apostolic era and the emergence of catholic [i.e., universal] Christianity, and he was deeply involved in the central issues and challenges of this critical era: the growing threat of persecution by the state, the emerging Gnostic movement (he is particularly known for his opposition to one of the movement's most charismatic and theologically innovative teachers, Marcion), the development of the monepiscopal form of ecclesiastical organization, and the formation of the canon of the New Testament. Polycarp's only surviving document[262] is a letter to the Philippians, written in response to a letter from them (cf. 3.1; 13.1). It reveals, in addition to a direct and unpretentious style and a sensitive pastoral manner, a deep indebtedness to the Scriptures (in the form of the Septuagint) and early Christian writings, including *1 Clement* (with which Polycarp seems to be particularly familiar).[263] While apparently no New Testament books are cited as 'Scripture' (the reference to Ephesians in 12.1 is a possible exception), the manner in which Polycarp refers to them indicates that he viewed them as authoritative documents.[264]

Christ "gave gifts to men." "He gave some as apostles, and some as prophets, and some as evangelists, and some as pastors and teachers" (Eph. 4:8, 11-13, NASB). The Father moved these inspired ones along by Holy Spirit, as they set forth God's Word for the Christian congregation, "to stir [them] up by way of reminder," repeating many things already written in the Scriptures (2 Pet. 1:12-13; 3:1; Rom 15:15). Thus, we have internal New Testament evidence from Second Peter circa 64 C.E. that "there were collections of a few Pauline letters before there was a collection of all of his letters." Outside of Scripture, we find evidence of a collection of at least

---

[262] The attempt by H. von Campenhausen ("Polykarp und die Pastoralen," repr. *Aus der Frühzeit des Christentums* [Tübingen: Mohr/Siebeck, 1963], 197–252) to show that Polycarp also authored the pastoral Epistles has met with little acceptance.

[263] Schoedel (*Polycarp*, 4–5) suggests that it is "fairly certain" that the letter "reflects more or less direct contact" with the following writings: Psalms, Proverbs, Isaiah, Jeremiah, Ezekiel, Tobit, Matthew, Luke, Acts, Romans, 1–2 Corinthians, Galatians, Ephesians, Philippians, 1–2 Timothy, 1 John, 1 Peter, and *1 Clement*. Metzger (*Canon*, 61–62) adds to the New Testament list 2 Thessalonians and Hebrews while deleting Acts and 2 Corinthians.

[264] Michael William Holmes, *The Apostolic Fathers: Greek Texts and English Translations*, Third ed. (Grand Rapids, MI: Baker Books, 2007), 272–273.

ten Pauline letters that were collected together by 90-100 C.E.[265] We can be certain that the early Christians were collecting the inspired Christian Scriptures as early as the middle of the first century C.E. to the early second century C.E.

Clement of Rome (c. 96 C.E.) was acquainted with Paul's letter to the church at Corinth and said that Paul wrote under the inspiration of the Spirit. Thus, we have Clement of Rome (c. 30-100 C.E.), Polycarp of Smyrna (69-155 C.E.), and Ignatius of Antioch (c. 35 C.E. – c. 108 C.E.), who wove Scripture of the Greek New Testament into their writings, showing their view of them as inspired Scripture. Justin Martyr, who died about 165 C.E., used the expression "it is written" when quoting from Matthew. Theophilus of Antioch, who died about 181 C.E., declared "concerning the righteousness which the law enjoined, confirmatory utterances are found both with the prophets and in the Gospels because they all spoke inspired by one Spirit of God."[266] Theophilus then used such expressions as "**says the Gospel**" (quoting Matt, 5:28, 32, 44, 46; 6:3) and "**the divine word** gives us instructions, in order that "we may lead a quiet and peaceable life."[267] And it teaches us to render all things to all,[268] "honour to whom honour, fear to whom fear, tribute to whom tribute; to owe no man anything, but to love all."[269]

Once we reach the middle to the end of the second century C.E., it comes down to whether those who came before **would stress the written documents as Scripture by**

- the apostles, who had been personally selected by Jesus (Matthew, John, and Peter),

- Paul, who was later selected as an apostle by the risen Jesus himself,

---

[265] Jack Finegan, "The Original Form of the Pauline Collection," *HTR* 49 (1956) 85–104. See also Walter Schmithals, "Zur Abfassung und ältesten Sammlung der pauli nischen Hauptbriefe" ["On the Composition and Earliest Collection of the Major Epistles of Paul"], *ZNW* 51 (1960) 225–45.

[266] Theophilus of Antioch, "Theophilus to Autolycus," in *Fathers of the Second Century: Hermas, Tatian, Athenagoras, Theophilus, and Clement of Alexandria (Entire)*, ed. Alexander Roberts, James Donaldson, and A. Cleveland Coxe, trans. Marcus Dods, vol. 2, The Ante-Nicene Fathers (Buffalo, NY: Christian Literature Company, 1885), 114.

[267] 1 Tim. 2:2

[268] Rom. 13:7, 8

[269] Theophilus of Antioch, "Theophilus to Autolycus," in *Fathers of the Second Century: Hermas, Tatian, Athenagoras, Theophilus, and Clement of Alexandria (Entire)*, ed. Alexander Roberts, James Donaldson, and A. Cleveland Coxe, trans. Marcus Dods, vol. 2, The Ante-Nicene Fathers (Buffalo, NY: Christian Literature Company, 1885), 115.

- the half-brothers of Jesus Christ (James and Jude),

- as well as Mark and Luke, who were close associates and traveling companions of Paul and Peter.

We can see from the above that this largely was the case. We know that major church leaders across the Roman Empire had done just that. We know, for example, that Irenaeus of Asia Minor (180 C.E.) fully accepted 25 of 27 books of the New Testament but had some doubt about Hebrews and uncertainty about James. We know that Clement of Alexandria (190 C.E.) fully accepted 26 of 27 books of the New Testament but may not have been aware of 3 John. We know that Tertullian of North Africa (207 C.E.) fully accepted 24 of 27 books but may not have been aware of 2 and 3 John, or Jude. We know that Origen of Alexandria (230 C.E.) and Eusebius of Palestine (320 C.E.) fully accepted all 27 books of the New Testament. It has been estimated that by the close of the second century C.E., there were over 60,000 copies of major parts of the Greek New Testament in existence. This is an enormous number, even if it was only one in every fifty professing Christians who possessed a copy.

However, would there be evidence that these church leaders, going back to the days of the apostles, would influence the copyists? Moreover, were the copyists professionals? In other words, even if some of the copyists did not see the documents as Scripture, would the church leaders, and long-standing traditions, motivate them to copy the documents with accuracy? In addition, would the professional scribe copy accurately even if he did not view them as Scripture? And if the scribe did view the texts as Scripture, the inspired Word of God, was it plenary inspiration (every word), or that the meaning was inspired? Generally speaking, from what we know about the Alexandrian scribes, they would have sought to reproduce an accurate copy regardless of their views. We can say that there were other scribes, who saw the message as inspired; thus, their focus was not on retaining every single word, nor word order. It seems that they felt they could alter the words without damaging the intended meaning of the author. These copyists added and removed words here and there, rearranged words, and substituted words, presumably in the hope of improving the text but not intending to alter the meaning. It also has to be acknowledged that there were some untrained copyists who simply produced inaccurate copies, regardless of how they viewed the text.

Then, there were scribes who willfully altered the text, with the intention of improving it. Some were seeking to harmonize the gospel accounts. An extreme example would be Tatian, a noteworthy, apologetic writer of the second century C.E. In an account of his conversion to nominal Christianity, Tatian states, "I sought how I might be able to discover the truth," which points to his intent. About 170 C.E., Tatian compiled a harmonized account of the life and ministry of Jesus Christ, combining the four Gospels into a single narrative (Diatessaron means "of the four"). Another who willfully revised the New Testament was Lucian of Antioch (c. 240-312 C.E.). Lucian produced the Syrian text, renamed the Byzantine text. About 290 C.E. some of his associates made various subsequent alterations, deliberately combining elements from earlier types of text, and this text was adopted about 380 C.E. At Constantinople it became the predominant form of the New Testament throughout the Greek-speaking world. The text was also edited, with parallel accounts harmonized, grammar corrected, and abrupt transitions modified to produce a smooth text. As a result, this was not a faithfully accurate copy. However, others willfully altered the text to have it support their doctrinal position. Marcion (c. 85-c. 160 C.E.), a semi-Gnostic of the second century C.E., is a leading example. In fact, the idea of forming a catalog of authoritative Christian writings did not come to mind until Marcion. One such catalog was the Muratorian Fragment, Italy (170 C.E.) The list shows 24 books of the New Testament being accepted without question as Scriptural and canonical, some uncertainty about 2 Peter, and Hebrews and James were not listed, possibly unknown. In the end, we must admit that there were heretics who altered the text to make it align with their doctrinal positions, but also Orthodox Christians who also altered the text to strengthen their doctrinal positions.

We must keep in mind that we are dealing with an oral society. Therefore, the apostles, who had spent three and a half years with Jesus, first published the Good News orally. The teachers within the newly founded Christian congregations would repeat this information until it was memorized. Thereafter, those who had heard this gospel would, in turn, share it with others (Acts 2:42, Gal 6:6). In time, they would see the need for a written record so Matthew, Luke, Mark, and John would pen the Gospels, and other types of New Testament books would be written by Paul, James, Peter, and Jude. We can see from the first four verses of Luke that **Theophilus**[270] was being given a written record of what he had already been taught orally. In verse 4, Luke says to Theophilus, "[My purpose is] that you may know the exact truth about the things you have been taught."

The appearance of the written record did not mean the end of the oral publication. Both oral and written would be used together. Most did

---

[270] **Theophilus** means "friend of God," was the person to whom the books of Luke and Acts were written (Lu 1:3; Ac 1:1). Theophilus was called "most excellent," which may suggest some position of high rank. On the other hand, it simply may be Luke offering an expression of respect. Theophilus had initially been orally taught about Jesus Christ and his ministry. Thereafter, it seems that the book of Acts, also by Luke, confirms that he did become a Christian. The Gospel of Luke was partially written to offer Theophilus assurances of the certainty of what he had already learned by word of mouth.

not read the written records themselves, as they would hear them read in the congregational meetings by the lector. Paul and his letters came to be used in the same way as he traveled extensively but was just one man and could only be in one place at a time. It was not long before he took advantage of the fact that he could be in one place and dispatch letters to other locations through his traveling companions. These traveling companions would not only deliver the letters but would know the issues well enough to address questions that might be asked by the leaders of the congregation to which they had been dispatched. In summary, the first century saw the life and ministry of Jesus Christ, the Son of God, as well as his death, resurrection, and ascension. After that, his disciples spread this gospel orally for at least 15 years before Matthew penned his gospel. The written was used in conjunction with the oral message.

In the first-century C.E., the Bible books were being copied individually. In the late first century or the beginning of the second century, they began to be copied in groups. At first, it was the four gospels and then the book of Acts with the four gospels, as well as a collection of the Apostle Paul's writings. Each of the individual books of the New Testament were penned, edited, and published between 44 and 98 C.E. A group of the apostle Paul's letters and the gospels were copied and published between 90 to 125 C.E. The entire 27 books of the New Testament were not published as a whole until about 290 to 340 C.E.

Thus, we have the 27 books of the New Testament that were penned individually in the second half of the first century. Each of these would have been copied and recopied throughout the first century. Copies of these copies would, of course, be made as well. Some of the earliest manuscripts that we now have indicate that a professional scribe copied them. Many of the other papyri provide evidence that a semi-professional hand copied them, while most of these early papyri give evidence of being made by a copyist who was literate and experienced at making documents. Therefore, either literate or semi-professional copyists produced the vast majority of our early papyri, with some being made by professionals. The first century Christians carried out their evangelism with a sense of urgency because the great apostasy was on the horizon, not so much that the end was nigh. So, yes, the spread of Christianity definitely had an impact on our efforts of ascertaining the original wording of the original text. The early Christians were seeking to evangelize the world because of the foretold apostasy that was coming, they viewed the books of the twenty-seven New Testament books as inspired in the same way that the Jews viewed the thirty-nine Old Testament books as inspired, and, again, literate or semi-professional copyists produced the vast majority of our early papyri, with some being made by professionals.

How Were the Scriptures Impacted by the Persecution of Early Christians?

Jesus had told his followers, "'a slave is not greater than his master.' If they persecuted me, they will also persecute you. If they kept my word, they will keep yours also.'" (John 15:20) Certainly, the growth of Christianity from 120 disciples on Pentecost 33 C.E. to over one million by the middle of the second century was a frightening thought to the pagan mind as well as Judaism. Thus, shortly after the death and resurrection of Jesus Christ, the pagan population, Judaism, and the Roman government began the very persecution of which Jesus had warned. However, it was in the fourth century, under the Roman Emperor Diocletian, that a program of persecution began with the intent of wiping out Christianity. In 303 C.E., Diocletian spread a series of progressively harsh edicts against Christians. This brought about what some historians have called "The Great Persecution."

Diocletian's first edict ordered the burning of copies of the Scriptures and the destruction of Christian houses of worship. Harry Y. Gamble writes, "Diocletian's edict of 303 ordering the confiscation and burning of Christian books is itself important evidence, in both its assumptions and results. At the start of the fourth century, Diocletian took it for granted that every Christian community, wherever it might be, had a collection of books and knew that those books were essential to its viability." (Gamble 1995, 150) Church historian Eusebius of Caesarea, in his *Ecclesiastical History*, reported, "all things in truth were fulfilled in our day, when we saw with our very eyes the houses of prayer cast down to their foundations from top to bottom, and the inspired and sacred Scriptures committed to the flames in the midst of the market-places." (Cruse 1998, VIII, 1. 9-11.1) The Christians who were most affected by the persecution lived in Palestine, Egypt, and North Africa. In fact, just three months after Diocletian's edict, the mayor of the North African city of Cirta, which was destroyed in the beginning of the 4th century and was rebuilt by the Roman Emperor Constantine the Great, is said to have ordered the Christians to give up all of their "writings of the law" and "copies of scripture." It is quite clear that the intent of Diocletian and local leaders was to wipe out the Word of God.

The authorities had many Christians who obeyed the decrees by handing over their copies of the Scriptures. Nevertheless, some refused to give up their copies of God's Word. Bishop Felix of Thibiuca (d. 303 C.E.) in Africa was martyred during the Great Persecution alongside Audactus, Fortunatus, Januarius, and Septimus.[271] Felix resisted the command of the

---

[271] These men may have been deacons but, apart from their joint martyrdom with Felix, more about their identities is unknown at the time of this writing.

local magistrate Magnillian (Lat. *Magnillianus*) to surrender his congregation's copies of the Christian Scriptures. One account had Felix and the others being taken to Carthage and decapitated on July 15, 303 C.E. Other Christian leaders deceived the leaders by handing in their pagan writings, safeguarding their Scriptures.

The Diocletian persecution was, in the end, unsuccessful. Many Christian libraries escaped the persecution of Diocletian. Two of the best collections today, the Beatty and Bodmer papyri, survived the fires. Alfred Chester Beatty (1875-1968), at the age of 32, had amassed a fortune. As a collector of books, he had over 50 papyrus codices, both religious and secular, which are dated earlier than the fourth century C.E. There are seven consisting of portions of Old Testament books, and three consisting of portions of the New Testament (P45 c. 250, P46 c. 175–225, and P47 c. 250-300). Martin Bodmer (1899-1971) was also a wealthy collector, who discovered twenty-two papyri in Egypt in 1952 which contained parts of the Old and New Testaments, as well as other early Christian literature. Particularly noteworthy are the New Testament Bodmer papyri, which consist of P66 dating to c. 200 C.E. and P75 dating to c. 175 C.E. Many in rural Egypt would have heard of the persecution in Alexandria, likely making great efforts to remove their manuscripts from their congregations, hiding them until the persecution was lifted.

The men known as the *readers* in the early Christian congregations, who read from the Scriptures during the meeting, carried the burden of preserving the Word of God beyond preserving accurate copies.[272] They also would have guarded them during times of persecution. Because of the mass persecution against Alexandria, Egypt,[273] we owe the primary preservation of our New Testament manuscripts to those congregations within rural Egypt. During times of persecution, manuscripts would not have been housed in the facilities of the congregation but rather would have been hidden in homes. Because of the dry sands of Egypt, the professional scribal practices, and the courage of the Christians, we not only owe the Egyptian Christians for the preservation of the New Testament but also for the original *words* that made up the New Testament. If we look at the manuscripts copied right after the Diocletian persecution (Codex Vaticanus and Sinaitic c. 350 C.E.), they are reflective of the manuscripts from rural Egypt that survived, such as P4, 64, 67 from Coptos, P13 from

---

[272] Some may have been scribes as well but not all. Retaining accurate, fresh copies for the congregation entailed reaching out to scribes or scriptoriums, to acquire copies for their congregation.

[273] This is not to say that no manuscripts survived the persecution in Alexandria; it is possible that some came through the flames.

Oxyrhynchus, and P[46] from Fayum, and P[75] from Abu Mana. (P. W. Comfort 1992, 16-17)

What we do know is that by the time we get to the era of the Diocletian persecution (February 23, 303 – July 25, 306.), the authorities were well aware that there were still many copies of the New Testament throughout the Roman Empire. Otherwise, there would have been no need on February 24, 303 for Diocletian's first "Edict against the Christians" to be published. Diocletian thought he could eradicate Christianity by destroying its sacred writings. After the persecution of Diocletian and Constantine succeeding his father on July 25, 306, Constantine immediately ended any persecutions that were ongoing at that time and offered Christians complete restitution of what they had lost under the persecution. When Constantine issued the Edict of Milan of **313 C.E.**, Christianity was legalized in the Roman Empire, at which point, the church would have seen the need to dramatically increase the number of copies of the Scriptures. Now that Christianity was no longer being persecuted, Christian scribes could openly make copies of the New Testament manuscripts.

In **331 C.E.**, Constantine had ordered Eusebius to prepare fifty copies of entire Bible to be written on prepared parchment for distribution to the churches he intended to build in Constantinople. (Eus., Vit. Const. 4.36.2) From this small order placed by Constantine, we can only imagine how many copies had been made in the churches throughout the entire Roman Empire. It has been estimated that there were some fifteen hundred to two thousand manuscripts of the Greek New Testament copied in the fourth century C.E. (J. Duplacy) While we certainly took a loss in the number of copies that may have come down to us today as a result of ongoing sporadic persecution of Christianity in those first two and a half centuries after the death of the apostle Paul at the hands of the Roman Emperor Nero in about 65 C.E. up unto Diocletian (303-306 C.E.), there is little doubt that the storehouse of Greek original language manuscripts (5836+) that we do possess are an envy of the secular historians, who have next to nothing in comparison.

CHAPTER 9 What Are Textual Variants [Errors] and How Many Are There?

The first part of this chapter will cover the gist of what is most often discussed in New Testament textual criticism today. After that, we will discuss what should be the primary focus of NTTC (New Testament Textual Criticism). It would seem that Bart D. Ehrman and other Bible critics of his persuasion have sent many textual scholars on a quest. These scholars have become obsessed with discussing how many variants there are, how to count the textual variants, and whether they are significant or insignificant. Below, we will cover what is being said about variants, as well as whether some are more significant than others, and then close the chapter with what actually is the most important mission in NTTC.

Some Bible critics seem, to begin with, the belief that if the originals were inspired of God and fully inerrant, the subsequent copies must continue to be inerrant in order for the inerrancy of the originals to have value. They seem to be asking, "If only the originals were inspired, and the copies were not inspired, and we do not have the originals, how are we to be certain of any passage in Scripture?" In other words, God would never allow the inspired, inerrant Word to suffer copying errors. Why would he perform the miracle of inspiring the message to be fully inerrant and not continue with the miracle of inspiring the copyists throughout the centuries to keep it inerrant? First, we must acknowledge that God has not given us the specifics of every decision he has made in reference to humans. If we begin asking, "Why did God not do this or do that," where would it end? For example, why didn't God just produce the books himself, and miraculously deliver them to people as he gave the commandments to Moses? Instead of using humans, why did he not use angelic messengers to pen the message, or produce the message miraculously? God has chosen not to tell us why he did not move the copyists along with the Holy Spirit, so as to have perfect copies, and it remains an unknown. However, it should be noted that if we can restore the text to its original wording through the science of textual criticism, i.e. to an exact representation thereof, we have, in essence, the originals.

We do know that the Jewish copyists and later Christian copyists were not infallible as were the original writers. The Holy Spirit inspired the original writers, while the most that can be said about the copyists is that they were **guided** by the Holy Spirit. However, do we not have a treasure-load of evidence from centuries of copies, unlike ancient secular literature? Regardless of the recopying, do we not have the Bible in a reliable critical text and trustworthy translations, with both improving all the time? It was only inevitable that imperfect copyists, who were not under inspiration, would cause errors to creep into the text. However, the thousands of copies that we have enable textual scholars to identify and reject these errors. How? For one thing, different copyists made different errors. Therefore, the textual scholar compares the work of different copyists. He is then able to identify their mistakes.

A Simple Example

Suppose 100 people were invited or hired to make a handwritten copy of Matthew's Gospel, with 18,345 words. Further suppose that these people fit in one of four categories as writers: **(1)** struggle to write and have no experience as a document maker; **(2)** skilled document makers (recorders of events, wills, business, certificates, etc.); **(3)** trained copyists of literature; and **(4)** the professional copyists. There is little doubt that these copyists would make some copying errors, even the professionals. However, it would be impossible that they would all make the same errors. If a trained textual scholar with many years of religious education, including textual studies, and decades of experience, were to compare the 100 documents carefully, he could identify the errors and restore the text to its original form, even if he had never seen that original.

The textual scholars of the last 250 years, especially the last 70 years have had over 5,800 Greek manuscripts at their disposal. A number of the manuscripts are portions dating to the second and third centuries C.E. Moreover, more manuscripts are always becoming known; technology is ever advancing, and improvements are always being made.

Hundreds of scholars throughout the last three centuries have produced what we might call a master text, by way of lifetimes of hard work and careful study. Are there places where we are not certain of the reading? Yes, of course. However, we are considering very infrequent places in the text of the Greek NT that contains about 138,020 words, which would be considered difficult in arriving at what the original reading was. In all these places the alternative readings are provided in the apparatus. Bible critics who exaggerate the extent of errors are misleading the public on several fronts. First, some copies are almost error-free and negate the critics, who claim, "We have only error-ridden copies."[274] Second, the vast majority of the Greek New Testament has no scribal errors. Third, textual scholarship can easily identify and correct the majority of the scribal errors. In addition, of the remaining errors, we can still say most are

---

[274] (Bart D. Ehrman, Misquoting Jesus: The Story Behind Who Changed the Bible and Why 2005, 7)

solved with satisfaction. Of the small number of scribal errors remaining, we can say that most are solved with some difficulty, and there remain very few errors of which textual scholarship continues to be uncertain about the original reading at this time.

400,000 to 500,000 Supposed Variants in the Manuscripts

With this abundance of evidence, what can we say about the total number of variants known today? Scholars differ significantly in their estimates—some say there are 200,000 variants known, some say 300,000, some say **400,000 or more!** We do not know for sure because, despite impressive developments in computer technology, no one has yet been able to count them all. Perhaps, as I indicated earlier, it is best simply to leave the matter in comparative terms. There are more variations among our manuscripts than there are words in the New Testament.[275]

Bart D. Ehrman has some favorite, unprofessional ways of describing the problems, which he stresses without qualification, in every interview he has for a lay audience or seminary students. Below are several, the first two from the quotation above:

- Scholars differ significantly in their estimates—some say there are 200,000 variants known, some say 300,000, some say **400,000 or more!**

- There are **more variations** among our manuscripts **than there are words** in the New Testament.

- We have only **error-ridden copies,** and the vast majority of these are centuries removed from the originals and different from them, evidently, in thousands of ways. (*Whose Word is It*, 7)

- We don't even have copies of the copies of the originals, or **copies of the copies of the copies of the originals.** (*Misquoting Jesus*, 10)

- **In the early Christian centuries, scribes were amateurs** and as such were more inclined to alter the texts they copied. (*Misquoting Jesus*, 98)

- **We could go on nearly forever** talking about specific places in which the texts of the New Testament came to be changed, either accidentally or intentionally. (*Misquoting Jesus*, 98)

- The Bible began to appear to me as a very **human book.** (*Misquoting Jesus*, 11)

---

[275] Ibid., 89-90

Each of the bullet points above claimed by Ehrman can be categorized as an exaggeration, misinformation, misleading, or just a failure to be truthful. Many laypersons-churchgoers have been spiritually shipwrecked in their faith by such unexplained hype. What the uninformed person hears is that we can never get back to the originals or even close, that there are hundreds of thousands of significant variants that have so scarred the text, we no longer have the Word of God, and it is merely the word of man. How such a knowledgeable man cannot know the impact his words are having is beyond this author.

Miscounting Textual Variants

In 1963, Neil R. Lightfoot penned a book that has served to help over a million readers, *How We Got the Bible*. It has been revised two times since 1963, once in 1988, and again in 2003. There is a "miscalculation" in the book which has contributed to a misunderstanding in how textual variants are counted. In fact, there are several other books repeating it. A leading textual scholar, Daniel B. Wallace, has brought this to our attention in an article entitled, *The Number of Textual Variants an Evangelical Miscalculation.*[276] World-renowned Bible apologist Norman L. Geisler has commented on it as well.

Lightfoot wrote,

> From one point of view, it may be said that there are 200,000 scribal errors in the manuscripts. Indeed, the number may well considerably exceed this and obviously will grow, as more and more manuscripts become known. However, it is wholly misleading and untrue to say that there are 200,000 errors in the text of the New Testament. (Actually, textual critics consciously avoid the word "error;" they prefer to speak of "textual variants.") This large number is gained by counting all the variations in all of the manuscripts (over 5,800). This means that if, for example, one word is misspelled in 4,000 different manuscripts, and it amounts to 4,000 "errors." Actually, in a case of this kind, only one slight error has been made, and it has been copied 4,000 times. But this is the procedure which is followed in arriving at the large number of 200,000 "errors."[277]

Wallace makes this observation in his article:

---

[276] http://bible.org/article/number-textual-variants-evangelical-miscalculation

[277] *How We Got the Bible* (Grand Rapids: Baker, 2003; p). Lightfoot says (53-54)

In other words, Lightfoot was claiming that textual variants are counted by the number of manuscripts that support such variants, rather than by the wording of the variants. This book has been widely influential in evangelical circles. I believe over a million copies of it have been sold. And this particular definition of textual variants has found its way into countless apologetic works." He goes on to clarify just what a textual variant is, "The problem is, the definition is wrong. Terribly wrong. A textual variant is simply any difference from a standard text (e.g., a printed text, a particular manuscript, etc.) that involves spelling, word order, omission, addition, substitution, or a total rewrite of the text. No textual critic defines a textual variant the way that Lightfoot and those who have followed him have done.

Geisler writes,

Some have estimated there are about 200,000 of them. First of all, these are not "errors" but variant readings, the vast majority of which are strictly grammatical. Second, these readings are spread throughout more than 5300 manuscripts, so that a variant spelling of one letter of one word in one verse in 2000 manuscripts is counted as 2000 "errors."[278]

Lightfoot evidently was thought to have erred by counting manuscripts, rather than the variants in the text. In fairness to Lightfoot, it should be pointed out that he deplored the system of counting "errors" by the number of manuscripts, as the quotation above reveals. He was simply saying that critics were doing this, not that it was proper. It is difficult to see why Wallace would attribute responsibility for the system to Lightfoot. Also, Wallace cited Lightfoot's 1963 edition that did not include the distinction between "error" and "textual variant."

Let me offer the reader an example for our purposes. First, we should underscore a few important points raised: 1) we have so many variants because we have so many manuscripts. 2) We do *not* count the manuscripts; we count the variants. 3) A variant is any portion of the text that exhibits variations in its reading between two or more different manuscripts. This is more precisely called a **variation unit**. It is important to distinguish variation units from variant readings. Variation units are the places in the text where manuscripts disagree, and each variation unit has at least two variant readings. Setting the limits and range of a variation unit is sometimes difficult or even controversial because some variant readings

---

[278] *Baker Encyclopedia of Christian Apologetics*, by Norm Geisler (Grand Rapids: Baker, 1998; p. 532)

affect others nearby. Such variations may be considered individually, or as elements of a longer single reading.

We should also note that the terms "manuscript" and "witness" may appear to be used interchangeably in this context. Strictly speaking, "witness" (see below) only refers to the content of a given manuscript or fragment, so the witness predates the physical manuscript on which it is written to a greater or lesser extent. However, the only way to reference the "witness" is by referring to the manuscript or fragment that contains it. In this book, we have sometimes used the terminology "witness *of* x or y manuscript" to distinguish the content in this way.

We begin by choosing our "base" or "standard text." We are using the *standard text* (critical or master text), Nestle-Aland (NA) Greek Text (28th edition) and the United Bible Society (UBS) Greek Text (5th edition). These two critical texts are actually the same. Therefore,

Note: When the acronym **NU** is used, N stands for Nestle-Aland, the U for United Bible Societies, since the texts are the same. The apparatuses are different, the UBS version designed primarily for translators (more on this below).

In this writer's opinion, the critical NU text is as close as we can get to what the original would have been like.[279] Therefore, we can use the reading in the critical text as the original reading, and anything outside of that in the manuscript history is a variant: spelling, word order, omission, addition, substitution, or a total rewrite of the text. Any difference in two different manuscripts is a variant, technically speaking.

Before going to our example, I want to emphasize that Bible critics, who grumble and repeat over and over again how there are 400,000 variants in the text of the New Testament, have only one agenda: they want to discredit the Word of God. They use the issue of variants as a misrepresented excuse for their having lost their faith, having shipwrecked their faith, or having had no faith from the start. These Bible critics are no different from the religious leaders Jesus dealt with in the first century. Jesus said of them, "Blind guides! You strain out a gnat, yet gulp down a camel!" (Matt. 23:24). They thrust aside 99.95 percent because 0.05 of one per

---

[279] It is true that some scholars, such as Philip Comfort, argue that the NU could be improved upon because in many cases it is too dependent on internal evidence, when the documentary evidence should be more of a consideration in choosing readings. It should be pointed out, however, that this is in only a relative handful of places, when one considers 138,020 words in the Greek New Testament, and it is hardly consequential. I would also mention that this writer would agree with Comfort in the matter of giving more weight to documentary evidence.

cent is in not absolutely certain! Now let's turn to our example, which comes from the Apostle Paul's letter to the Colossians.

Example of a Textual Variant

Colossians 2:2 Updated American standard Version (UASV)

[2] that their hearts may be comforted, having been knit together in love, and into all riches of the full assurance of understanding, and that they may have a complete knowledge[280] of the mystery **of God**, namely **Christ**, [τοῦ θεοῦ Χριστοῦ; tou theou Christou]

See the chart below.

Variants	Variant	MSS or Versions
NU[281]	of the God of Christ	Standard Text
1	of the God	10 MSS[282]
2	of the Christ	1 MS
3	of the God who is Christ	4 MSS
4	of the God who is concerning Christ	2 MSS
5	Of the God in the Christ	2 MSS
6	of the God in the Christ Jesus	1 MS
7	of the God and Christ	1 MS
8	Of God the father Christ	4 MSS
9	Of God the father of Christ	5 MSS
10	Of God and Father of Christ	2 MSS
11	Of God father and of Christ	4 MSS
12	Of God father and of Christ Jesus	3 MSS
13	Of God father and of Lord of us Christ Jesus	2 MSS
14	Of God and father and of Christ	38 MSS
Total 14	14 Variants in 79 MSS	79 MSS

---

[280] *Epignosis* is a strengthened or intensified form of *gnosis* (*epi*, meaning "additional"), meaning, "true," "real," "full," "complete" or "accurate," depending upon the context. Paul and Peter alone use *epignosis*.

[281] Recall that NU is an acronym for two critical manuscripts: (1) Nestle-Aland Greek Text (28th ed.) and (2) United Bible Societies Greek Text (5th ed.)

[282] This is only a partial list of the manuscripts, as we are just offering an example, to see how we count the variants.

These variants are found in 79 MSS. Thus, we have 14 variants in 79 manuscripts, not 79 variants. We do not count manuscripts, as most textual scholars know. In trying to paint a picture about the trustworthiness of the text, this author does not think talking about variants is really helpful, and it can confuse the layperson. It is important for the churchgoer to know what a variant is and the general extent of the variants, but in the long run, it is the places in the text that are affected by variants that most matter, and what we have as our text in the end.

The United Bible Society's "A" "B" "C" and "D" ratings are fine, and the definitions by UBS, i.e., [A] **certain**, [B] **almost certain**, [C] **difficulty in deciding**, and [D] **great difficulty in arriving at**, are helpful but should be better qualified, with some numbers of what percentage of the text fall under each area.

All Variant Units (Places)

What we need to talk about is how many **places** there are where we find variants. What percentage is this of the entire New Testament text?

We can then discuss:

- What percentage of the text is untouched by variants?
- Of the percentage affected, how much can we say or surmise to be given an "A" rating, a "B" Rating, a "C," or "D" rating?

Variant Reading and Variation Unit

This section is based in large part on the work by Eldon Jay Epp and Gordon D. Fee, *Studies in the Theory and Method of New Testament Textual Criticism* (Grand Rapids, MI: Eerdmans, 1993), wherein Eldon J. Epp expands on the brief 1964 article of Ernest C. Colwell (1901–74) and Ernest W. Tune on "Variant Readings: Classification and Use."

Again, what we need to discuss is how many variation units (places) there are where we find variations. Before doing so, let us define some terms.

SIGNIFICANT AND INSIGNIFICANT READINGS AND OR VARIANTS: Below we have what are commonly described as significant and insignificant variants. *Significant* would mean any reading that has an impact on the transmission history of a variant unit. For example, it would apply to how we determine the relationship of the manuscripts to one another, such as where a particular manuscript would fall in the history and transmission of the manuscripts. It would also be impactful if the reading could help the textual scholar establish the original. Therefore, *insignificant* would mean just the opposite, referring to a reading that has very little to no impact at all in *many* aspects of a transmission history. The reason we stop at "many" aspects here is that all readings in a manuscript play a role in some aspects of the transmission history, such as the characteristics of the manuscript it is in and the scribal activity within that individual manuscript.

Insignificant—Nonsense Reading: As Epp points out, a nonsense reading is "a reading that fails to make sense because it cannot be construed grammatically, either in terms of grammatical/lexical form or in terms of grammatical structure, or because in some other way it lacks a recognizable meaning. Since authors and scribes do not produce nonsense intentionally, it is to be assumed (1) that nonsense readings resulted from errors in transmission, (2) that they, therefore, cannot represent either the original text or the intended text of any MS or alert scribe, and (3) that they do not aid in the process of discerning the relationships among MSS."[283] It should also be stated that the original did not contain any nonsense readings, as the writers were led by the Holy Spirit. The inspired author before publication would have corrected any error by a scribe such as Tertius or Silvanus.

Insignificant—Certainty of Scribal Errors: while these errors "can be construed grammatically and make sense," there is a certainty on the part of textual scholars that these are scribal errors. These are not nonsense readings but rather readings that make sense, which are scribal errors beyond all reasonable doubt. These would "be certain instances of haplography and dittography, cases of harmonization with similar contexts, hearing errors producing a similar-sounding word, and the transposition of letters or words with a resultant change in meaning."[284] The problem that we sometimes encounter here is that what may be *certainty* of scribal error to one scholar may instead be an *almost certainty* to another, and even less so to another. The key element here in determining a reading that is understandable as insignificant is that it can be "demonstrated" so by the scholar making such a claim.

Insignificant—Incorrect Orthography (Greek for "correct writing"): this term is used loosely to refer to the spelling of words, which (for Greek) can include breathing and accent marks. Thus, one can refer to variations in the orthography of a word, or even to incorrect orthography. When a variation in orthography is due merely to dialectical or historical changes in spelling for variant readings, the variations are often ignored in the decision process because the reading in question is identical to another

---

[283] Eldon Jay Epp and Gordon D. Fee, *Studies in the Theory and Method of New Testament Textual Criticism* (Grand Rapids, MI: Eerdmans, 1993), 58.

[284] Ibid. 58.

reading, once the orthographical differences are factored in (*mutatis mutandis*). Epp writes, "Mere orthographic differences, particularly itacisms and nu-movables (as well as abbreviations) are 'insignificant' as here defined; they cannot be utilized in any decisive way for establishing manuscript relationships, and they are not substantive in the search for the original text. Again, the exception might be the work of a slavish scribe, whose scrupulousness might be considered useful in tracing manuscript descent, but the pervasive character of itacism, for example, over wide areas and time-spans precludes the 'significance' of orthographic differences for this important text-critical task."[285]

Insignificant—Singular Readings: a singular reading is technically a variant reading that occurs only once in only one Greek manuscript and is therefore immediately suspect. There is some quibbling over this because critics who reject the Westcott and Hort position on the combination of 01 (Sinaiticus) and 03 (Vaticanus) might call a reading "nearly singular" if it has only the support of these two manuscripts. Moreover, it is understood that not all manuscripts are comparable. Thus, for example, one would comfortably reject a reading found only in a single late manuscript, while many critics would not find it so easy to reject a reading supported uniquely by 03. Some also give more credit to singular readings that have additional support from versions. Singular readings that are insignificant would be nonsense readings, transcriptional errors, meaningless transpositions, and itacisms.

Significant Variants: a *significant* reading/variant is any reading that has an impact on any major facet of transmission history of a variant unit. One approach to identifying these is to remove the insignificant variants first: nonsense readings, determined (without doubt) scribal errors, incorrect orthography, and singular readings. Those readings that cannot be ruled out in this process are probably significant.

Number of Variants, Significant and Insignificant Variants vs. Level of Certainty

It would seem that some scholars have lost sight of the most important goal of textual criticism, namely, reconstructing the original. There is little doubt that agnostic Bible scholar Dr. Bart D. Ehrman has led the conversation on how many textual variants exist. The author of this publication are focusing their attention on the initial goal of textual criticism, returning to the original. We believe that even now the Greek New Testament completely reliable. However, there are some 2,000

---

[285] Ibid. 58.

textual places within the New Testament that need to be dealt with because the witnesses and internal evidence require consideration and deliberation.

Level of Certainty

The level of certainty charts below is generated from A TEXTUAL COMMENTARY ON THE GREEK NEW TESTAMENT (Second Edition), A Companion Volume to the UNITED BIBLE SOCIETIES' GREEK NEW TESTAMENT (Fourth Revised Edition) by Bruce M. Metzger.

The letter {A} signifies that the text is certain.

The letter {B} indicates that the text is almost certain.

The letter {C} indicates that the Committee had difficulty in deciding which variant to place in the text.

The letter {D}, which occurs only rarely, indicates that the Committee had great difficulty in arriving at a decision. In fact, among the {D} decisions sometimes none of the variant readings commended itself as original, and therefore the only recourse was to print the least unsatisfactory reading.

The word count below is taken from the Nestle-Aland Novum Testamentum Graece using Logos Bible Software.[286] While this author has compiled the numbers regarding the level of certainty of readings from Metzger's Textual Commentary, he has not gone to the point of counting the letters or words at each variant place. We will just offer the reader the general statement that almost all textual variants in the commentary were based on a letter or a few letters in a Greek word, to two-three words. Seldom was it an entire sentence or verse, very rarely several verses like the long ending of Mark. Therefore, we have chosen three words as the average to multiply the total number of variants, so that the reader can see the truly small number of variants that are even worthy of consideration, as opposed to the total number of words in the New Testament. For example, Matthew has 18,346 words with a mere 153 places where we find variants selected for the GNT, affecting about 459 words.

We need to add and emphasize, that all of the variants counted were selected by the GNT editors as relevant for translation, and the total does not include other variant units that were not considered relevant for that purpose. A good number of these additional variants can be found in the NA apparatus, but only with considerable difficulty in many cases because the same variants are frequently handled differently in the GNT and NA apparatuses. The author of this book do consider all variant units relevant

---

[286] Word Counts for Every Book of the Bible ..., http://overviewbible.com/word-counts-books-of-bible/ (accessed April 20, 2017).

even if a good number of them are difficult or virtually impossible to represent in translation (depending on the target language), and we recommend that the reader adjust the figures offered below by multiplying the numbers of variants by a factor of two, which should compensate for any variants that are not reported in the GNT text. We see no reason to assume a significantly different outcome in the ratings that might have been assigned to these variants if they had been included in the GNT, except possibly where no decisions might be possible in the cases of competing readings that were fully acceptable (rather than difficult).

For readers who have a working knowledge of NT Greek, it may be informative simply to select a few random pages of corresponding text from the GNT and NA and compare the apparatuses to see what is missing from the GNT relative to the NA apparatus. We believe that our suggestion of multiplying the variant figures below by a factor of two will appear more than reasonable; however, even using a factor of three or four will still leave a relatively minute percentage of "C" and "D" readings, as revealed below.

So then, if we look at Matthew and first multiply the GNT variant units by three for an average three words a variant, we have 459 words. Of the 153 variant units found in Matthew, we are certain of about 32 of them, almost certain about 70, have a little difficulty deciding on 50, and great difficulty deciding on only one variant unit. When we say that we have difficulty deciding, this does not mean that we cannot decide, as we can. Moreover, a good translation will list the alternative reading in a footnote. So, in the entirety of the Gospel of Matthew, there is only one variant place (Matt 23:26) which we would count as about three out of 18,346 words, where there was great difficulty in deciding the original. As it turns out, in this case, the GNT apparatus handles it as a variant of eight words, while NA breaks it into two variants, thus illustrating our point about the difficulty of comparing the two apparatuses. Some translations have incorporated the variant (ESV, NASB, NIV, TNIV, NJB, and the NLT), viewing it as the original, while other translations (NRSV, NEB, REB, NAB, CSB, and the UASV) see the variant as an addition taken from the previous verse.

Matthew 23:26 Blind Pharisee, cleanse first the inside of the cup,[287] so that the outside of it may also become clean. (UASV)

NU has καθάρισον πρῶτον τὸ ἐντὸς τοῦ ποτηρίου, ἵνα γένηται καὶ τὸ ἐκτὸς αὐτοῦ καθαρόν "first cleanse the **inside of the cup, that the outside**

---

[287] The NU (D Θ f¹ itᵃ·ᵉ syrˢ) has the above reading. A variant, WH and Byz (ℵ (B²) C L W 0102 0281 Maj) add "and of the dish." The variant is an addition taken from the previous verse.

of it may also become clean," which is supported by D Θ f¹ it^{a.e} <u>syr</u>^s (bold mine).

Variant/Byz WH καθαρισον πρωτον το εντος του ποτηριου και της παροψιδος ινα γενηται και το εκτος αυτων καθαρον have "first cleanse the **inside of the cup [and the dish], that the outside** of them may also become clean," which is supported by ℵ (B²) C L W 0102 0281 Maj.

Looking at the above support alone, it would seem that the witnesses for the longer reading ("and the dish") are weightier, making the longer reading the likely original. Then, when we consider the presence of a few manuscripts (B* f¹³ 28 *al*) that are not listed for the shorter reading because they have the longer reading ("and the dish"), the weight shifts over to the shorter reading's being the original. Why? Because these few manuscripts have the singular αυτου instead of αὐτῶν, even though they have the longer reading. This tells us that the archetype text was the shorter reading. Clearly, the copyist added ("and the dish") from the previous verse, Matthew 23:25, which reads, "Woe to you, scribes and Pharisees, hypocrites! because you cleanse **the outside of the cup and of the dish**, but inside they are full of greediness and self-indulgence."

Below, we will look at all of the numbers, the total words in the Greek New Testament, the number of A, B, C, and D variants in each book as they were selected by the GNT committee, followed by the total number of variants listed in Metzger's textual commentary.

The Entire New Testament (138,020 Words)

{A-D}	New Testament
{A}	505
{B}	523
{C}	354
{D}	10
Total Var.	1,392
Words	138,020

The Gospels (64,767 Words)

{A-D}	Matt	Mark	Luke	John
{A}	32	45	44	44
{B}	70	49	73	62
{C}	50	45	44	41

{D}	1	1	0	2
Total Var.	153	140	161	149
Words	18,346	11,304	19,482	15,635

The Acts of the Apostles (18,450 Words)

{A-D}	Acts
{A}	74
{B}	82
{C}	40
{D}	1
Total Var.	197
Words	18,450

Paul's Fourteen Epistles (37,361 Words)

{A-D}	Rom	1 Cor	2 Cor	Gal.	Eph.	Php	Col.
{A}	39	21	12	16	16	10	8
{B}	19	22	17	3	11	7	12
{C}	20	15	10	8	7	3	8
{D}	1	1	0	0	0	0	0
Total Var.	79	59	39	27	34	20	28
WORDS	7,111	6,830	4,477	2,230	2,422	1,629	1,582

{A-D}	1 Th	2 Th	1 Tim	2 Tim	Tit	Phm.	Heb.
{A}	9	3	15	2	2	2	20
{B}	2	3	2	6	1	3	11
{C}	3	2	2	1	1	0	12
{D}	0	0	0	0	0	0	0
Total Var.	14	8	19	9	4	5	43
WORDS	1,481	823	1,591	1,238	659	335	4,953

The General Epistles (7,591 Words)

{A-D}	Jam	1 Pet	2 Pet	1 Jn	2 Jn	3 Jn	Jude
{A}	7	21	8	18	4	1	9
{B}	12	9	7	7	1	1	0
{C}	4	7	6	4	0	0	3
{D}	0	0	1	0	0	0	1
Total Var.	23	37	22	29	5	2	13
WORDS	1,742	1,684	1,099	2,141	245	219	461

The Book of Revelation (9,851 Words)

{A-D}	Revelation
{A}	23
{B}	31
{C}	18
{D}	1
Total Var.	73
Words	9,851

As noted above, the author of this publication maintain that all variation units or places where variations occur are significant because we are dealing with the Word of God, and reconstructing the original wording is of the utmost importance. Recall Lightfoot once more. "What about the significance of these variations? Are these variations immaterial or are they important? What bearing do they have on the New Testament message and on faith? To respond to these questions, it will be helpful to introduce three types of textual variations, classified in relation to their significance for our present New Testament text. 1. Trivial variations which are of no consequence to the text. 2. Substantial variations which are of no consequence to the text. 3. Substantial variations that have bearing on the text."[288]

Whether we are talking about the addition or omission of such words as "for," "and," and "the," or different forms of similar Greek words, differences in spelling, or the addition of a whole verse or even several verses, the importance lies **not with the significance of impact** on the meaning of the text but rather **the certainty** of the wording in the original. What we want to focus on is the certainty level of reconstructing every single word that Matthew, Mark, Luke, John, Paul, Peter, James, and Jude penned.

We will use Lightfoot's example of Matthew 11:10-23, that is, fourteen verses of 231 words; we have eleven variants in verses 10, 15, 16, 17, 18, 19(2), 20, 21, and 23(2). This may seem worrisome to the churchgoer or someone new to textual criticism. However, while all of the variants are found in the NA28 critical apparatus (2012), pp. 31–32,[289] the following sources below only covered seven of them because four are not even an

---

[288] *How We Got the Bibles*, by Neil R. Lightfoot (Grand Rapids: Baker, 1998; p. 95-103)

[289] Eberhard Nestle and Erwin Nestle, *Nestle-Aland: NTG Apparatus Criticus*, ed. Barbara Aland et al., 28. revidierte Auflage. (Stuttgart: Deutsche Bibelgesellschaft, 2012), 31–32.

issue. Why are they not an issue? We know what the original reading is with absolute certainty. The seven that have some uncertainty are mentioned in the textual commentaries below.

- Comfort *New Testament Text and Translation* covers verses 15 and 19

- Comfort *Commentary on the Manuscripts* and Text *of the New Testament* covers verses 12 and 19

- Metzger's *Textual Commentary on the Greek New Testament* covers 15, 17, 19, and 23.

Immediately we need to note that verse 12 is absolutely certain as to the original words as well. Verse 19a is mentioned in Comfort's textual commentary because he is drawing attention to the "Son of Man" being written as a nomen sacrum ("sacred name" that is abbreviated) in two early manuscripts (‭א‬ W), as well as in L. Therefore, verse 19a is absolutely certain as well. We are now down to five variants. The original readings of verses 15, 17, 19a and the two in verse 23 where variants occur are almost certain. The textual scholars on the committees for four leading semi-literal and literal translations (ESV, LEB, CSB, and the NASB) agree on ten of the eleven variants. There is disagreement on **Matthew 11:15**. Even so, the reader has access to the original and alternatives in the footnote.

"He who has ears to hear, let him hear." (ESV, NASB, UASV)

The variant is ο εχων ωτα ακουειν ακουετω "the one having ears to hear let him hear," which is supported by ‭א‬ C L W Z Θ f¹·¹³ 33 Maj syrᶜ·ʰ·ᵖ cop

"The one who has ears to hear, let him hear!" (LEB, cf. CSB)

WH and NU have ὁ ἔχων ὦτα ἀκουέτω "the one having ears let him hear," which is supported by B D 700 itᵏ syrˢ

As is usually the case in more difficult decisions, the variant readings are divided in their support between the leading Alexandrian manuscripts. One reading has 01 (Sinaiticus) on its side, the other has 03 (Vaticanus). This tends to cancel out the weight of documentary evidence.

Now, we return to the charts above. There are 138,020 words in the New Testament. Just 1,392 textual variants deemed relevant for translation have enough of an issue to even be considered in the textual commentary. Again, if we average three words per variant, this amounts only to about 3.026 percent of the 138,020 words, or about 6 percent when we compensate for variant units ignored by the GNT editors. We can also remove the 505 {A} ratings because they are certain. Then, we really have no concerns about the {B} ratings because they are almost certain as well.

This means that out of 138,020 words in the Greek New Testament, we only have 364 variants (1,092 words by our average) with which we have difficulty, a mere 10 of which involve great difficulty in deciding which reading to put in the text. Our average would make these variants 0.791 percent of the text without accounting for any difficult variants not included because they were considered irrelevant for translation.

We need not be disturbed or distracted by worries of how many variants there are, or whether they are significant or insignificant. We need only to deal with the certainty of each variation unit, endeavoring to determine the original reading. We should also be concerned with the role textual criticism plays in apologetics. There is no possibility of apologetics if we do not have an authoritative and true Word of God. J. Harold Greenlee was correct when he wrote, "Textual criticism is the basic study for the accurate knowledge of any text. New Testament textual criticism, therefore, is the basic biblical study, a prerequisite to all other biblical and theological work. Interpretation, systemization, and application of the teachings of the NT cannot be done until textual criticism has done at least some of its work."[290] We would add apologetics to that list for which textual criticism is a prerequisite. How are we to defend the Word of God as inspired, inerrant, true, and authoritative, if we do not know whether we even have the Word of God? Therefore, when Bible critics try to muddy the waters of truth with misinformation, it is up to the textual scholar to correct the Bible critic's misinformation.

Again, it is true that Lightfoot erred if he was counting the manuscripts instead of the variants. However, we need not count variants either but rather variation units, namely, the places where there are variations. The above Colossians 2:2 example of variations that are found in 79 manuscripts was seen to have 14 variants in 79 manuscripts, not 79 variants. While this is true, it is also true that this is simply one variation unit, i.e. one place, where a variation occurs. This may sound as though we are trying to rationalize a major problem of hundreds of thousands of variants. However, it is actually the other way around. The Bible critic is misrepresenting the facts, trying to talk about an issue without giving the reader or listener all of the facts. We need to consider Benjamin Disraeli's words on statistics: "There are three types of lies: lies, damn lies, and statistics."

---

[290] *Introduction to New Testament Textual Criticism*, by J. Harold Greenlee (Peabody: Hendrickson Publishers, 1995; p. 7)

Certainty of the Original Words of the Original Authors

Virgil (70-19 B.C.E.) wrote the *Aeneid* between 29 and 19 B.C.E. for which there are only five manuscripts dating to the fourth and fifth centuries C.E.[291] Jewish historian Josephus (37-100 C.E.) wrote *The Jewish Wars* about 75 C.E., for which we have nine complete manuscripts, seven of major importance dating from the tenth to the twelfth centuries C.E.[292] Tacitus (59-129 C.E.) wrote *Annals of Imperial Rome* sometime before 116 C.E., a work considered vital to understanding the history of the Roman Empire during the first century, and we have only thirty-three manuscripts, two of the earliest that date 850 and 1050 C.E. Julius Caesar (100-44 B.C.E.) wrote his Gallic Wars between 51-46 B.C.E.,[293] which is a firsthand account in a third-person narrative of the war, of which we have 251 manuscripts dating between the ninth and fifteenth centuries.[294]

On the other hand, New Testament textual scholars have over 5,800 Greek manuscripts, not to mention ancient versions such as Latin, Coptic, Syriac, Armenian, Georgian, and Gothic, which number into the tens of thousands. We have many early and reliable manuscripts in Greek and the versions, a good number that cover almost the entire New Testament dating within 100 years of the originals. Therefore, reconstructing the original Greek New Testament is a realistic goal for Bible scholars. This belief and goal that we could anticipate a time when we would recover the original wording of the Greek New Testament had its greatest advocates in the nineteenth century, in Samuel Tregelles (1813-75), B. F. Westcott (1825-1901), and F. J. A. Hort (1828-92). While they acknowledged that we would never recover every word with absolute certainty, they knew that it was always the primary goal to come extremely close to the original. When we entered the twentieth century, there were two textual scholars

---

[291] Preface | Dickinson College Commentaries. (April 25, 2017) http://dcc.dickinson.edu/vergil-aeneid/manuscripts

[292] Honora Howell Chapman (Editor), Zuleika Rodgers (Editor), 2016, A *Companion to Josephus* (Blackwell Companions to the Ancient World), Wiley-Blackwell: p. 307.

[293] Carolyn Hammond, 1996, Introduction to *The Gallic War*, Oxford University Press: p. xxxii.

Max Radin, 1918, The date of composition of Caesar's Gallic War, *Classical Philology* XIII: 283–300.

[294] O. Seel, 1961, *Bellum Gallicum*. (Bibl. Teubneriana.) Teubner, Leipzig.

W. Hering, 1987, *C. Iulii Caesaris commentarii rerum gestarum, Vol. I: Bellum Gallicum.*(Bibl. Teubneriana.) Teubner, Leipzig.

Virginia Brown, 1972, *The Textual Transmission of Caesar's Civil War*, Brill.

Caesar's Gallic war - Tim Mitchell. (April 25, 2017) http://www.timmitchell.fr/blog/2012/04/12/gallic-war/

who have since stood above all others, Kurt Aland and Bruce Metzger. These two men carried the same purpose with them, as they were instrumental in bringing us the Nestle-Aland and the United Bible Societies critical editions, which are at the foundation of almost all modern translations.

From the days of Johann Jacob Griesbach (1745-1812), to Constantin Von Tischendorf (1815-1874), to Samuel Prideaux Tregelles (1813-1875), to Fenton John Anthony Hort (1828-1892), to Kurt Aland (1915-1994), to Bruce M. Metzger (1914-2007),[295] we have been blessed with extraordinary textual scholars. These scholars have devoted their entire lives to providing us the transmission of the New Testament text and the methodologies by which we can recover the original words of the New Testament authors. They did not construct these histories and methodologies from textbooks or in university classrooms. No, they spent decades upon decades in working with manuscripts and putting their methods of textual criticism into practice, as they provided us with one improved critical edition after another. As their knowledge grew, the number of manuscripts which they had to work with fortunately grew as well.

Samuel Tregelles stated that it was his purpose to restore the Greek New Testament text "as nearly as can be done on existing evidence."[296] B. F. Westcott and F. J. A. Hort declared that their goal was "to present exactly the original words of the New Testament, so far as they can now be determined from surviving documents."[297] Metzger said that the goal of textual criticism is "to ascertain from the divergent copies which form of the text should be regarded as most nearly conforming to the original."[298] Sadly, after centuries, textual criticism is losing its way, as new textual scholars have begun to set aside the goal of recovering and establishing the original wording of the Greek New Testament. They have little concern for the certainty of a reading as to whether it is the original.

---

[295] These textual scholars provided us with histories of the transmission of the New Testament text and methodologies. However, we have had dozens of textual scholars who have given their lives to the text of the New Testament. To mention just a few, we have Brian Walton (1600-1661), John Fell (1625-1686), John Mill (1645-1707), Edward Wells (1667-1727), Richard Bentley (1662-1742), Johann Albert Bengel (1687-1752), Johann Jacob Wettstein (1693-1754), Johann Salomo Semler (1725-1791), Johann Leonard Hug (1765-1846), Johann Martin Augustinus Scholz (1794-1852), Karl Lachmann (1793-1851), Erwin Nestle (1883-1972), Allen Wikgren (1906-1998), Matthew Black, (1908-1994), Barbara Aland (1937-present), and Carlo Maria Martini (1927-2012).

[296] Tregelles, *An Account of the Printed Text of the Greek New Testament*, 174.

[297] Westcott and Hort, *Introduction to the New Testament in the Original Greek*, 1.

[298] Metzger, *The Text of the New Testament*, v.

In speaking of the positions of agnostic Bart D. Ehrman (author of *The Orthodox Corruption of Scripture*) and David Parker (author of *The Living Text of the Gospels*), Elliott overserved, "Both emphasize the living and therefore changing text of the New Testament and the needlessness and inappropriateness of trying to establish one immutable original text. The changeable text in all its variety is what we textual critics should be displaying."[299] Elliott then reflects further on his goals within textual criticism: "Despite my own published work in trying to prove the originality of the text in selected areas of textual variation ... I agree that the task of trying to establish the original words of the original authors with 100% certainty is impossible. More dominant in text critics' thinking now is the need to plot the changes in the history of the text. That certainly seemed to be the consensus at one of the sessions of the 1998 SBL conference in Orlando, where the question of whether the original text was an achievable goal received generally negative responses."[300]

We strongly disagree. The goal of textual criticism had been and still should be **to restore** the New Testament Greek text **in every word that was originally penned** by the New Testament authors, in a critical edition. If we are aiming only "to plot the changes in the history of the text," as Elliott put it, we are unable to do so precisely at the time when we have the greatest need to see what happened, i.e. soon after the NT books were first published, if we actually deny and rob ourselves of any chance to recover the original. Then we must admit either that we can never have the complete word of God (the new position), or that any and potentially every quality Greek witness must be considered the word of God. The latter might even be said of a quality version, or at least of readings clearly inferred from such a version. In reality, however, any manuscript that departs from the original in its witness is more or less damaged goods.

We obviously do not think such pessimism is the necessary or inevitable response. In looking at the numbers above as to the certainty level of the restoration of the original Greek New Testament, we have come a long way since John Fell (1625-1686). A spot comparison of changes in ratings between GNT5 and previous GNT editions indicates that the level of certainty is increasing in most cases, and when it does not, the preference tends toward the earliest and most reliable manuscripts.[301] To set aside the

---

[299] J. K. Elliott, *New Testament Textual Criticism: The Application of Thoroughgoing Principles: Essays on Manuscripts and Textual Variation*, 592.

[300] Ibid. 592.

[301] Sample comparisons of the General Epistles in GNT5 with previous GNT editions led to this conclusion. When the level of certainty decreased–which was infrequent compared to the reverse–the trend seemed to be that more weight was being given to 03 and/or 01 in

primary goal of textual criticism now would be an insult to the lives of many textual scholars who preceded us, not to mention to the authors who penned the New Testament books and the Almighty God who inspired them.

---

opposition to internal factors. It is also expected that certainty levels will increase with the use of the CBGM (discussed in detail below).

Bibliography

Abbot, Nabia. 1938. *STUDIES IN ANCIENT ORIENTAL CIVILIZATIONS.* Chocago: The University of Chicago Press.

Aland, Kurt, and Barbara Aland. 1995. *The Text of the New Testament.* Grand Rapids: Eerdmans.

—. 1987. *The Text of the New Testament.* Grand Rapids: Eerdmans.

Aland, Kurt, Matthew Black, and Carlo M. Martini. 1993; 2006. *The Greek New Testament, Fourth Revised Edition (Interlinear With Morphology).* Deutsche Bibelgesellschaft: United Bible Society.

Arndt, William, Frederick W. Danker, and Walter Bauer. 2000. *A Greek-English Lexicon of the New Testament and Other Early Christian Literature. 3rd ed. .* Chicago: University of Chicago Press.

Baer, Daniel. 2007. *The Unquenchable Fire.* Maitland, FL: Xulon Press.

Bagnall, Roger S. 2009. *The Oxford Handbook of Papyrology (Oxford Handbooks).* Oxford: Oxford University Press.

Bagnall, Roger S. 2012. *Everyday Writing in the Græco-Roman East.* Berkeley and Los Angeles, CA: University of California Press.

Balz, Horst, and Gerhard Schneider. 1978. *Exegetical Dictionary of the New Testament.* Edinburgh: T & T Clark Ltd.

Barnett, Paul. 2005. *The Birth of Christianity: The First Twenty Years (After Jesus, Vol. 1) .* Grand Rapids, MI: Wm. B. Eerdmans .

Bercot, David W. 1998. *A Dictionary of Early Christian Beliefs.* Peabody: Hendrickson.

Black, David Alan. 1994. *New Testament Textual Criticism: A Concise Guide.* Grand Rapids, MI: Baker Books.

—. 2002. *Rethinking New Testament Textual Criticism.* Grand Rapids: Baker Books.

Bock, Darrell L, and Daniel B Wallace. 2007. *Dethroning Jesus: Exposing Popular Culture's Quest to Unseat the Biblical Christ.* Nashville: Thomas Nelson.

Borgen, Peder. 1997. *Philo of Alexandria: An Exegete for His Time.* Leiden, Boston: Brill.

Bowman, Alan K. 1998. *Life and Letters on the Roman Frontier: Vindolanda and its People.* London and New York: Routledge.

Brand, Chad, Charles Draper, and England Archie. 2003. *Holman Illustrated Bible Dictionary: Revised, Updated and Expanded.* Nashville, TN: Holman.

Brown, Virginia. 1972. *The Textual Transmission of Caesar's Civil War.* Leiden: Brill.

Capes, David B, Rodney Reeves, and E. Randolph Richards. 2007. *Rediscovering Paul: An Introduction to His World, Letters and Theology.* Downers Grove: IVP Academic.

Carson, D. A, and Douglas J Moo. 2005. *An Introduction to the New Testament.* Grand Rapids, MI: Zondervan.

Carson, D. A. 1994. *New Bible Commentary: 21st Century Edition. 4th ed.* Downers Grove: Inter-Varisity Press.

Clayton, Joseph. 2006. *Luther and His Work.* Whitefish: Kessinger Publishing.

Cmfort, Philip Wesley. 2015. *A Commentary On the Manuscripts and Text of the New Testament.* Grand Rapids: Kregel Publications.

Colwell, E. C. 1969. *Methods in Evaluating Scribal Habits: A Study of P45, P66, P75, in Studies in Methodology in Textual Criticism of the New Testament.* Leiden and Boston: Brill.

Colwell, Ernest C. 1965. *Scribal Habits in Early Papyri: A Study in the Corruption of the Text.* Grand Rapids: Eerdmans.

Comfort, Philip. 2005. *Encountering the Manuscripts: An Introduction to New Testament Paleography and Textual Criticism.* Nashville: Broadman & Holman.

Comfort, Philip W. 2008. *New Testament Text and Translation Commentary.* Carol Stream: Tyndale House Publishers.

Comfort, Philip Wesley. 1992. *The Quest for the Original Text of the New Testament.* Eugene: Wipf and Stock.

Comfort, Philip, and David Barret. 2001. *The Text of the Earliest New Testament Greek Manuscripts.* Wheaton: Tyndale House Publishers.

Cruse, C. F. 1998. *Eusebius' Eccliatical History.* Peabody, MA: Hendrickson.

Deissmann, Adolf. 1910. *LIGHT FROM THE ANCIENT EAST: The New Testament Illustrated by Recently Discovered Texts of the Graeco-Roman World.* New York and London: Hodder and Stoughton.

Dell'Orto, Luisa Franchi. 1990. *Riscoprire Pompei (Rediscovering Pompeii).* Italy: L'Erma di Bretschneider.

Durant, Will & Ariel. 1950. *The Story of Civilization: Part IV—The Age of Faith.* New York, NY: Simon & Schuster.

Ehrman, Bart D. 2005. *Misquoting Jesus: The Story Behind Who Changed the Bible and Why.* New York: Harper One.

—. 2006. *Peter, Paul and Mary Magdalene: The Followers of Jesus in History and Legend.* Oxford: Oxford University Press.

Ehrman, Bart D, and Michael W. Holmes. 2012. *The Text of the New Testament in Contemporary Research: Essays on the Status Quaestionis. Second Edition.* Leiden and Boston: Brill.

Ehrman, Bart D. Holmes, Michael W. 1995. *The Text of the New Testament in Contemporary Research: Essays on the Status Quaestionis .* Grand Rapids, MI: Eerdmans.

Ehrman, Bart D. 2003. *Lost Christianities: The Battles for Scripture and the Faiths We Never Knew .* New York: Oxford University Press.

Elliott, J. K. 2010. *New Testament Textual Criticism: The Application of Thoroughgoing Principles: Essays on Manuscripts and Textual Variation (Novum Testamentum, Supplements).* Leiden: Brill.

Epp, Eldon J. 1993. *Studies in the Theory and Method of New Testament Textual Criticism.* Grand Rapids: Wm. B. Eerdmans Publishing Co.

—. 1989. *Textual Criticism.* Atlanta: Scholars Press.

Evans, Craig A. 2002. *Fabricating Jesus: How Modern Scholars Distort the Gospels.* Downers Grove, IL: InterVaristy Press.

—. 2012. *Jesus and His World: The Archaeological Evidence.* Louisville: Westminster John Knox Press.

Fahlbusch, Erwin (Editor), Jan Milic (Editor) Lochman, John (Editor) Mbiti, Jaroslav (Editor) Pelikan, and Lukas (Editor) Vischer. German 1986, 1989, 1992, 1996, 1997; English 1999, 2001, 2003, 2005. *The Encyclopedia of Christianity (Vol. 1-3).* Grand Rapids: Eerdmans Publishing Company and Koninklijke Brill NV.

Fee, Gordon D. 1993. *P75, P66, and Origen: The Myth of Early Textual Recension in Alexandria, in: E. J. Epp & G. D. Fee, Studies in the*

Theory & Method of NT Textual Criticism. Grand Rapids: Wm. Eerdmans.

Fee, Gordon D. 1974. *P75, P66, and Origen: The Myth of the Early Textual Recension in Alexandria.* Grand Rapids: Zondervan.

—. 1979. *The Textual Criticism of the New Testament.* Grand Rapids: Zondervan.

Ferguson, Everett. 2003. *Backgrounds of Early Christianity.* Grand Rapids, MI: Wm. B. Eerdmans.

Freeman, James M. 1998. *THE NEW MANNERS & CUSTOMS OF THE BIBLE.* Gainesville: Bridge-Logos.

Gamble, Henry Y. 1995. *Books and Readers in the Early Church: A History of Early Christian Texts.* New Haven: New Haven University Press.

Geisler, Norman L, and William E Nix. 1996. *A General Introduction to the Bible.* Chicago: Moody Press.

Geisler, Norman, and David Geisler. 2009. *CONVERSATION EVANGELISM: How to Listen and Speak So You Can Be Heard.* Eugene: Harvest House Publishers.

Goldberg, Sander M. 2005. *Constructing Literature in the Roman Republic (1st Ed.).* Cambridge: Cambridge University Press.

Greenlee, J Harold. 1995. *Introduction to New Testament Textual Criticism.* Peabody: Hendrickson.

—. 2008. *The Text of the New Testament.* Peabody: Henrickson.

Guthrie, Donald. 1990. *Introduction to the New Testament (Revised and Expanded).* Downers Grove, IL: InterVarsity Press.

Haines-Eitzen, Kim. 2000. *Guardians of Letters: Literacy, Power, and the Transmitters of Early Christian Literature.* New York, NY: Oxford University Press.

Hammond, Carolyn. 1996. *Introduction to The Gallic War.* Oxford: Oxford University Press.

Harris, William V. 1989. *Ancient Literacy.* Cambridge, MA: Harvard University Press.

Hatch, William Henry Paine. 45. "A Recently Discovered Fragmrnt of the Epistle to the Romans." *Harvard Theological Review* 81-85.

Head, Peter M. 2004. "The Habits of New Testament Copyists Singular Readings in the Early Fragmentary Papyri of John." *Biblica, Vol. 85, No. 3* 399-408.

Hezser, Catherine. 2001. *Jewish Literacy in Roman Palestine (Texts and Studies in Ancient Judaism)* . Tübingen, Germany: Mohr Siebeck.

Hill, Charles E., and Michael J. Kruger. 2012. *The Early Text of the New Testament.* Oxford: Oxford University Press.

Holmes, Michael W. 1989. *New Testament Textual Criticism.* Grand Rapids: Baker.

—. 2007. *The Apostolic Fathers: Greek Texts and English Translations.* Grand Rapids: Baker Academics.

Hurtado, Larry. 1989. *New International Bible Commentary: Mark. .: .* Peabody, Mass: Hendrickson.

Hurtado, Larry. 1998. "The Origin of the Nominal Sacra." *Journal of Biblical Literature* 655-673.

Jeffers, James S. 1989. *The Greco-Roman World of the New Testament Era: Exploring the Background of Early Christianity.* Downers Grove, IL: InterVarsity Press.

Johnson, William A. 2012 (Reprint). *Readers and Reading Culture in the High Roman Empire: A Study of Elite Communities (Classical Culture and Society).* Oxford, New York: Oxford University Press.

Johnson, William A, and Holt N Parker. 2011. *Ancient Literacies: The Culture of Reading in Greece and Rome.* Oxford: Oxford University Press.

Jones, Timothy Paul. 2007. *Misquoting Truth: A Guide to the Fallacies of Bart Ehrman's Misquoting Jesus.* Downer Groves: InterVarsity Press.

Komoszewski, J. Ed, James M. Sawyer, and Daniel Wallace. 2006. *Reinventing Jesus .* Grand Rapids, MI: Kregel Publications.

Kyrtatas, Dimitris J. 1987. *The Social Structure of the Early Christian Communities.* Brooklyn, NY: Verso.

Lane Fox, Robin. 2006. *Pagans and Christians: In the Mediterranean World from the Second Century AD to the Conversion of Constantine.* City of Westminster, London: Penguin.

Lea, Thomas D., and Hayne P. Griffin. 1992. *The New American Commentary, vol. 34, 1, 2 Timothy, Titus.* Nashville: Broadman & Holman Publishers.

Lightfoot, Joseph Barber, and J. R Harmer. 1891. *The Apostolic Fathers.* London: Macmillan and Co.

Lightfoot, Neil R. 1963, 1988, 2003. *How We Got the Bible.* Grand Rapids, MI: Baker Books.

Malherbe, Abraham J. 1986. *Social Aspects of Early Christianity (2nd ed).* Eugene, OR: Wipf & Stock Pub.

McCarthy, Dan, and Charles Clayton. 1994. *Let the Reader Understand: A guide to Interpreting and Applying the Bible.* Wheaton, Illinois: BridgePoint.

McKenzie, John L. 1975. *Light on the Epistles: A Reader's Guide.* Chicago, IL: Thomas More Press.

McRay, John. 2003. *Paul: His Life and Teaching.* Grand Rapids: Baker Academics.

Meeks, Wayne A. 2003. *The First Urban Christians: The Social World of the Apostle Paul (2nd ed.).* New Haven, CT: Yale University Press.

Metzger, Bruce M. 1964, 1968, 1992. *The Text of the New Testament: Its Transmission, Corruption, and Transmission.* New York: Oxford University Press.

Metzger, Bruce M. 1994. *A Textual Commentary on the Greek New Testament.* New York: United Bible Society.

Metzger, Bruce M., and Bart D. Ehrman. 2005. *The Text of the New Testament: Its Transmission, Corruption, and Restoration (4th Edition).* New York: Oxford University Press.

Metzger, Bruce. 1981. *Manuscripts of the Greek Bible: An Introduction to Palaeography .* New York, NY: Oxford University Press.

Millard, Alan. 2000. *READING AND WRITING IN THE TIME IF JESUS.* New York, NY: NYU Press.

Milnor, Kristina. 2014. *Graffiti and the Literary Landscape in Roman Pompeii.* Eugene, OR: Oxford University Press.

Mounce, Robert H. 2001. *The New American Commentary.* Nashville, TN: Broadman & Holman Publishers.

Mounce, William D. 2006. *Mounce's Complete Expository Dictionary of Old & New Testament Words.* Grand Rapids, MI: Zondervan.

Myers, Allen C. 1987. *The Eerdmans Bible Dictionary .* Grand Rapids, Mich: Eerdmans.

Nestle, Eberhard, and Erwin Nestle. 2012. *Nestle-Aland: NTG Apparatus Criticus, ed. Barbara Aland et al., 28. revidierte Auflage (Revised Edition).* Stuttgart: Deutsche Bibelgesellschaft.

Ohlson, Kristin. 2010. *Smithsonian.com.* July 26. Accessed March 27, 2019. https://www.smithsonianmag.com/history/reading-the-writing-on-pompeiis-walls-1969367/.

Orchard, Bernard (Editor), Longstaff, Thomas R. W. (Editor). 2005. "J. J. Griesbach: Synoptic and Text - Critical Studies 1776-1976." *Society for New Testament Studies Monograph Series (Book 34)* xi.

Orchard, Bernard. 1776-1976, 2005. *J. J. Griesbach: Synoptic and Text - Critical Studies .* Cambridge: Cambridge University Press.

Parker, David C. 1992. *Codex Bezae: An Early Christian Manuscript and its Text.* Cambridge: Cambridge University Press.

Parker, David C. 1997. *The living Text of the Gospels.* Cambridge: Cambridge University Press.

Price, Randall. 2007. *Searching for the Original Bible.* Eugene: Harvest House.

Richards, E. Randolph. 2004. *Paul And First-Century Letter Writing: Secretaries, Composition and Collection.* Downers Grove: InterVarsity Press.

—. 1990. *The Secretary in the Letters of Paul.* Tübingen: J.C.B. Mohr.

Roberts, C. H. 1970. *Books in the Graeco-Roman World and in the New Testament in the Cambridge History of the Bible, Vol. 1, From the Beginnings to Jerome .* Cambridge: Cambridge University Press.

Roberts, Colin H. 1979. *Manuscript, Society, and Belief in Early Christian Egypt.* London: Oxford University Press.

Roberts, Colin H., and Theodore C. Skeat. 1987. *The Birth of the Codex.* London: Oxford University Press.

Robertson, A. T. 1925. *An Introduction to the Textual Criticism of the New Testament.* London: Hodder & Stoughton.

Royse, James R. 2008. *Scribal Habits in Early Greek New Testament Papyri (New Testament Tools and Studies) (New Testament Tools, Studies and Documents).* Leiden & Boston: Brill Academic Pub.

Schaff, Philip, and David Schley Schaff. 1910. *History of the Christian Church, vol. 2.* New York: Charles Scribner's Sons.

Schurer, Emil. 1890. *A HISTORY OF THE JEWISH PEOPLE IN THE TIME OF JESUS CHRIST (Volume II).* Edinburgh: T. & T. Clark.

Scott, Julius J. Jr. 1995. *Jewish Backgrounds of the New Testament.* Grand Rapids, MI: Baker Academic.

Souter, Alexander. 1913. *The Text and Canon of the New Testament.* New York: Charles Scribner's Sons.

Starr, Raymond J. 1987. "The Circulation of Literary Texts in the Roman World." *The Classical Quarterly* 213-223.

Theissen, Gerd. 2004. *The Social Setting of Pauline Christianity.* Eugene, OR: Wipf & Stock Pub.

Towns, Elmer L. 2006. *Concise Bible Dictrines: Clear, Simple, and Easy-to-Understand Explanations of Bible Doctrines.* Chattanooga: AMG Publishers.

Tregelles, Samuel Prideaux. 1854. *An Account of the Printed Text of the Greek New Testament: With Remarks on Its Revision Upon Critical Principles.* London: S. Bagster and Sons.

Tuckett, Christopher M. 2001. "P52 and Nomina Sacra." *New Testament Study* 544-48.

Wachtel, Klaus, and Michael W Holmes. 2011. *The Textual History of the Greek New Testament: Changing Views in Contemporary Research, Text-Critical Studies.* Atlanta: Society of Biblical Literature.

Wallace, Daniel B. 2011. *Revisiting the Corruption of the New Testament: Manuscript, Patristic, and Apocryphal Evidence.* Grand Rapids, MI: Kregel Publications.

Wallace, Daniel. 2011. *The Reliability of the New Testament: Bart Ehrman and Daniel Wallace in Dialogue.* Minneapolis, MN: Fortress Press.

Wegner, Paul D. 2006. *A Student's Guide to Textual Criticism of the Bible: Its History Methods & Results.* Downers Grove: InterVarsity Press.

—. 1999. *The Journey from Text to Translation.* Grand Rapids: Baker Academic.

Westcott, B. F., and F. J. A. Hort. 1882. *Introduction to the New Testament in the Original Greek.* New York: Harper & Brothers.

—. 1882. *The New Testament in the Original Greek, Vol. 2: Introduction, Appendix.* London: Macmillan and Co.

Whiston, William. 1987. *The Works of Josephus.* Peabody, MA: Hendrickson.

Wright, Brian J. 2016. *"Ancient Rome's Daily News Publication With Some Likely Implications For Early Christian Studies," TynBull 67.1 (2016): 145-160.* Accessed March 22, 2017. https://www.academia.edu/18281056/_Ancient_Romes_Daily_Ne

ws_Publication_With_Some_Likely_Implications_For_Early_Christi
an_Studies_TynBull_67.1_2016_145-160.

Yonge, Charles Duke. 1995. *With Philo of Alexandria, The Works of Philo:
Complete and Unabridged.* Peabody, MA: Hendrickson.

Zuntz, Gunther. 1953. *The Text of the Epistles: A Disquisition upon the
Corpus Paulinum.* London: Oxford University Press.

47379561R00128

Printed in Poland
by Amazon Fulfillment
Poland Sp. z o.o., Wrocław